D1083789

Psychology of Language

An Introduction to Sentence and Discourse Processes

Murray Singer
University of Manitoba

LEA LAWRENCE ERLBAUM ASSOCIATES, PUBLISHERS
1990   Hillsdale, New Jersey   Hove and London

Copyright © 1990 by Lawrence Erlbaum Associates, Inc.
All rights reserved. No part of this book may be reproduced in
any form, by photostat, microform, retrieval system, or any other
means, without the prior written permission of the publisher.

Lawrence Erlbaum Associates, Inc., Publishers
365 Broadway
Hillsdale, New Jersey 07642

Library of Congress Cataloging-in-Publication Data
Singer, Murray.
    Psychology of language : an introduction to sentence and discourse
processes / by Murray Singer.
      p. cm.
    ISBN 0-8058-0005-0
    1. Psycholinguistics. I. Title.
    [DNLM: 1. Cognition. 2. Language. 3. Psycholinguistics. BF 455
S617p]
P37.S46   1990
401'.9—dc20
DNLM/DLC
for Library of Congress   89-23457
                                         CIP

Printed in the United States of America
10 9 8 7 6 5 4 3

Dedicated with gratitude to my mother,
the late Sarah Singer, and to my father, Eddy Singer

Contents

Preface

The contemporary study of language processes emerged around 1970 from the psycholinguistic tradition of the 1960s, which in turn had been stimulated by twin revolutions in cognitive psychology and linguistics in the 1950s. The pace of progress in this field has been striking. Over the past two decades, the initial proposals concerning the representation of discourse meaning have begun to converge on a paradigm for studying these issues. There is growing consensus, for example, that discourse understanding results in the construction of representations of the form and idea content of a message, and of the situation to which it refers. The mental processes that act upon these representations are viewed as those that apply as well in other realms of complex information processing, including problem solving, reasoning, and learning. The study of language processes, furthermore, is recognized as an interdisciplinary endeavor, pursued within the framework of cognitive science.

I began to give serious consideration to writing this book in 1985. Few textbooks on the psychology of language had been introduced during the first half of the decade. There was a growing body of literature on discourse processes, spanning 15 years, which had not been subjected to systematic integration in textbook form. The prospect of writing a textbook on language processes was appealing, particularly as I anticipated that the project would stimulate me to examine the literature in a fashion that daily demands usually preclude. On a pragmatic dimension, my impending sabbatical of 1986–87 offered a block of time during which to concentrate on the project.

The resulting book addresses the central issues of sentence and discourse processes, with particular emphasis on reading and listening comprehension. Throughout, I have strived to make the material accessible to upper level undergraduate students. In this regard, I have tried to identify the logic of the specific experimental manipulations that are described, and of the more general on-line and memory measures that are frequently invoked. Hundreds of numbered and unnumbered verbal examples are intended to flesh out the principles that are presented in the text. The tables and figures are likewise meant to make the presentation as concrete as possible.

The material is presented in 10 chapters. Chapters 2, 3, 5, and 8 are the longest ones, and might make appropriate 2-week reading assignments. I have adopted a variety of conventions to make a clear distinction between utterances and the ideas that they convey. These conventions are described at the end of chapter 1.

I am very grateful to the many individuals who have generously shared their insights and suggestions about this project. Lyle Bourne and my former colleague, Dan Perlman, offered helpful advice concerning the initial organization of the project. I am indebted to Gordon Bower, Herb Clark, Fernanda Ferreira, Art Graesser, Ely Kozminsky, Gail Singer, and several anonymous reviewers who each read and evaluated one or more chapters. The work greatly benefited from the efforts of Morton Ann Gernsbacher, who read the complete manuscript and identified many issues that needed clarification or correction. Herb Clark and Gail Singer provided invaluable guidance about how best to make the content accessible to the reader. Nancy Black and Colleen Singbeil assisted with several technical phases of the project. Students in several undergraduate and graduate courses provided me with helpful feedback.

Thanks are due to the staff at Lawrence Erlbaum Associates for their help. Larry Erlbaum and Judi Amsel answered my numerous inquiries patiently and promptly. Stacy Cain, John Eagleson, and Art Lizza provided needed guidance during different phases of the project.

The research projects of mine that are cited in this book have been supported by operating grant A9800 from the Natural Sciences and Engineering Research Council of Canada. I have also benefited from two Leave Fellowships from the Social Sciences and Humanities Research Council of Canada, and from grants from both the Research Grants Committee and the U of M and SSHRC Fund Committee of the University of Manitoba.

I would like to take this opportunity to acknowledge the many teachers and colleagues who have shaped my understanding of the issues addressed in this book. Al Bregman at McGill taught me my first course in cognitive psychology and was instrumental in my decision to pursue graduate studies at Carnegie Mellon University. At Carnegie, I was influenced by numerous teachers and advisors, including the late Bill Chase, John R. Hayes, Herbert Simon, fellow graduate student, Richard Young, and Charles Perfetti from University of Pittsburgh. Two fruitful sabbaticals, at the University of Colorado and at Stanford, have provided excellent opportunities for professional development. It was at Stanford that most of the chapters of this volume were written. Walter Kintsch, Ely Kozminsky, and Jim Miller at Colorado and Herb Clark and Gordon Bower at Stanford provided noteworthy hospitality, generosity, and encouragement in those settings. Other colleagues, too numerous to mention, have guided my understanding of the issues addressed in this book. It is my hope that the end product does justice to the insights and analyses of all of these individuals.

Finally, I would like to thank my wife, Gail, for her support, encouragement, and advice during all phases of this project.

Murray Singer

1

Introduction

Human beings live and function in an environment of language. From the moment of birth, a child encounters a steady stream of speech. Some of this speech is aimed directly at the infant, and some at other people. By the age of three, the child is capable of participating in complex and useful conversations. In mature adults, the ability to produce and understand language is taken for granted, and most likely seldom pondered.

The apparently effortless way in which people understand language is revealed by the following sentence from a magazine article.

> Fortunately for the earth's current inhabitants, the sun is enjoying a stable middle age, about halfway between its formation some 4.5 billion years ago and its demise about 5 billion years hence ("The Fate of the Sun," 1987).

To understand this ordinary sentence, the reader must perform many tasks. First, the written symbols must be recognized as representing familiar letters and words. The meaning of each of those words must be retrieved from memory. For each ambiguous word, such as *earth*, *current*, and *stable*, the correct sense must be selected. Pronouns, such as *its*, must be related to their corresponding concepts, such as SUN. Because the form of a sentence has a large impact on its meaning, the reader must perform a grammatical analysis of the sentence. In this regard, superficially similar sentences, such as **The patient was in the doctor's waiting room**, and **The patient doctor waited in the room,**

1

have very different meanings. The list of comprehension subtasks is very lengthy.

The easy of comprehension is all the more amazing in view of the speed with which it is accomplished. College students can read technical material at approximately 200 words per minute. The speech rate of adults is about 3 words per second, and listeners have no trouble following a message delivered at this rate. Indeed, the rate of both spoken and written comprehension can be increased without an undue loss of comprehension (Miller, 1981). For example, it has been reported that television advertisers sometimes speed up spoken messages by 20% in order to make more efficient use of a 30-second slot. Thus, language comprehension presents the paradox of a task that is tremendously complex, and yet poses few difficulties for most adults and children. Is it possible to reconcile these two observations?

The pervasiveness of language use in human activities is reflected by many practical questions. Why does one school child learn to read relatively effortlessly whereas another struggles for years with this basic, essential skill? Why does one advertising message convince us to acquire a product, whereas another fails? Why is one college textbook easy and even pleasurable to read, and another, frustrating and boring? It is only by a scientific examination of language comprehension that we may approach answers to such questions.

PSYCHOLOGY AND LANGUAGE

What is language? At one level, it is a symbolic system that merits study and description by linguists and other scientists. Viewed in another way, language is a medium of communication, which permits ideas to be conveyed among members of a social community. The study of language is a psychological problem because language is a product of the human mind, and psychology is the science of the mind. The psychological study of language has many branches, a reflection of the complexity of language itself.

Table 1.1 presents a two-dimensional analysis of several branches of the psychology of language, with emphasis on oral-auditory communication. The first dimension is language function, namely, input versus output. The second dimension contrasts the manipulation of physical signals, such as speech sounds, with the processing of the abstract symbols of thought. According to this scheme, the decoding of incoming speech signals by the auditory system is called *speech perception*. The output of the physical signal, by means of the speech organs, is called *articulation*. The mental analysis of incoming symbols of meaning is

TABLE 1.1
Some Subfields of the Psychology of Language

Language Function	Information	
	Physical	Abstract
Input	Speech Perception	Comprehension
Output	Articulation	Production

called *comprehension*. Finally, formulating messages in the mind prior to articulation, including stages such as syntactic planning and word choice, is called *production*. There is sufficient understanding of each of these areas of the psychology of language that entire textbooks are frequently devoted to just one of them (e.g., Crowder, 1982; Miller, 1981). The present volume is predominantly concerned with comprehension, and deals also with some issues of language production.

This book focuses on the processing of sentences and discourse. The *sentence* is a familiar linguistic unit whose precise definition is elusive (Sells, 1985, p. 5). *Discourse* refers to any extended, coherent message. This includes narrative and expository texts, speeches, poetry, conversation, and many other familiar types of communication.

Furthermore, this book concentrates on the concepts, methods, and findings that experimental psychologists have presented in the study of language comprehension. However, the study of language is increasingly an interdisciplinary task, of interest to linguists, computer scientists, philosophers, anthropologists, sociologists, and students of literature, as well as to psychologists. Progress in each of these disciplines, particularly linguistics and computer science, has had a considerable impact on the study of the psychology of language since 1950. The interdisciplinary study of cognition, of which language is one essential aspect, is known as *cognitive science*.

The next three sections of this chapter describe the contributions of human information processing, linguistics, and computer science to the psychology of language. Subsequent sections compare reading and listening, and examine the experimental methods of the psychology of language. Finally, some notes on the use of this book are presented.

THE ROLE OF HUMAN INFORMATION PROCESSING

Cognitive psychology refers to the study of the basic processes of thought, including those of perception, memory, and attention. In combination, these processes permit people to perform an unlimited variety of complex mental tasks, including problem solving and reasoning, the learning of new ideas and skills, and the use of language.

The 1950s witnessed the beginning of the cognitive revolution in modern psychology (e.g., Baars, 1986). Between 1915 and 1955, North American psychology was dominated by the behaviorist school of thought. According to this position, behavior was to be understood in terms of the regularities of the *responses* evoked by patterns of environmental *stimuli*, such as a pigeon's peck in response to the appearance of a grain of corn. Behaviorists considered thinking to fall outside the domain of psychology, following the argument that thoughts are not directly observable. Therefore, little progress was achieved in the study of thinking during the behaviorist era, particularly in North America.

Several factors contributed to the reemergence of the study of cognition. First, many behavioral phenomena could not be readily explained without reference to thinking (e.g., Hebb, 1949; Lashley, 1951; Tolman, 1948). A second factor was the appearance, in the late 1940s, of electronic computers and the academic discipline of computer science. Computer science offered to psychology an important metaphor of the mind: that of *information processing* (e.g., Gentner & Grudin, 1985). Computers, like human beings, are capable of decoding, storing, manipulating, and retrieving information. Accordingly, psychologists began to address people's information processing capabilities: How much information can a person store? How long will it remain intact? How quickly may it be retrieved? The new information processing approach soon resulted in numerous landmark findings concerning the nature of human memory and problem solving (e.g., Miller, 1956; Newell, Shaw, & Simon, 1958; Peterson & Peterson, 1959). The cognitive revolution quickly gained momentum.

A complete theory of cognition requires the analysis of the *representation of knowledge*, and of the *mental processes* that operate on those representations. The goal of this section is to outline the representation and processing principles of cognitive psychology, emphasizing the concepts most relevant to the psychology of language.

Representation

When people hear a sentence, such as (1), they analyze its content and store this content in memory.

(1)   The ants on the wooden table ate the sweet jelly.

Likewise, upon seeing the Mona Lisa, people encode the image of a woman smiling enigmatically in front of a picturesque landscape. However, people neither routinely memorize the string of 10 words of sentence (1) (Bransford & Franks, 1971; Jarvella, 1971; Sachs, 1967), nor retain the fine detail of the Mona Lisa (Norman & Rumelhart, 1975, p. 25). This section addresses the nature of the memory representations that people extract from complex stimuli.

Propositional Representation.   The fact that people can understand sentence (1) and remember its meaning prompted researchers to identify the basic unit of meaning conveyed by language messages. Underlying every sentence are one or more elementary ideas, called *propositions* (Anderson & Bower, 1973; Clark, 1969; Kintsch, 1972; Norman & Rumelhart, 1975; Schank, 1972; Winograd, 1972). Each proposition consists of a *predicate* plus one or more *arguments*. For example, underlying the sentence, **The children broke the lamp,** is the proposition (BREAK, CHILDREN, LAMP) (see Kintsch, 1974). It consists of the predicate, BREAK, and the arguments, CHILDREN and LAMP. Predicates and arguments are abstract concepts rather than words. However, these concepts often correspond to familiar words.

The predicate of a proposition is usually derived from a *verbal unit* in a sentence, such as a verb, an adverb, or an adjective. The predicate BREAK in our example corresponds to the verb of **The children broke the lamp.** For the sentence, **John is thin,** the predicate is derived from the adjective, *thin.* The proposition in question is (THIN, JOHN), with the predicate, THIN.

The arguments of a proposition are the concepts that are related to the predicate. The arguments are usually derived from the nouns of the sentence, and there may be one, two, three, or more of them in a single proposition. (THIN, JOHN) has one argument, namely JOHN. (BREAK, CHILDREN, LAMP) has two arguments, CHILDREN and LAMP. Underlying the sentence, **The pilot painted the fence with the brush,** is the proposition, (PAINT, PILOT, FENCE, BRUSH). This proposition has three arguments, PILOT, FENCE, and BRUSH.

Many sentences convey several propositions. For example, the propositional content of **The ants on the wooden table ate the sweet jelly** is (EAT, ANTS, JELLY), (LOCATION:ON, ANTS, TABLE), (WOODEN, TABLE), and (SWEET, JELLY). The propositions extracted from complex messages are organized to form an integrated network (e.g., Anderson, 1976; Bransford & Franks, 1971; Kintsch, Kozminsky, Streby, McKoon, & Keenan, 1975; Norman & Rumelhart, 1975). Figure 1.1 shows one system for portraying the network that results upon understanding **The ants on the wooden table ate the sweet jelly** (Kintsch, 1974). Further details about propositional representation are presented in Chapter 2.

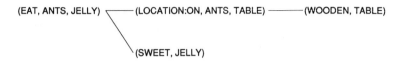

FIG. 1.1.   Network of propositions underlying the sentence, **The ants on the wooden table ate the sweet jelly.**

The Knowledge Schema.   People's knowledge is usually organized around specific topics, rather than consisting of random sets of facts. An organized knowledge structure is called a *schema* (plural "schemata") (e.g., Anderson, Spiro, & Anderson, 1978; Bartlett, 1932; Bobrow & Norman, 1975; Charniak, 1975; Dooling & Lachman, 1971; Minsky, 1975; Rumelhart & Ortony, 1977; Schank & Abelson, 1977). For example, one type of schema, called a *script*, refers to people's organized knowledge about familiar, stereotyped situations, such as washing clothes, a child's birthday party, and eating in a restaurant.

Table 1.2 shows an outline of the RESTAURANT MEAL script that was derived from the judgments of a large sample of people (Bower, Black, & Turner, 1979). This script includes props, such as a MENU and FOOD; roles, such as CUSTOMER and WAITER; entry conditions, such as the customer being hungry; and results, such as the customer's hunger being satisfied. The script also includes propositions expressing a *causal chain* of the usual events of eating in a restaurant. These events are in turn organized into *scenes*. Some of the events in the chain are optional. For example, it is possible to order at a restaurant without consulting the menu.

There are schemata about many sort of concepts. For example, people know the usual form of plans for accomplishing a goal, and of familiar types of texts, such as the story. All of these schemata play an important role in language processing, because they provide a framework for organizing complex ideas.

Image Representations.   Most people report that they can construct and inspect images of visual scenes. Consider the following demonstration: The top of a 3-inch cube is painted red, and two sides that are adjacent to the top and opposite to one another are painted blue. The cube is then cut into twenty-seven 1-inch cubes. Now, please answer the following question. How many small cubes have exactly one red face and one blue face?

Quite amazingly, many people quickly give the correct answer, "six" (Guilford, Fruchter, & Zimmerman, 1952). When asked how they have arrived at the answer, they typically claim that they manipulated and inspected a visual image. They report determining the final answer by

TABLE 1.2
Restaurant Script

Name:	Restaurant		
Props:	Tables	*Roles:*	Customer
	Menu		Waiter
	Food		Cook
	Bill		Cashier
	Money		Owner
	Tip		
Entry Conditions:		*Results:*	Customer has less money
	Customer hungry		Owner has more money
	Customer has money		Customer is not hungry
Scene 1:	*Entering*		
	Customer enters restaurant		
	Customer looks for table		
	Customer decides where to sit		
	Customer goes to table		
	Customer sits down		
Scene 2:	*Ordering*		
	Customer picks up menu		
	Customer looks at menu		
	Customer decides on food		
	Customer signals waitress		
	Waitress comes to table		
	Customer orders food		
	Waitress goes to cook		
	Waitress gives food order to cook		
	Cook prepares food		
Scene 3:	*Eating*		
	Cook gives food to waitress		
	Waitress brings food to customer		
	Customer eats food		
Scene 4:	*Exiting*		
	Waitress writes bill		
	Waitress goes over to customer		
	Waitress gives bill to customer		
	Customer gives tip to waitress		
	Customer goes to cashier		
	Customer gives money to cashier		

Source: Bower, Black, & Turner, 1979, Table 1, p. 179. Reprinted by permission.

"counting" the cubes that fit the requested description. Indeed, it is difficult to see how one could answer so quickly if one had to rely on a purely propositional representation of the problem statement.

There is considerable evidence that people can construct and manipulate visual images. For example, people can mentally rotate and compare complex figures (Cooper & Shepard, 1973; Shepard & Metzler, 1971), mentally compare the shapes of American states (Shepard &

Chipman, 1970), and make judgments about memorized geometric shapes (Brooks, 1968; Palmer, 1977). Contrary to people's intuitions, visual images do not reliably capture the full detail of the original scene (Bower, 1972; Norman & Rumelhart, 1975). However, it appears that images are more effective than propositional representations in preserving information about shape, and of the spatial relations among objects in a scene (Anderson, 1983; Simon, 1972).

In the realm of sentence processing, theorists have mainly focused on the propositional representation. Many sentences, however, also suggest visual images. For example, sentence (2) may evoke a vivid scene, whereas sentence (3) is less likely to do so.

(2) The sailboat sped across the bay.
(3) Bill's luck saved the day.

In particular, messages that describe the relative spatial arrangements of objects appear to result in the construction of both a propositional and an image representation (Bransford, Barclay, & Franks, 1972; Ehrlich & Johnson-Laird, 1982; Paivio, 1971; Perrig & Kintsch, 1985).

Declarative Versus Procedural Knowledge. People can articulate much of their knowledge. Most factual knowledge can be put into words, such as, **Information processing psychology began in the 1950s.** It is more difficult, but possible, to verbally describe abstract concepts and images (Anderson, 1980). However, knowledge of skilled behavior typically cannot be stated in words. For example, you cannot teach someone to swim by describing a set of arm and leg movements. This is partly because even an expert swimmer is not generally aware of the fine details of the skill. The term *declarative knowledge* refers to information that can be expressed in words, and *procedural knowledge* refers to knowledge that cannot be articulated.

An important feature of procedural knowledge is that executing a procedure is much less demanding of a person's mental energy, or *cognitive resources* (Bobrow & Norman, 1975), than is the expression of declarative knowledge. For example, riding a bicycle does not prevent a skilled cyclist from thinking about other matters or carrying on a conversation.

Motor skills, such as typing, playing a musical instrument, and riding a bicycle, provide the most common examples of procedural knowledge. However, the native speaker's knowledge of language is also procedural in nature. For example, most people can distinguish between the grammatical and ungrammatical sentences of their native language, but it takes a trained linguist to state the rules of grammar.

Cognitive Processes

Memory. Memory is such an integral aspect of thinking that it is difficult to conceive of an organism possessing a mind but not a memory. The tasks of walking across a room, recognizing a familiar face, solving an algebra problem, and understanding a sentence differ greatly from one another. However, they all depend on one's ability to remember facts, experiences, and skills.

One general account of memory function states that incoming information passes through a series of memory systems. First, sensory input, be it the sound of someone's voice or a touch on the arm, is temporarily recorded in *sensory memory* (e.g., Sperling, 1963). The analysis of the contents of sensory memory results in the identification of familiar units of information. For example, the analysis of speech permits the recognition of a series of speech sounds, and hence whole words. These units are deposited in *working memory*, where they undergo further analysis. At this stage, the grammatical structure and propositions of a spoken sentence might be extracted. Finally, the contents of working memory are, with some probability, transferred to a more permanent memory system, called *long-term memory*.

The principles of working memory and long-term memory are of central concern in this book. Table 1.3 compares the characteristics of these two systems. Working memory holds only two to eight familiar units of meaning, known as *chunks*. Accordingly, most adults can repeat, in perfect order, a string of six digits, such as 6-4-2-7-0-0, but not 12 digits, such as 9-1-1-3-2-2-1-9-9-9-5-9. The contents of a chunk, however, vary with expertise. For chess experts, for example, familiar patterns of chess pieces constitute chunks. Therefore, after studying a chess position for 5 seconds, the expert can replace almost 20 pieces in their correct positions. This is because a chess position consists of just a few chunks. In contrast, the novice player can replace only 4 or 5

TABLE 1.3
Working Memory Versus Long-term Memory

Characteristic	Working Memory	Long-Term Memory
Unit	Chunk	No restrictions
Capacity	2 to 8 chunks	Indefinitely large
Retrieval	Easy, fast	Effortful, slow
Duration	30 seconds	Indefinitely long
Forgetting	Decay and interference	Little evidence of information loss
Other	Role of rehearsal	

pieces (Chase & Simon, 1973). Long-term memory, on the other hand, appears to have no effective capacity limitations. Rather, it holds the accumulated knowledge of a lifetime.

The *duration* of information in working memory is only about 18 to 30 seconds (e.g., Peterson & Peterson, 1959; Reitman, 1974). Beyond that limit, the contents of working memory decay and cannot be retrieved. However, information can be maintained indefinitely in working memory by repeating it over and over, an activity known as *rehearsal*. In contrast, information that is stored in long-term memory can be retrieved after 40 years or more (Bahrick, Bahrick, & Wittlinger, 1975), although forgetting does occur at a slow rate. Forgetting in long-term memory is primarily due to *interference* among similar memories, and to the use of the wrong memory cue. There is little evidence that information is completely lost from long-term memory.

In general, the retrieval of information from working memory is easy and fast. Upon hearing the phone number, 964-2700, it is likely that you can quickly repeat it. Retrieval from long-term memory can be time-consuming and effortful. To illustrate, please take a moment to answer the question, **What did you have for dinner last Thursday evening?** Most people can answer this question, but it frequently takes them several dozen seconds to do so.

Two other characteristics of working memory deserve mention. First, working memory functions as the active workspace of the mind. For example, both the chunks extracted from sensory memory and ideas retrieved from long-term memory are delivered to the working memory system. Only when ideas occupy working memory can elementary mental operations, such as comparison, be applied to them. Second, information is not automatically transferred from working memory to long-term memory. Transfer to long-term memory is promoted by *elaborative processing* (Craik, 1981; Craik & Watkins, 1973), which requires that a person consider the contents of working memory in relation to other knowledge.

Activation.   The cognitive units in memory vary in their levels of *activation*. From its resting, or baseline, level of activation, a unit may be activated as a result of perceptual processing, including language processing. For example, the concept JELLY can become activated if one sees some jelly, or hears or sees the word *jelly* (Anderson, 1983, p. 28). The concept of activation provides one definition of working memory, as follows: *Active units may be thought of as occupying working memory.*

Activation spreads in propositional networks, from active concepts to related ideas. The spread of activation may be either *automatic* or *controlled.* Activation spreads automatically from one concept to another in a variety of memory networks. This has been demonstrated using a task called *lexical decision,* in which people are asked to decide whether letter strings, such as "butter" and "scarl," form English words. Correct judgment time for a word string, such as "butter," is faster when it immediately follows a related word, such as "bread," than when it follows an unrelated one, such as "nurse" (e.g., Meyer & Schvaneveldt, 1971; Schvaneveldt, Meyer, & Becker, 1976). The presentation of "bread" is said to automatically *facilitate* the lexical decision about "butter."

The spread of activation can also be *controlled.* For example, when people are presented with one category name, they can strategically direct their attention to a different category. On each trial of a study designed to demonstrate this, people viewed one of the category names, BIRD, BUILDING, or BODY. Then, they had to make a lexical decision about a letter string. The subjects were told that, when the word "building" appeared, they should focus their attention on the category of BODY PARTS, and vice versa. Under these conditions, people needed less time to judge that *elbow* is a word when preceded by the category name BUILDING than when it was preceded by the neutral cue, "XX-XXX" (Neely, 1977). In other words, the subjects controlled the spread of activation from the concept BUILDING to the category of BODY PARTS.

The automatic and controlled spread of activation differ on several dimensions (Anderson, 1976, 1983; Anderson & Pirolli, 1984; Neely, 1977; Posner & Snyder, 1975; Ratcliff & McKoon, 1981a, 1981b; Schneider & Shiffrin, 1977). Automatic facilitation occurs within about one-twentieth of a second, but decays within three-quarters of a second. Furthermore, activation spreads automatically regardless of the strategy that one adopts. That is, even if one intends to think of body parts upon the presentation of the word "building," decisions about building names are nevertheless facilitated for about three-quarters of a second. Controlled facilitation takes a lot longer to take effect than automatic facilitation: about ½ second. However, controlled facilitation may be maintained as long as one focuses attention on the relevant category.

Another difference is that the controlled spread of activation places high demands upon one's cognitive resources, whereas automatic processing is of relatively low cost (Posner & Snyder, 1975; Schneider & Shiffrin, 1977). People possess only a limited supply of cognitive resources, which may be devoted to a single mental task, or divided among two or more tasks (Kahneman, 1973; Norman & Bobrow, 1975). There are certain sets of tasks that one can perform simultaneously: For example it is possible to drive along the highway, converse with a passenger in the car, and listen to the radio. In contrast, it is difficult if not impossible to effectively attend to the meaning of two conversations at once (Broadbent, 1958; Treisman, 1960).

When two or more tasks can be performed simultaneously, only one of them can involve an extensive degree of controlled processing. However, tasks become increasingly automatic as a function of practice (Anderson, 1983). Accordingly, the experienced driver, who may have spent thousands of hours behind the wheel, can execute the skilled operations of guiding the vehicle with minimal resource demands. However, if the traffic suddenly gets heavy, or a highway leads through a large city, the need to attend to the stimuli of driving might make it necessary to suspend the conversation for a while.

The distinction between automatic and controlled processing is directly relevant to the ability to understand ordinary language. At the beginning of this chapter, it was emphasized there are numerous subtasks underlying language comprehension. However, people tend to be so experienced in language use that the tasks of word recognition, grammatical analysis, and meaning retrieval are automatic in nature, and demand a minimum of one's cognitive resources. This, coupled with the procedural nature of language skills, may partly explain why comprehension generally proceeds smoothly.

THE ROLE OF LINGUISTICS

The study of language was traditionally pursued primarily within the disciplines of philosophy and linguistics. Before 1900, one of the main goals of linguistics was a *prescriptive* one: That is, linguists informed people about how to speak and write. A prescriptive linguist might propose that one should say, **Gail and I went to the movies** rather than **Gail and me went to the movies.**

Since the turn of the century, language *description* has supplanted prescription as the primary goal of modern linguistics. Upon examining naturally occurring languages, linguists describe them by identifying their underlying rules. From this point of view, the use of the word *ain't* becomes a phenomenon for the linguist to describe, rather than a behavior to tell people to avoid.

Linguistics has provided inventories, or *taxonomies*, of the parts of language (e.g., Lyons, 1968). Languages can be analyzed in several ways. There are *grammatical units*, such as the word, phrase, clause, and sentence. There are sets of *grammatical categories*. For example, there are numerous parts of speech, including the noun, pronoun, verb, adverb, adjective, preposition, conjunction, and exclamation. The *gram-

matical functions of language include the subject and predicate of the sentence. These concepts are the basic building blocks upon which any successful theory of language must be based.

The discipline of linguistics consists of numerous subfields. *Phonology* is the study of the speech sounds that form the basic units of spoken language. *Syntax* refers to those grammar rules that specify the acceptable form of sentences. For example, it is a syntactic issue that **The plumber bought the car** is a grammatical sentence but **Car plumber bought the the** is not. *Semantics* refers to the study of language meaning. One semantic problems is illustrated by the famous sentence, **Colorless green ideas sleep furiously.** This sentence is an *anomaly:* That is, it is grammatical in form, but it violates principles of the way in which meanings can be combined (Chomsky, 1957). Likewise, semantics addresses the issues of what makes sentence (4) ambiguous, sentence (5) self-contradictory, and sentences (6a) and (6b) synonymous (Bierwisch, 1970).

(4)   The farmer filled the pen.
(5)   My aunt is married to a bachelor.

(6)   a.   The square is above the circle.
      b.   The circle is below the square.

The area of *pragmatics* examines the relations between messages and their linguistic and nonlinguistic context. The largest unit of language inspected in most areas of linguistics is typically the sentence. In contrast, pragmatics addresses larger units, including texts and conversations. A central problem of pragmatics is the purpose or *speech act* of utterances (Grice, 1957, 1975; Searle, 1975). For example, people can produce utterances in order to convey a new fact, ask a question, issue a command, or declare a state of affairs, such as, **This bridge is now open.** Pragmatics also considers the impact of context on sentence meaning. For example, in the sequence **The farmer's goats were hungry. The farmer filled the pen,** the reader is not likely to conclude that the word *pen* refers to a writing implement.

To achieve the goal of describing natural language, linguists must identify grammar rules that capture the form of the sentences of the language. These rules must distinguish between grammatical and ungrammatical sentences, a difference that is subtle. This is illustrated by sentence pairs (7) through (9).

(7)   a.   Alan seems sick.
      b.   *Alan seems sleeping.

(8) a. Sue ran.
     b. *Sue convinced.

(9) a. Phil saw the picture that the cavemen painted.
     b. *Phil saw the picture that the cavemen painted the picture.

The *a* version of each pair is grammatical, but the corresponding *b* version is readily judged to be unacceptable. Following a linguistic convention, ungrammatical sentences are marked with asterisks. The problem facing the linguist is to account for these judgments.

In linguistics, a grammar of a natural language is viewed as constituting a theory of language. Grammars must describe, or "account for," the appearance of every grammatical sentence of a language and none of the ungrammatical ones. The latter part of this criterion is important, because without it, even the trivial "grammar" that states that any string of English words is a grammatical sentence would succeed. If any string of words was grammatical, then both the *a* and the *b* forms of (7)–(9) would be legal English sentences.

The modern relationship between cognitive psychology and linguistics was stimulated by progress in linguistics in the 1950s, especially that due to Chomsky (1957, 1965). Advances in linguistics helped psychologists to frame useful research questions about the psychology of language. For example, according to the linguistic technique of *immediate constituent analysis*, sentences are analyzed into several levels of subunits, called constituents. For example, in Fig. 1.2, the sentence, **Phil saw the painting,** is analyzed into a noun phrase and a verb phrase. These phrases, in turn, are further analyzed into parts of speech, and

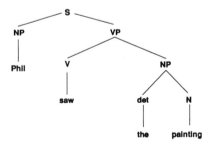

Key : S - Sentence
       NP - Noun Phrase
       VP - Verb Phrase
       N - Noun
       V - Verb
       det - Determiner

FIG. 1.2. Immediate constituent analysis of **Phil saw the painting.**

ultimately into words. This technique prompted psychologists to determine that the linguistic constituent is a psychologically useful concept (e.g., Caplan, 1972; Carroll, 1978; Fodor & Bever, 1965).

Equally influential was Chomsky's (1957) proposal that the application of *transformational rules* to the simple sentence, **The lawyer typed the letter,** accounts for the appearance of the relatively complex sentences, (10a)–(10c).

(10) a. Did the lawyer type the letter?
      b. The letter was typed by the lawyer.
      c. The lawyer did not type the letter.

Psychologists conducted experiments to determine whether there are mental operations corresponding to linguistic transformations, such as the interrogative, the passive, and the negative (e.g., Gough, 1966; Miller & McKean, 1964; Wason, 1965). This research indicated that people do not appear to produce complex sentences by applying mental transformations to simple sentences. However, the finding that the linguistic transformation is not a psychologically valid concept was a relatively minor setback in psycholinguistics. More importantly, research in the 1960s established that there are problems of mutual interest to psychologists and linguists, and that the two fields possess methods needed to study these problems. The interaction between the two disciplines will be apparent in many of the analyses presented in this book.

THE ROLE OF COMPUTER SCIENCE

Almost since the advent of the electronic computer in the late 1940s, it has been a goal of computer scientists to create computer systems capable of language production and comprehension. Such a system would permit untrained individuals to ask the computer questions, and even to program the computer. The first major natural-language task undertaken by computer scientists was machine translation. In spite of initial optimism, efforts during the 1950s resulted in programs that produced infamous errors. For example, one system translated the English proverb, **The spirit was willing but the flesh was weak,** into the Russian, **The vodka was good but the meat was rotten.** The reason for these failures has been summarized succinctly: "Language moves in a common sense world" (Feigenbaum & McCorduck, 1984). Without a representation of common sense ideas, of the meaning of concepts, and of the grammatical structure of sentences, the computer had no "understanding" of the material it was translating. The computer pursued its task simply by translating each word from the source language to the target language, using a computerized dictionary.

In reaction to this failure, computer scientists in the 1960s concentrated on the subtasks of language processing. For example, techniques were devised for representing the meaning of concepts by means of networks of related ideas (Quillian, 1968). In this system, the concept BIRD appeared in a network that identified it as a type of animal, with *instances* such as ROBIN and CANARY, and with properties such as FLYING, SINGING, and LAYING EGGS. The strategy of dividing language into its component tasks culminated in the landmark SHRDLU system of Winograd (1972). SHRDLU could converse sensibly about a "world" of children's building blocks. It was based on numerous separate programs. Each program was devoted to a subtask, including syntax, the representation of concept meaning, and the representation of the current arrangement of the blocks. Table 1.4 presents a brief conversation between SHRDLU and a person.

What does computer understanding have to do with the psychology of language? First, progress in computer science alerted cognitive psychologists to the distinction between representation and process, and the usefulness of measuring the information processing characteristics of cognitive systems. Second, in certain respects, a running computer program represents a theory of behavior. In this regard, it is useful to distinguish between the realms of *artificial intelligence*, and the *computer simulation* of human cognition (Newell & Simon, 1972; Simon & Newell, 1971). Consider a complex task such as playing chess. The artificial intelligence approach to chess would use the full speed and memory capabilities of the computer to play the best possible game. In contrast, a program created to simulate human chess playing would include a representation of human limitations. This program might have

TABLE 1.4
A Conversation with SHRDLU (Computer Statements in Capitals)

1. pick up a big red block.
   OK.
2. grasp the pyramid.
   I DON'T KNOW WHICH PYRAMID YOU MEAN.
3. find a block which is taller than the one you are holding and put it into the box.
   OK.
4. what does the box contain?
   THE BLUE PYRAMID AND THE BLUE BLOCK.
5. what is the pyramid supported by?
   THE BOX.

Source: Winograd, 1972. Reprinted by permission.

a working memory of about five chunks, and be permitted to consider only a dozen or so alternative moves on each turn, rather than the thousands permitted by the computer's astounding speed. If the simulation program played a passable game, and if its choice of moves resembled those selected by people, then it would express a theory of human chess playing. Likewise, it is possible to simulate human language comprehension.

The exchange of information between psychology and computer science has been bidirectional. Computer science has provided psychology with many principles of information processing, and with powerful techniques for expressing psychological theory. Psychological evidence has guided the development of certain computational systems. For example, certain psychological studies revealed that people draw only a limited set of conclusions during the comprehension of a message (see chapter 7). This suggested to computer scientists that machine understanding systems should likewise be restricted in their generation of inferences. Earlier systems, which had not been constrained in this fashion, got bogged down in the *inferential explosion* that results from computing all of the probable conclusions of a message. In some sense, the computer got "lost in thought."

Throughout this book, principles of computer science and computer simulations of language processing are applied to the problems at hand. Chapter 10 inspects the principles of machine understanding in more detail. It also describes several representative simulation systems.

READING VERSUS LISTENING

There are two predominant *modes* of encoding language messages: by listening and by reading.[1] The oral-auditory mode of linguistic communication is the primary one: Human beings, as a species, have probably spoken for hundreds of thousands of years, but have written for less than ten thousand years. As individuals, children likewise speak long before they read and write. These observations raise the possibility that there are substantive differences between listening and reading comprehension. However, recent analyses discourage this conclusion.

One obvious difference between listening and reading is that the initial encoding processes are different: Listening requires the phonological interpretation of speech sounds, and reading depends on the orthographic analysis of written symbols. However, similarities between listening and reading are equally apparent. In both modes, the

---

[1] Like written language, sign language, such as American Sign Language for the hearing impaired, is encoded visually.

understander encounters sequences of words. To comprehend these sequences, it is necessary to retrieve the meaning of each word, analyze the syntax of the sequences, and extract the propositions conveyed by the message. It is therefore possible that the similarities between listening and reading might outweigh the differences.

The conclusion that listening resembles reading is supported by at least three types of study. First, studies of reading and listening frequently reveal comparable complex patterns of comprehension and memory. For example, in both modes, people integrate related sets of ideas into networks (Bransford & Franks, 1971; Singer & Rosenberg, 1973). Likewise, both readers and listeners remember a higher proportion of the ideas of short discourses than long ones (Kintsch et al., 1975). Second, the information processing characteristics of listening and reading appear to be similar. In this regard, the working memory capacity of both listeners and readers is approximately two simple sentences of an ongoing message (Glanzer, Dorfman, & Kaplan, 1981). Likewise, the fundamental processes of word recognition are similar in listening and reading (Bradley & Forster, 1987). Third, reading problems frequently are indicative of general comprehension deficits: In other words, there is one general comprehension facility underlying listening and reading (Just & Carpenter, 1984). For example, young unskilled readers have the same working memory capacity as skilled readers, but show deficits in memory functions that depend on the ability to organize the ideas underlying a message (Perfetti & Goldman, 1976). Of course, there do exist deficits particular to the ability to *encode* spoken or written language, such as difficulty in distinguishing the written letters *b* and *d*, or *p* and *q*.

In spite of these similarities, there are reasons to expect some systematic differences between listening and reading comprehension. First, readers can slow down, or even backtrack to an earlier part of a message, whereas listeners often have to keep up with the source of the message. Second, there are many distinct comprehension *orienting tasks*: For example, people process language in social conversations, for entertainment, to learn, and to proofread. The orienting task of the understander has been shown to affect the representation that is extracted from discourse (e.g., Cirilo, 1981; Kieras, 1981a; Mayer & Cook, 1981; Walker & Meyer, 1980). Now, listening and reading are associated with different orienting tasks. For example, understanding conversations is usually achieved by listening, whereas understanding recipes is most often accomplished by reading. Therefore, apparent differences between listening and reading might actually be due to differences between their associated orienting tasks.

In this book, the terms *speaker* and *listener* are used in the context of studies of listening comprehension, and *writer* and *reader* refer to reading. Occasionally, the more general term, *understander*, is used. Unless otherwise specified, it is assumed that the findings of reading experiments generalize to listening comprehension, and vice versa.

RESEARCH METHODS OF LANGUAGE PROCESSES

Since 1950, experimental psychologists have developed an extensive battery of techniques for the study of the psychology of language. Of course, many of these methods can be applied to other cognitive problems. As is true in every area of psychology, research methods can be as varied as the creativity and ingenuity of the scientist permit.

Memory versus On-Line Measures of Comprehension

Memory Measures.   The experimental study of human memory is almost as old as experimental psychology itself (e.g., Ebbinghaus, 1885). Upon the emergence of modern psycholinguistics, investigators applied the research methods of memory to the study of language comprehension. It is easy to justify studying sentence and discourse memory: If a person encodes a message, then it is likely that at least part of the message will be remembered. Therefore, examining people's memory of messages ought to reflect the nature of comprehension.

The relation between what is encoded and what is remembered is far from simple. For example, having heard a passage titled "Helen Keller," people confidently reported one week later that they recognized the test sentence, **She was deaf, dumb, & blind** (Sulin & Dooling, 1974). This was in spite of the fact that the original passage made no reference to Helen Keller's disabilities. The recognition of this test sentence resulted from people's retrieval of relevant general knowledge rather than their memory for the passage.

There are many ways to test people's memory for sentences and discourse. In *free recall,* people are simply asked to write or state as much of the original information as possible. In *cued recall,* part of the original stimulus is provided as a retrieval hint. For example, the phrase, **Helen Keller,** might be provided as a cue for a passage encountered earlier. In *recognition,* one is asked to judge whether specific words, phrases, or sentences appeared in a preceding list or message. People's memory performance differs as a function of the method that is used. For example, recognition memory is systematically better than free recall.

Memory measures have certain shortcomings. First, memory performance does not directly expose the processes of comprehension. Rather, it reveals the product of comprehension. Second, as a result of forgetting, memory measures may provide a distorted picture of comprehension. Third, people may report remembering only what they believe the experimenter wants them to report. The use of on-line measures of comprehension helps to address these deficiencies.

On-Line Measures. As the label suggests, on-line measures examine language processing during the course of comprehension. Using these procedures, the researcher either measures people's behavior continuously during comprehension, or occasionally interrupts the understander in order to examine the progress of comprehension.

One relatively straightforward on-line measure of reading comprehension is reading time. In a typical arrangement, a message is displayed on a television screen, one unit at a time. A unit can be a single word, a phrase, a sentence, or even longer portions of a message. The reader is instructed to examine each segment until it is understood, and to press a button to view the next segment. The researcher can deduce the processing demands of different language constructions from the time needed to read the segments.

To illustrate, consider sequences (11) and (12):

(11)   a.   Racing down the hill, Joey fell off his bike.
       b.   The next day his body was covered with bruises.

(12)   a.   Joey went to a neighbor's house to play.
       b.   The next day his body was covered with bruises.

To understand the sentence, **The next day his body was covered with bruises,** the reader needs to discover how the event it describes was caused by the preceding events. This ought to be easier to accomplish in the context of (11a) than (12a), because the causal connection with (12a) is not obvious. Reading time data confirmed that people took longer to read the b sentence after (11a) than after (12a) (Keenan, Baillet, & Brown, 1984). This example is typical of the way that reading time is used to test hypotheses about language processing.

A sophisticated technique for charting reading processes is to measure the position and the duration of people's eye fixations upon the text (e.g., Just & Carpenter, 1980; McConkie & Rayner, 1975; Rayner, 1983a). To accomplish this, an invisible infrared beam of light is bounced off the lens of the reader's eye as a text is read. A videocamera receives the reflected beam, and a computer is used to gauge the location of the reader's fixation upon the text. Furthermore, these measurements can be made dozens of times per second. As a result, a record is made of every fixation performed by the reader.

The measurement of eye fixations tells the researcher exactly where in a unit of text a reader is looking, as well as how long is spent reading the unit. This permits the evaluation of hypotheses that could not be tested using reading time alone. For example, reading time might reveal that a person needed 3.5 sec to report understanding, **The old man's glasses were filled with wine.** Fixation data might add to this the information that, upon reaching the end of the sentence, the reader looked back at the word *glasses.* This *regressive fixation* would suggest that the reader reevaluated the interpretation of the ambiguous word, **glasses.**

Researchers have identified several assumptions underlying the interpretation of eye fixation data. For example, it has been proposed that the analysis of every word in a text is performed immediately upon fixation, rather than in a delayed manner (Just & Carpenter, 1980). Another assumption is that the reader continues to fixate a word as long as it is being analyzed (Ehrlich & Rayner, 1983; Just & Carpenter, 1980).

Some on-line measures of comprehension are intermittent rather than continuous. According to this procedure, people read or listen to a message, and are occasionally interrupted to make a judgment about a test stimulus. The accuracy or time of the judgment reflects the nature of the comprehension processes that were executed up to the point of interruption. Consider the following example: The phrase **landing planes** is ambiguous: It can refer to planes that are landing or the activity of landing airplanes. In one study, people listened to sentence fragments, such as **If the pilot is required to attend flight school, landing planes . . .** , and then saw the test word **is** or **are** on a TV screen. The task was to read the test word out loud. For the present example, people needed more time to read **are** than **is.** This outcome indicated that the grammatical construction of the present example, up to the point of interruption, created a bias to expect the singular, *is* (Townsend & Bever, 1982).

One drawback of on-line measures of comprehension is that they have the potential to change the behavior they are intended to chart. For example, having to press a button to signal the understanding of each word in a text might change the character of the reading process (Danks, 1986). Requiring a reader to make a judgment about a word that does not fit the ongoing sentence context may have a similar impact (Masson, 1984). Researchers always have to weigh the merits of a method against its pitfalls in the selection of an experimental procedure.

The Laboratory Study of Language Processes

Experimental psychologists always need to consider whether their laboratory findings generalize to the natural setting (e.g., Neisser, 1976). Critics of laboratory research state that laboratory behavior differs systematically from naturally occurring behavior. In the realm of language understanding, when people comprehend ordinary language messages, they typically are motivated to learn, to interact socially, or to be entertained. Because participants in laboratory experiments may have none of these motivations, laboratory comprehension may differ from that observed in natural contexts.

There are a variety of ways of addressing this critique. First, certain features of human cognition, such as the capacity of working memory and the mechanisms of allocating cognitive resources, are unlikely to be influenced by the setting. Therefore, it is likely that laboratory experiments can generate useful knowledge about the information processing characteristics of comprehension.

Second, a general strategy of experimental psychology is to demonstrate agreement among different measures of the same phenomenon. For example, in the study of anxiety, it would be useful to demonstrate that rating scales, physiological measures, and the judgments of an observer all generate consistent scores: A person who is detected as being very anxious by one measure should not appear very calm according to another. In the study of language comprehension, memory and on-line measures ought to support the same conclusions. The convergence of laboratory measures of comprehension would suggest that the experimental observations are valid, although it would not guarantee that the findings generalize to the natural setting.

Third, it is possible to directly compare comprehension in the laboratory and the natural setting. In one study of this sort, I recruited students who had reported that they frequently read a campus newspaper. In the laboratory, tests were made of the students' memory for newspaper articles that they had read *before they were recruited for the study.* Other students were asked to read the same articles on TV monitors in the laboratory. Comparisons revealed highly similar profiles of recall and recognition between the natural and laboratory readers (Singer, 1982; see also Graesser, Higgenbotham, Robertson, & Smith, 1978). This outcome supported the usefulness of laboratory studies of language processes, but more studies of this sort are needed.

A more general argument in favor of laboratory investigations is summarized in the following quotation:

> If it were true [that communicative skills can only be adequately understood by studying them in the natural conversational context], the study

of . . . language would be radically different from the rest of science, where nature has to be pushed or pulled out of its normal course before it reveals its secrets. Studies of spontaneous speech have their place, though they tend to prove useful only to those who have sharp questions to put to the data. (MacNamara, 1987, p. 305).

This book presents experimental evidence derived from a vast battery of scientific techniques. To understand each method, it is necessary to consider its logic, rationale, assumptions, and pitfalls. The logic of a method is a statement of how a particular pattern of results supports a corresponding conclusion. The rationale addresses the issue of why this method was chosen over others. The assumptions are the conditions under which the method can be considered valid. The pitfalls of a method are the ways in which it can produce results that appear to mean one thing when they in fact mean something else.

SOME NOTES ON USING THIS BOOK

The Table of Contents of this book identifies the major sections of each chapter. The reader will notice that many sections of the text are further subdivided. Attention to the heading structure will help the reader grasp the organization of each chapter. Consider the section of Chapter 1 titled, "The Role of Human Information Processing." This section consisted of the subsections, *Representation* and *Cognitive Processes*. Each subsection was further subdivided. This organization was conveyed by three levels of headings, namely centered headings, left-adjusted headings, and paragraph headings. The complete set of headings for that section was as follows:

THE ROLE OF HUMAN INFORMATION PROCESSING
Representation
Propositional Representation.
The Knowledge Schema.
Image Representations.
Declarative versus Procedural Knowledge.
Cognitive Processes
Memory.
Activation.

Several conventions are adopted in order to distinguish between words and sentences, on the one hand, and the ideas that they convey, on the other. Sample sentences that are presented in the text will appear in bold print. However, if it is necessary to refer to a sample sentence on several occasions, then this sentence will appear as a numbered example, such as (7a), Alan seems sick.

To refer to the meaning of (7a), its underlying propositions may be listed, such as P1 (SEEM, P2), P2 (SICK, ALAN). Another way of accomplishing the same thing will be to present the sentence in uppercase letters, such as ALAN SEEMS SICK. This has the merit of making the text a little easier to read. Likewise, when referring to the abstract concept underlying a word such as *sick*, the uppercase, SICK, will be presented.

Italics will be used to introduce technical terms, such as *procedural knowledge*. Double quotation marks (") will fulfill three functions: To identify quotations, to introduce an ironic or otherwise unusual sense of a phrase, and to mention the titles of example stories and other discourses.

Each chapter ends with a summary, intended to help the reader review the main ideas that were presented. The reader is strongly encouraged to also read the summary *before* beginning the chapter. This may provide a frame of reference for integrating the new material.

SUMMARY

Language is a complex symbolic system that permits communication among members of human societies. The psychology of language is studied within the framework of cognitive psychology, with emphasis on an information processing analysis. The content of sentences and discourse is captured by propositions consisting of a predicate plus one or more arguments. The propositions underlying a message are organized by the understander into networks. People's knowledge about familiar concepts is represented in structures called schemata. People also store and manipulate image representations extracted from their sensory experiences.

To comprehend a spoken or written message, one must first record the stimulus in sensory memory. The analyzed products of sensory memory are transferred to working memory, the active workspace of the mind. Working memory has a capacity of two to eight familiar chunks. Without rehearsal, information decays from working memory within about 30 seconds. The transfer of new information from working memory to long-term memory is enhanced by elaborative processing: That is, the examination of the relations between the information and other ideas.

Concepts in propositional networks may be activated beyond their normal resting levels. A concept may be directly activated by its corresponding environmental stimulus or word. Activation spreads among concepts, both automatically and in a controlled fashion. The automatic spread of activation places low demands upon one's cognitive resources, whereas controlled processing has a high cost. As a result, one can perform only a single controlled task at a time. It takes relatively little effort to understand spoken and written messages because most of the subtasks of comprehension are highly practiced, and therefore have become automatic.

In the study of language processes, there is extensive exchange of ideas between psychology and the disciplines of linguistics and computer science. An important goal of linguistics is to identify rules that account for the appearance of the grammatical sentences of a language. Sets of rules of this sort form grammars. Linguistic problems are studied in subfields such as phonology, syntax, semantics, and pragmatics. Computer scientists have identified many concepts and principles that carry suggestions about how people process information. Computer programs for understanding natural language have highlighted the many levels of language processing that theorists need to analyze.

Listening and reading frequently result in similar patterns of comprehension and memory, and encoding difficulties in the two modes have been shown to go hand-in-hand. Furthermore, the information processing characteristics of the two modes are similar. However, systematic differences between the goals of listening and reading tasks may lead to comprehension differences.

Memory measures of comprehension help to identify the information that the understander has extracted from a message. Memory measures can be misleading if the memory of the message changes between understanding and testing. On-line measures, such as reading time and eye fixations, provide more direct indexes of comprehension. However, on-line measures have the potential of altering the understander's behavior. In general, any laboratory study may lack validity, but there is some evidence that language processing is similar in the laboratory and the natural setting.

2

Language and Meaning: Representing and Remembering Discourse

LEVELS OF REPRESENTATION

People use language mainly for the purpose of communication with one another. To communicate effectively, a person must arrange words into sequences that obey a variety of complex rules of grammar, and that observe the constraints of human information processing. The aim of the understander is to identify those ideas that the speaker intends to convey. Understanding discourse appears to result in several levels of mental representation. These levels include the representation of the precise, or *verbatim*, form of the message, the syntactic organization of the sentences, an integrated network of the propositions underlying the message, and a model of the situation to which the message refers.

The multi-level nature of discourse representation is probably due to the fact that every stage of language processing results in distinct memories. Consider sentence (1).

(1)   The burglar opened the window.

To completely understand this sentence, the listener must analyze its speech sounds, identify its words, make use of its grammatical cues, and evaluate its accuracy using higher reasoning processes. Figure 2.1 is meant to suggest that each of these processes yields its own distinct representation.

Consider, by analogy, the sequence of operations applied to a tree, from the time that it is cut down until it is manufactured into an article

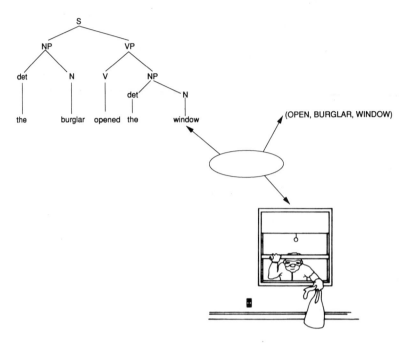

FIG. 2.1. Multi-level representation of **The burglar opened the window.**

of furniture and sold to a consumer. Like a sentence, the tree is subjected to successive "stages of analysis": It is felled by a logger, milled into planks, carved into furniture parts and assembled by a carpenter, and ultimately sold by a retailer. At each stage, the "processor"—logger, miller, carpenter, and salesperson—records the operations performed on the tree, and the purchase and sale prices of the products. As a result, a trace of the processing of the tree is left at every level. One oversimplification of this metaphor is that it is likely that phonological, lexical, syntactic, and semantic processes are overlapping rather than sequential operations.

The multi-level representation of discourse has several implications. First, people's memory for discourse can reflect the different levels of representation. Providing people with different experimental instructions, such as "try to remember the message in its exact form," or "try to remember the general sense of the message," can influence them to retrieve information from one level of representation or another (Anderson & Pichert, 1978; Hasher & Griffin, 1978; Reder, 1982). Second, as mentioned earlier, the understander works simultaneously on the construction of the different representations. Therefore, each level can guide the analysis performed at every other level (see chapter 3). In general, this book emphasizes those representations that reflect the meaning of discourse: namely, propositional networks and situation models.

SENTENCE FORM VERSUS MEANING

Following the influence of advances in linguistics (Chomsky, 1957, 1965), much of the psycholinguistic research of the 1960s emphasized problems of syntax. Toward the end of that decade, the focus began to shift to semantic issues, for several reasons. First, psychologists were eager to address the central function of language, which is to communicate ideas. Second, a reformulation of the theory of transformational grammar stated that complex sentences, such as passives, are not derived by applying transformations to the simpler "kernel" form of those sentences (Chomsky, 1965). This theoretical change diminished the importance assigned to the role of syntax in language processing. Third, psychologists demonstrated that sentence meaning has more impact on people's judgments than does syntax (e.g., Blumenthal & Boakes, 1967; Gough, 1966; Slobin, 1966). The next section presents several well-known studies that consolidated the switch in emphasis in psycholinguistics from form to meaning.

Memory for Sentence Meaning and Form

The relative strength of the memory for form and meaning of sentences was evaluated by Sachs (1967). People heard tape-recorded passages about a variety of topics, and occasionally were interrupted with test sentences to recognize. For example, one passage included the sentence, **He sent a letter about it to Galileo, the great Italian scientist.** The listener later heard one of the following test sentences.

(2) a. He sent a letter about it to Galileo, the great Italian scientist. (identical)

b. Galileo, the great Italian scientist, sent him a letter about it. (semantic change)

c. A letter about it was sent to Galileo, the great Italian scientist. (voice change)

d. He sent Galileo, the great Italian scientist, a letter about it. (formal change)

Test sentence (2a) was *identical* to the original sentence, (2b) introduced a semantic change, (2c) changed the *voice* of the sentence from active to passive, and (2d) presented a superficial *formal* change. Therefore, the correct answer was "identical" for (2a) and "changed" for (2b), (2c), and (2d). The effect of the amount of intervening text on people's memory was also examined. There were either 0, 80, or 160 syllables of text between a sentence and its recognition item.

For the present purposes, the voice change and formal change conditions may be grouped into a *syntactic change* category. With 0 intervening syllables, the identical, semantic change, and syntactic change test sentences were all judged correctly about 90% of the time. The situation was quite different after 80 and 160 intervening syllables: Accuracy was about 80% for semantic-change sentences, but only about 60% in the identical and syntactic-change conditions. These results indicated that after the initial memory representation of a sentence has faded, people cannot remember its exact form. Therefore, people cannot accurately state whether a test sentence has the same or different form as a sentence that appeared in the text. In contrast, people remember the meaning or gist of a sentence: The listeners detected semantic changes 80% of the time. Sachs (1967) concluded that people remember the meaning of a sentence better than its form.

In another study, people heard a set of related sentences, such as (3)–(6), interspersed among other sentences in a list (Bransford & Franks, 1971).

(3)   The old car pulled the trailer.
(4)   The hill was steep.
(5)   The car pulling the trailer climbed the steep hill.
(6)   The old car climbed the hill.

Shortly afterwards, the participants rated their confidence of *recognizing* test sentences, such as (7) and (8).

(7)   The old car pulling the trailer climbed the steep hill. (new)
(8)   The old car climbed the hill. (old)

These test sentences varied in their complexity: That is, they conveyed between one and four propositions or idea units.

Several features of the results were notable. First, people incorrectly reported recognizing those new test sentences that were consistent with the meaning of the original items. For example, people frequently recognized sentence (7) even though it had not occurred in the original list. Second, people's recognition confidence ratings depended mainly on the complexity of the test sentences, and not on whether they were old or new. For example, complex new sentences, such as (7), were recognized more confidently than simple old sentences, such as (8). One might have expected people to be more accurate for short, simple sentences.

The interpretation of these results is that, upon understanding sentences (3)–(6), people integrate the underlying ideas into a network (Bransford & Franks, 1971). During recognition, the meaning of a test sentence is compared with this network. Recognition confidence is mainly a function of the overlap between the propositional content of the test sentence and the network. This accounts for the high recognition ratings of complex, new test sentences: Namely, they closely resembled the stored network. These findings supported the view that meaning predominates over form in sentence memory.

Findings of this sort prompted many psycholinguists to focus their attention on language meaning. The next section examines the representation of discourse meaning. Particular emphasis will be placed on the propositional representation of discourse ideas. The last two sections of the chapter respectively examine the form and situation representations that are extracted from discourse.

PROPOSITIONAL CONTENT OF SENTENCES AND DISCOURSE

Propositional Notation

The basic principles of the propositional representation of discourse were introduced in chapter 1. To briefly review, the idea content of every sentence consists of one or more units of meaning, called propositions. For example, consider sentence (9).

(9)   The pilot painted the fence with the brush.

Underlying this sentence is the proposition, (PAINT, PILOT, FENCE, BRUSH). The proposition consists of the predicate, PAINT, plus three arguments, PILOT, FENCE, and BRUSH. The predicate and arguments of a proposition are abstract concepts, but they frequently correspond closely to familiar words.

The complexities of language meaning demand special conventions in the propositional notation. Consider sentence (10):

(10)   Bill's unlocking the door annoyed Sue.

Upon reflection, it can be seen that sentence (10) describes the relation between two simple ideas. Sentence (10) may be propositionally represented as follows:

P1 (UNLOCK, BILL, DOOR)
P2 (ANNOY, P1, SUE)

To capture the meaning of sentence (10), proposition P1 appears as an argument embedded in proposition P2.

Some language functions are typically not shown in propositions. These include features such as verb tense (e.g., present, future) and verb mood (e.g., declaration, question, command). Most theorists assign these *modal* characteristics to a component separate from the propositional content of a sentence (Fillmore, 1968; Frederiksen, 1985; Kintsch, 1974).

In general, the propositional representation of discourse is a complicated technical problem that has received careful attention (e.g., Kintsch, 1974; Meyer, 1975; Turner & Greene, 1978). Additional details of this procedure will be introduced throughout the book as they are needed.

Semantic Cases

Each argument in a proposition fills one of several possible semantic roles, or *cases*, in relation to its predicate. The following cases are ones that appear in most theoretical analyses (Chafe, 1970; Fillmore, 1968, pp. 24–25). In each sample sentence, the noun in capital letters exemplifies the case being defined.

AGENT—the animate instigator of the action identified by the verb (e.g., **The CATCHER threw the ball**)

INSTRUMENT—the inanimate force or object causally involved in an action or state (e.g., **The child broke the window with the ROCK; The SAW cut the wood**)

LOCATIVE—the location or spatial orientation of the state or action identified by the verb (e.g., **The banker walked in the PARK**)

OBJECT—the case of anything representable by a noun whose role is identified by the semantic interpretation of the verb; the most neutral case (e.g., **The pilot painted the FENCE**)

BENEFACTIVE—the person who benefits from the action (e.g., **Tom gave the gift to MARY**)

It is usually possible to identify a unique case for each argument in a proposition. For example, in the representation of **The pilot painted the fence with the brush, pilot** occupies the agent case, **fence** is an object, and **brush** is an instrument. The proposition underlying this sentence can be written, (PAINT, AGENT:PILOT, OBJECT:FENCE, INSTRUMENT:BRUSH). However, the cases are usually omitted when they are obvious.

The semantic case of a word-concept does not depend on the position of the word in the sentence. This is readily seen in the following pairs of sentences:

(11) a. The tailor cut the cloth.
      b. The scissors cut the cloth.

(12) a. Wendy opened the door.
      b. The door opened.

The words **tailor** and **scissors** occupy exactly the same surface positions in sentences (11a) and (11b), respectively, but most adults and children would agree that TAILOR is an agent whereas SCISSORS is an instrument (e.g., Braine & Wells, 1978). Conversely, *door* appears in different surface positions in (12a) and (12b), but plays the role of the object in both sentences (Fillmore, 1968, p. 27).

Many verbs have several senses. For example, **to run** has the senses of hurrying; and of conducting something, such as a meeting. Each sense of every verb is associated with a distinct set of semantic cases. For example, among the cases of both **to eat** and **to buy** are the agent and the object. This means that there cannot be an instance of eating without some object being eaten (Schank, 1972). It is interesting to note, however, that even when a case is *conceptually* required, it does not always have to appear in the surface form of the corresponding sentence. To illustrate, both sentences (13) and (14) omit the conceptually required object case.

(13) *Alice bought.
(14) Alice ate.

Although (13) is ungrammatical, (14) is acceptable.

In our use of propositional notation, only those cases that are explicitly mentioned in a sentence will be shown in the corresponding proposition. For example, for the sentence, **The dentist ate with the fork,** we will write the proposition, (EAT, AGENT:DENTIST, INSTRUMENT:

FORK), rather than (EAT, AGENT:DENTIST, OBJECT:X, INSTRU-MENT:FORK) (see Kintsch, 1974).

Reference

Many spoken and written sentences *refer* to particular entities, such as objects or people. To fully understand a sentence, the listener must be able to identify the entities to which the sentence refers (Frege, 1892; Lyons, 1977). For example, sentence (15) makes an assertion about a particular architect, rather than architects in general.

(15)   The architect watched *Star Wars*.

Therefore, understanding sentence (15) requires the retrieval of the memory representation of that particular architect, and the relating of this new information to that representation.

The entities to which a message refers are called its *referents*. In ordinary discourse, different expressions may have identical referents. For example, in sequence (16), the expressions **lawyer** and **attorney** both refer to the same individual.

(16)   Anne consulted the lawyer. The attorney accepted the case.

Likewise, in sequence (17), **architect** and *he* both refer to the same person, and **Star Wars** and **it** refer to the movie STAR WARS.

(17)   The architect watched *Star Wars*. He enjoyed it.

Speakers may use different expressions to refer to the same entities for stylistic reasons.

On other occasions, identical expressions in a discourse may have different referents. In sequence (18), the first instance of **alligator** refers to the abstract concept ALLIGATOR, whereas the second one refers to a particular alligator (Haviland & Clark, 1974).

(18)   Ed wanted an alligator for his birthday. The alligator was his favorite present.

The arguments of a proposition typically denote specific entities. Accordingly, it is reasonable to represent **The architect watched Star Wars. He enjoyed it** as P1 (WATCH, ARCHITECT, STAR-WARS), P2, (ENJOY, ARCHITECT, STAR-WARS) (Kintsch, 1974). The arguments of P2, ARCHITECT and STAR-WARS, denote the referents of *he* and *it*, respectively. In view of the fact that people may know several architects, it would be even more precise to designate the architect in question by an arbitrary number, such as ARCHITECT$_{411}$ (Winograd, 1972). However, for most of the present purposes, this convention will not be necessary.

Network Representation of Propositions

Propositions are frequently depicted using network notations, such as those introduced in the field of artificial intelligence (Anderson, 1976, 1983; Norman & Rumelhart, 1975; Schank, 1972). The network consists of positions, or *nodes*, and links. Figure 2.2a illustrates the network that expresses the proposition underlying **The pilot painted the fence with**

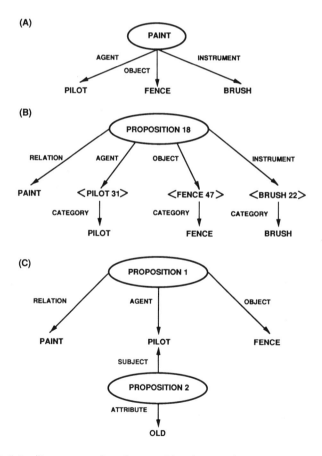

FIG. 2.2.   Some examples of propositional networks.

the brush, namely (PAINT, AGENT:PILOT, OBJECT:FENCE, INSTRU-MENT:BRUSH). The ellipse in Fig. 2.2a represents the predicate of the proposition, namely PAINT. The predicate is connected to its arguments by links, each of which bears an arrow showing its direction. Each link carries the label of a different semantic case.

Although Fig. 2.2a presents a convenient notation, it obscures the fact that propositional arguments are typically specific entities rather than general categories. A more precise propositional representation of **The pilot painted the fence with the brush** is shown in Fig. 2.2b. The arguments in Fig. 2.2b are specific instances of the concepts in question, such as PILOT$_{31}$ and FENCE$_{47}$. The fact that the entity, PILOT$_{31}$, is a member of the category, PILOT, is expressed by a link connecting PILOT$_{31}$ and PILOT. In this notation, the ellipse represents the proposition as a whole, and so is assigned an arbitrary proposition number. The ellipse is connected to its predicate by a *relation* link.

Networks can be used to identify the interrelations among two or more propositions. Figure 2.2c represents the two propositions underlying the sentence, **The old pilot painted the fence.** In graphs such as 2.2c, there is typically one ellipse for each proposition.

In some systems of network representation of propositions, concepts are routinely analyzed into their semantic elements (e.g., Norman & Rumelhart, 1975; Schank, 1972). Consider the semantic analysis that states that **to frighten** means CAUSE TO BE AFRAID (e.g., Katz & Fodor, 1963). According to this view, there are two propositions underlying **Mary frightened John:** P1 (CAUSE, MARY, P2) and P2 (AFRAID, JOHN). However, although people are capable of decomposing the meaning of the words they use, there is evidence that comprehension does not require the identification of semantic elements (Fodor, Garrett, Walker, & Parkes, 1980; Kintsch, 1974). It is likely that this is because the meanings of most common words form chunks of familiar information (Miller, 1956; Simon, 1974). Therefore, these meanings can be manipulated without analyzing them into their elements. As a result, we will treat the propositional representation of **Mary frightened John** as (FRIGHTEN, MARY, JOHN).

The propositional approach to language representation has emerged as the favored view because it has enjoyed considerable success in addressing many basic phenomena of language comprehension. The next section describes studies that indicate the merits of the propositional analysis of text.

PSYCHOLOGICAL REALITY OF PROPOSITIONS

Memory for Ideas

A scientific concept is considered to have psychological validity if it is reflected in people's behavior. Numerous tests of the psychological validity of the propositional representation of discourse have been performed. One hypothesis stated that if propositions are units of meaning, then sentence reading time will increase with the number of underlying propositions, holding sentence length constant (Kintsch & Keenan, 1973). For example, sentence (19) conveys three propositions, (LOUD, MUSIC), (PLEASE, MUSIC, CROWD), and (HAPPY, CROWD), whereas sentence (20) conveys only one proposition, (EAT, MOUSE, WATERMELON).

(19)   The loud music pleased the happy crowd.
(20)   What ate the watermelon was the mouse.

However, sentences (19) and (20) each have seven words. If encoding propositions is time-consuming, then people should take longer to read (19) than (20).

In an experiment designed to test this hypothesis, people read brief texts that were 16 or 17 words long, but which varied from four to nine underlying propositions (Kintsch & Keenan, 1973). Sentence reading time increased with the number of sentence propositions that the readers could recall. Figure 2.3 indicates that it took people about 1.5 seconds to encode each additional proposition. This outcome supports the psychological validity of the proposition.

A related study examined the impact of propositional arguments on reading time (Kintsch et al., 1975). Texts conveying equal numbers of propositions may vary in the total number of different arguments that they introduce. For example, sequences (21) and (22) each have two underlying propositions.

(21)   The customer ordered a salad. She ate it.
(22)   The customer ordered a salad. The waiter brought it.

However, (21) introduces only two arguments, CUSTOMER and SALAD, whereas (22) introduces three arguments, CUSTOMER, SALAD, and WAITER.

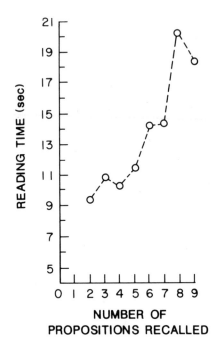

FIG. 2.3.   Mean reading time as a function of the number of text propositions recalled by participants. *Source:* Adapted from Kintsch & Keenan, 1973, Figure 1, p. 262. Adapted by permission.

It was predicted that, holding the number of propositions constant, reading time would increase with the number of different arguments. The reasoning was as follows: The appearance of each new argument requires the identification of a referent. This referent may either be previously familiar to the reader, or not. If the argument, CUSTOMER, of sentence (21), refers to a familiar entity, the reader must access it in memory. If CUSTOMER refers to an unfamiliar entity, then it is necessary to assign a new memory node to represent that entity. Because accessing old nodes and assigning new ones are time-consuming processes, it is likely that reading time will increase with the total number of different arguments.

In the experiment, people read passages that were equated for length and number of propositions, but that included FEW or MANY different arguments (Kintsch et al., 1975). As predicted, reading time was greater in the MANY condition. This was the case both for short and long texts, and both for simple (history) and complex (science) subject matters. These results supported the hypothesis that the number of different arguments in a text affects reading time (see also Graesser, Hoffman, & Clark, 1980; Haberlandt & Graesser, 1985).

The propositional representation of a message results in some arguments being grouped into the same propositions, and others being assigned to different propositions. For example, the representation of **The customer at the counter noticed the pie** is (LOCATION:AT, CUSTOMER, COUNTER), (NOTICE, CUSTOMER, PIE). PIE and CUSTOMER appear together in one proposition, but PIE and COUNTER do not. The psychological validity of this grouping was tested by Ratcliff and McKoon (1978: McKoon & Ratcliff, 1980a, 1980b).

In one experiment, people read sets of four sentences, followed by a series of test words (Ratcliff & McKoon, 1978). The readers indicated whether they recognized each test word: that is, whether each test word had appeared in the preceding set of four sentences. Recognition time was faster when a test word was immediately preceded by another test word from the same proposition, than by a word from a different proposition. Using the *pie* example, recognition time for *pie* was faster when it was preceded by *customer*, which appeared in the same proposition as *pie*, than when it was preceded by *counter*, which did not. In the terminology of chapter 1, this showed that concepts activate other concepts that appear in the same proposition. This outcome was not due to the physical distance of the words in the sentences nor to the similarity of the meanings of the words. These findings provided a measure of the organization of discourse propositions.

Organization of the Text Base

The propositions extracted from a message are organized by the understander into a hierarchical tree or graph, called the *text base* (Kintsch, 1974). According to this view, there is a single proposition at the top of the tree, and one or more propositions at lower levels. One method for constructing hierarchical text bases can be explained with reference to the text shown in Table 2.1 (Kintsch et al., 1975). First, the proposition that best captures the theme of the text is assigned to the top level of the tree. For the present text, (LOVE, GREEKS, ART) is the Level 1 proposition. A coherent text base is constructed by linking subsequent propositions to ones with which they share an argument. In particular, each successive proposition is assigned at *one level below the highest proposition with which it shares an argument.* For example, (BEAUTIFUL, ART) is assigned to Level 2 because it shares the argument ART with (LOVE, GREEKS, ART). Propositions P3 and P4 are likewise assigned to Level 2. Each step of indentation in Table 2.1 denotes the next level of the hierarchy.

Proposition P5, (WHEN, P3, P4), is of special interest. It is assigned to Level 3 not because it shares an argument with P3, but because P3 is embedded in it. That is, the predicate WHEN expresses a temporal (time) relation among two ideas. The two ideas in question are represented by

TABLE 2.1
Hierarchical Text Base of a Brief Passage

The Greeks loved beautiful art. When the Romans conquered the Greeks, they copied them, and thus, learned to create beautiful art.

P1	(LOVE, GREEKS, ART)
P2	(BEAUTIFUL, ART)
P3	(CONQUER, ROMANS, GREEKS)
P4	(COPY, ROMANS, GREEKS)
P5	(WHEN, P3, P4)
P6	(LEARN, ROMANS, P8)
P7	(CONSEQUENCE, P3, P6)
P8	(CREATE, ROMANS, P2)

Source: Adapted from Kintsch et al., 1975, Table 2, p. 198. Adapted by permission.

the propositions P3 (CONQUER, ROMANS, GREEKS) and P4 (COPY, ROMANS, GREEKS). Embedding, and the sharing of arguments, are two types of direct link between propositions. Finally, propositions P6, P7 and P8 are also Level 3 propositions, because each one shares an argument with a Level 2 proposition.

The proposal of a hierarchical text base generated several important hypotheses: First, it was predicted that higher level propositions in a text will be recalled better. This pattern, known as the *levels effect* has received consistent experimental support (e.g., Kintsch & Keenan, 1973; Kintsch et al., 1975; McKoon, 1977). Figure 2.4 shows the levels effect observed by Kintsch et al. (1975).

Second, in hierarchically organized text bases, it is possible to compute the distances between propositions. For example, in the text base shown in Table 2.1, P1 and P2 are separated by one link, and P1 and P5 are separated by two links. McKoon and Ratcliff (1980a) predicted that the smaller the distance between two propositions in the text base, the more they will activate one another. To test this hypothesis, they asked people to read passages of six sentences. After each one, the participants judged whether each of a series of test words came from the passage. Judgment time was less for words that were immediately preceded by words that were close in the text base, than for those preceded by distant text base words. This outcome, coupled with the levels effect, supports the psychological validity of an organized text base.

Conclusions

Propositional analysis is an effective technique for representing the ideas conveyed by discourse. Experimental studies support the hypothesis that propositions form a psychological unit of meaning. The propo-

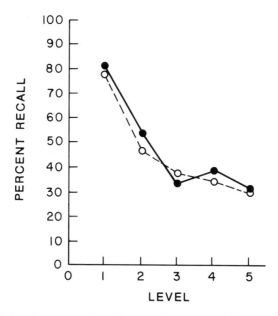

FIG. 2.4. The levels effect: Percent of text propositions recalled as a function of text base hierarchical level. *Source:* Kintsch et al., 1975, Figure 2, p. 203. Reprinted by permission.

sitions extracted from a message are integrated into an organized, hierarchical network called the text base.

It has been proposed that the text base of a message includes a second structured network called the *macrostructure* (Kintsch & van Dijk, 1978). The macrostructure consists of propositions that capture the main idea, or theme, of a message. For that reason, the processes of constructing the macrostructure will be examined in chapter 6, "Theme."

REPRESENTATION OF THE FORM OF DISCOURSE

Memory for Discourse Form Diminishes Rapidly

The next level of discourse representation that we consider is surface form. Every utterance and written sentence presents a string of words that conform precisely or loosely with the grammar of a natural language. It is conceivable that people store the *verbatim* (word-for-word) form of the sentences they comprehend. However, people exhibit poor memory for sentence form, particularly in contrast with their robust memory for sentence meaning (Bates, Masling, & Kintsch, 1978; Bransford & Franks, 1971; Sachs, 1967). As discussed earlier, after only 80 syllables of intervening text, people recognize about 80% of meaning changes in test sentences, but only 60% of form changes (Sachs, 1967). This outcome is consistent with the notion that people store the meaning of sentences, but not their form.

Several studies have provided evidence that people forget the surface form of sentences very shortly after comprehension has been completed. In one study, people listened to lengthy passages. They were occasionally interrupted and asked to recall the end of the current passage. Two different versions of one passage are illustrated by (23a) and (23b) (Jarvella, 1971).

> (23)   a.   The tone of the document was threatening. *Having failed to disprove the charges,* Taylor was later fired by the president.
> b.   The document had also blamed him for *having failed to disprove the charges.* Taylor later was fired by the president.

The last 13 words in (23a) and (23b) are identical. However, the italicized section of (23a) occurs in the final sentence of its passage, whereas the same words in (23b) appear in the second-to-last sentence. During testing, people exhibited verbatim recall of the italicized section of (23a) 54% of the time, as compared with only 21% for (23b). This suggests that the form of a sentence is forgotten when one proceeds to the following sentence.

In a comparable study (Caplan, 1972), people read or listened to sentences, and, after each one, decided whether or not a test word had occurred in the sentence. Test words, such as *snow,* occurred either before the last *major clause boundary* (identified by the slash "/"), as in (24), or after it, as in (25).

> (24)   Although we still have not had any snow,/storms are expected.
> (25)   Because the weather is cold and damp,/snow storms are expected.

A *clause* is a group of words with its own subject and predicate that appears in a larger sentence (Lyons, 1968, p. 171).

People took more time to recognize test words that appeared before the last major clause boundary than those appearing after it. This outcome was not affected by whether people read or listened to the sentences, nor by whether the last major clause boundary had occurred three, four, or five words before the end of the sentence. These findings, coupled with the results of Jarvella (1971), indicate that the words of the current sentence are retained in working memory. Once the sentence has been analyzed, the representation of sentence form is deleted, in order that the next sentence may be considered.

In conclusion, there is extensive evidence that people quickly forget the form of the sentences they understand (see also Clark & Sengul, 1979; Gernsbacher, 1985; Jarvella, 1979; McKoon, 1977; McKoon & Keenan, 1974). Furthermore, the phenomenon of surface information loss is not restricted to sentences. For example, Gernsbacher (1985) reported that people quickly forget the left-right orientation of pictures that convey a story.

Some Features of Discourse Form are Remembered

Although memory for the surface form of messages diminishes rapidly, there is evidence that this information is not lost completely. Even those procedures that reflect the predominance of discourse meaning over form also indicate that some details of surface form are remembered. For example, detecting 60% of form changes after 80 and 160 syllables of intervening material (Sachs, 1967) distinctly exceeds the chance level of 50% (see also Reynolds & Flagg, 1976; Soli & Balch, 1976).

In some studies of memory for discourse form, experimental sentences have been embedded in ordinary messages (Bates et al., 1978; Bates, Kintsch, Fletcher, & Giuliani, 1980; Keenan, MacWhinney, & Mayhew, 1977; Kintsch & Bates, 1977). In one study, for example, students heard experimental sentences, such as **Freud was working with Joseph Breuer, studying the method of free association,** in a classroom lecture (Kintsch & Bates, 1977). The students did not know that they were participating in an experiment. Two days later, a rated recognition task was administered. For each experimental sentence, the students received either an identical, paraphrase, or meaning-change test item, illustrated by (26a), (26b), and (26c), respectively.

(26) a. Freud was working with Joseph Breuer, studying the method of free association. (identical)
b. Freud learned the method of free association from Joseph Breuer. (paraphrase)
c. Freud spent time with Jean Charcot studying hypnosis as a clinical method. (meaning-change)

The results of this and other similar studies are that, even 1 to 5 days after a message is encountered, identical test sentences receive higher recognition ratings than their paraphrases. This reveals that people remember some details of sentence form. In contrast, items that change the meaning of the original are usually rejected, reflecting people's robust memory for sentence meaning. Memory for surface form is particularly pronounced for statements that are conspicuous in a message, such as jokes in a classroom lecture (Kintsch & Bates, 1977), and statements that reflect the relationship between the speaker and the listeners (Keenan et al., 1977).

There are systematic differences in the ability to remember the surface form of different language constructions. In one study, a comparison was made of verbatim memory for different referring expressions, such as names versus pronouns (e.g., *Bill* versus *he*), and names versus roles (e.g., *Ada* versus *his wife*) (Bates et al., 1978). Several results are notable. First, consistent with other studies of memory for discourse form, people reliably selected the original sentence over its paraphrase for all language functions examined. Second, verbatim memory was always better for the most specific form. That is, *his wife* was better than *Ada*, which in turn was better than *her*. This indicates that certain expressions and constructions may have an inherent advantage in being remembered verbatim.

Representation of Discourse Form: Grammatical, Lexical, and Order Information

What features of discourse form do people retain? People might store the precise words that are encountered in a message, the grammatical structure of the sentences, or information about the order of the words. In fact, there is evidence that all of these factors contribute to people's ability to remember surface form.

People's memory for the grammatical construction of a sentence was examined by Anderson (1974a). People studied sentences in the active and passive voice, and then had to judge the truth of test sentences in the same or opposite voice. The test occurred either immediately after study or about 2 minutes later. For example, after studying the active sentence, **The sailor protected the painter,** the participant could receive an identical test sentence, or its passive, **The painter was protected by the sailor.** Both of these sentences were true. Other test sentences, such as **The sailor was protected by the painter,** were false.

The results revealed that the identical test sentences were judged faster than sentences in the other voice, both in immediate and delayed testing, although the difference was smaller in the delayed condition (Anderson, 1974a). In a comparable study, it was found that, 6 minutes after study, correct judgments about test sentences in the same voice were about one-fifth of a second faster than for the opposite voice (Anderson & Paulson, 1977). Figure 2.5 illustrates that the judgment-

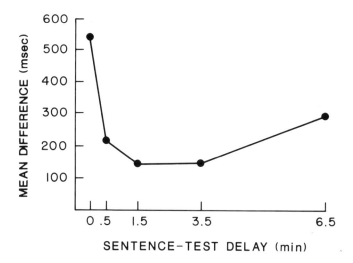

SENTENCE-TEST DELAY (min)

FIG. 2.5.   Mean judgment-time difference between true sentences that matched study sentences and those that did not, plotted as a function of the delay between study and test. *Source:* Adapted from Anderson & Paulson, 1977, Figure 3, p. 445. Adapted by permission.

time advantage of identical sentences declines systematically from immediate testing to testing after a 6.5-minute delay. However, even after 6.5 minutes, identical sentences are still judged about ¼ second faster than are ones in the opposite voice.

People have likewise been shown to retain information about the particular words that appear in a message. In one study, people studied experimental sentences and then had to distinguish identical test sentences from ones that substituted synonyms of the original wording. For example, **scared** was replaced by **frightened,** and **hid** by **concealed.** The identical test sentences received higher recognition ratings than synonym test sentences (Hayes-Roth & Hayes-Roth, 1977). This may indicate that people remember the particular string of words of a message. Alternatively, this outcome may be a result of the fact that the predicates and arguments of propositions correspond closely to words. For example, the proposition underlying **Mary frightened John** is (FRIGHTEN, MARY, JOHN). Having encoded this proposition, one might be more likely to accept **Mary frightened John** than **Mary scared John** in a recognition test.

Finally, there is evidence that people retain word-order information (see Anderson, 1983, for a review). In one study, people read stories that described sets of events. The stories presented these events in their chronological order, as illustrated by sentence (27a), or as a flashback, as illustrated by (27b) (Baker, 1978).

(27) a. Dan dropped a filing cabinet and then broke a lamp.
      b. Before Dan broke a lamp he dropped a filing cabinet.

After reading, the subjects had to judge whether pairs of test events, such as *dropped cabinet—broke lamp*, matched the chronological order of events conveyed by the story. The answer for this test item is *true* in the context both of (27a) and (27b). However, people needed more time to judge test items in relation to flashback descriptions than chronological ones. This shows that, in addition to extracting the meaning of the story, people retain information about its superficial order.

Reconstruction and Surface Memory

Which of sentences (28) and (29) seems more natural to you?

(28) On the first day of the baseball season, the mayor threw out the first ball.
(29) On the first day of the baseball season, the mayor threw the first ball out.

Suppose that a group of experimental subjects heard a broadcast of a baseball game that included sentence (28). Imagine further that, in a subsequent memory test, these individuals gave a higher recognition rating to alternative (28) than (29). One might be inclined to interpret this outcome as evidence for memory for surface form. However, there is an alternative explanation for such a result. If people find the phrase **The mayor threw out the first ball** more natural than **The mayor threw the first ball out,** then they might simply *assume* that the broadcast included (28) rather than (29).

In fact, people do not express equal preferences for all surface expressions of an idea. For example, people prefer the sentence, **The hi-fi fanatic turned up the volume,** over **The hi-fi fanatic turned the volume up;** and **The magician touched the girl and she disappeared** over **The magician touched the girl and the girl disappeared** (Bock & Brewer, 1974; see also Bates et al., 1978). Such preferences permit people to guess, or *reconstruct*, the original form of a message.

Because of this, researchers must distinguish between evidence for surface memory and evidence for reconstructive preferences. Bates has used two techniques to address this problem. In one study, the recognition preferences of people who had heard the dialogue of a soap opera were compared with those of others who had not heard the dialogue at all. The latter group simply had to guess which of the alternatives was more likely to appear in a soap opera (Bates et al., 1978). In another study, two different versions of the stimulus discourse used the alternative surface forms under investigation (Bates et al., 1980). The results of these studies were clear: People exhibit a distinct ability to remember some of the surface details of a discourse. This outcome cannot be completely attributed to reconstructive preferences.

To briefly summarize, memory for discourse form diminishes rapidly after the discourse has been processed. However, people retain some of the surface features of messages. This is due to the fact that some details of the grammar, choice of words, and order of words is remembered. Above-chance memory for discourse form cannot be completely attributed to people's reconstructive preferences.

REPRESENTATION OF SITUATION MODELS

To achieve a complete grasp of the communicative intentions of a speaker, the understander must construct a mental representation of the situation to which the speaker is referring. Such representations, alternately known as *situation, cognitive,* and *mental* models (Johnson-Laird, 1980, 1983; van Dijk & Kintsch, 1983), form a level of discourse representation distinct from surface form and from the text base. A discourse can describe any topic or situation. Therefore, the range of situations models resulting from discourse understanding is unlimited. They include the representation of people, events, episodes, the spatial arrangement of objects and locations, the steps of performing a task, and of problems to be solved.

Situation models integrate discourse ideas with pertinent general knowledge. For example, a story set in an airport will result in the construction of a situation model that combines the central events of the story with one's scriptal knowledge of airports. Representing situation models during comprehension is a dynamic process. The model guides the interpretation of each successive sentence or utterance in the discourse. Those sentences, in turn, continually update the model (van Dijk & Kintsch, 1983).

In contrast with the situation model, the text base representation captures the organization of the ideas directly expressed by the message. The situation model, on the other hand, may or may not refer to the particular propositions of the message. Indeed, situation models may be extracted from nonverbal stimuli, such as pictures, and do not depend on the presentation of a verbal message at all (Schmalhofer & Glavanov, 1986).

An example helps to illustrate the distinction between the situation model and the text base. In one study, people read messages that ordered familiar concepts and nonsense syllables on dimensions such as size (Potts & Peterson, 1985). For example, one sequence of sentences said, **A JAL is larger than a TOC. A TOC is larger than a pony. A beaver is larger than a CAZ.** The propositions of the text base of this message are (LARGER-THAN, JAL, TOC), (LARGER-THAN, TOC, PONY), and (LARGER-THAN, BEAVER, CAZ.). A situation model that can be extracted from this message represents the relative size of the concepts in question. Most importantly, by using one's knowledge that ponies are larger than beavers, a complete ordering can be constructed: namely, JAL > TOC > PONY > BEAVER > CAZ. This model does not indicate which comparisons were expressed in the message. It is constructed by integrating text ideas and general knowledge.

Representing and Remembering Situations

To show that situation models are extracted from discourse, it is necessary to demonstrate that discourse retrieval cannot be explained simply in terms of people's memory for the surface form and propositional content of a message. Because many messages identify the spatial arrangement of objects, the representation of spatial situations has received considerable attention (e.g., Bransford, Barclay, & Franks, 1972; Ehrlich & Johnson-Laird, 1982; Mani & Johnson-Laird, 1982). For example, in the study of Bransford et al. (1972), people heard lists of sentences including items such as (30) or (31).

(30)   Three turtles rested on a floating log, and a fish swam beneath them.

(31)   Three turtles rested beside a floating log, and a fish swam beneath them.

In a subsequent test, the readers of (30) frequently incorrectly recognized the identical sentence with the word them replaced by it; that is, **Three turtles rested on a floating log, and a fish swam beneath IT.** In contrast, the readers of (31) seldom reported recognizing **Three turtles rested beside a floating log, and a fish swam beneath IT.** One explanation of this outcome is that the understander constructs a model of the spatial situation, perhaps in the form of a visual image. For example, the model derived from (30) represents the turtles on top of the log, and the log over the fish. Changing the word **them** to **it** in (30) yields a sentence that is consistent with the model, because when the fish swims beneath it (the log), it also swims beneath the turtles, as stated in (30). As a result, it is recognized. In contrast, **Three turtles rested beside a**

floating log, and a fish swam beneath it is not consistent with the situation model of (31), and therefore it is not recognized.

This outcome cannot be explained in terms of people's memory for surface form, because both sentences (30) and (31) differed from their corresponding test sentences in exactly the same way: that is, by the replacement of **them** by **it.** Likewise, both recognition-test sentences introduced the same propositional change; that is, the replacement of the argument TURTLES by LOG in the proposition, (BENEATH, FISH, TURTLES). If this propositional change were sufficient to permit people to reject the altered form of (31), then they should likewise reject the changed form of (30).

The construction of spatial situation models also contributes to narrative understanding. Narratives frequently focus on the activities of a main character, or *protagonist*. Therefore, narrative understanding may depend on tracing the movements of the protagonist through the story realm. To examine this issue, Morrow, Greenspan, and Bower (1987) asked people to memorize the layout of a building that was the setting for a story. The subjects learned the spatial arrangement of the rooms, and memorized four objects that appeared in each room. Subsequently, the subjects read a story that took place in this setting. Crucial sentences, such as (32) and (33), described the protagonist moving from one room to another.

(32)   Wilbur walked from the library into the reception room.

(33)   Wilbur walked into the reception room from the library.

In both (32) and (33), the protagonist moves from the *source room*, the library, to the *goal room*, the reception room. It was predicted that, because the current location of the protagonist is the focus of the reader's attention, it should affect the accessibility of story information. To test this hypothesis, sentences such as (32) and (33) were followed by test probes presenting pairs of objects, such as **lamp clock.** The subject's task was to judge whether or not the two objects were in the same room, based on their memorized list. Decision time was less if the two objects were in the goal room than the source room, supporting the contention that the current location of the protagonist is the focus of attention. This was true whether the goal room had been mentioned most recently, as in (32), or not, as in (33). This outcome reflects the reader's construction and use of a situation model that combines spatial information with narrative functions.

Spatial information is only one of many types of information that contribute to situation models. Researchers have also studied situation models that order objects along a dimension (Potts, 1972; Potts & Peterson, 1985), that represent a problem or puzzle to be solved (Hayes & Simon, 1974; Kintsch & Greeno, 1985; van Dijk & Kintsch, 1983), and that organize the directions for performing certain actions (Baggett, 1986; Dixon, 1982). These studies support the proposal that people combine text knowledge and general knowledge to form representations of the situations described by discourse.

Representation of Conversational Situations

> (Bliss) walked into the pilot room and said, "There you are."
> Trevize looked up and said, "No need for surprise. We could scarcely have left the ship, and a thirty-second search would be bound to uncover us inside the ship, even if you couldn't detect our presence mentally."
> Bliss said, "The expression was purely a form of greeting and not meant to be taken literally, as you well know." (Asimov, 1986, p. 175)

Every utterance that a speaker makes is intended to serve a particular function, called its *speech act* or *illocutionary act* (Austin, 1962). The speech act of an utterance can be separated from its propositional content. Consider, for example, sentences (34), (35), and (36).

(34)   The wind-chill factor is −40 degrees today.
(35)   The *Psychological Abstracts* lists many articles about your topic.
(36)   There will be a Student Council meeting on Thursday.

At one level, sentences (34), (35), and (36) each present simple assertions. In the appropriate contexts, however, sentence (34) functions as a warning, sentence (35) as advice, and sentence (36) as an announcement. Other sentences may serve functions such as telling, hinting, contradicting, misleading, commanding, vowing, and offering. For a conversation to succeed, the listener must correctly identify the speech act of every utterance that is encountered. In so doing, the listener develops a cognitive model of the goals and intentions of the speaker (Clark, 1982; Grice, 1957; Strawson, 1964).

Speech act theorists have addressed the problem of how people determine one another's communicative intentions. One advance in this field has been the organization of speech acts into the categories of representative, directive, commisive, expressive, and declaration (Searle, 1975). The category of *representatives* refers to speech acts of informing, such as telling, hinting, advising, warning, and announcing. By uttering a *directive*, the speaker attempts to get the listener to do something. This can be accomplished by requesting, demanding, and ordering. Likewise, by the directive of asking, the speaker urges the listener to provide certain information. *Commissives*, such as promising, offering, and pledging, oblige a speaker to perform a certain action at a later time. *Expressive* speech acts, such as **I'm confused,** or **That annoys me,** identify the state of mind of the speaker. Finally, *declarations* are those statements, which by their very utterance, change a state of affairs. When a public official says, **May the Games begin,** then the Games have officially started.

The form of an utterance may provide information about its speech act. For example, in the category of directives, one frequently uses the interrogative form to convey asking, and the imperative form for demanding and ordering. Furthermore, one can expand any utterance to make its speech act explicit. That is, by stating, **I warn you that the wind-chill factor is −40 degrees today,** the speaker explicitly identifies the speech act of the utterance as a warning. More often, however, this is not done: Rather, speakers usually assume that their listeners can infer the speech act of an utterance. How this is accomplished is a central problem of speech act theory.

Determining the speech act of an utterance is seriously complicated by the fact that grammatical constructions that are typically associated with one category of speech act may be used to convey others. For example, sentences (37a), (37b), and (37c) have the superficial forms of requesting, asking, and telling, respectively.

(37) a   Please get me a drink.
      b. Can you get me a drink?
      c. I'm thirsty.

In the appropriate contexts, however, (37b) and (37c) might, like (37a), function as requests.

How then is a listener able to determine the speech act intended by the speaker? The *principle of cooperation* between speaker and listener provides the framework for a solution to this problem (Grice, 1975). According to this view, cooperative speakers and listeners comply with four *conversational maxims*. The *maxim of quantity* states that the speaker should make each contribution neither less nor more informative than required. According to the *maxim of quality*, the speaker should make only true utterances. The *maxim of manner* pertains to how an idea should be expressed: The speaker should be brief and orderly, and should avoid obscurity and ambiguity. Finally, the *maxim of relation* is succinctly summarized by Grice (1975). It states, "Be relevant."

Successful communication requires that the speaker and listener embrace the cooperative principle. For example, violations of the maxim of quality result in false utterances, and are clearly uncooperative. The role of the other maxims is more subtle, but no less important. Consider sequence (38):

(38)   a.   Would you like a slice of pie for dessert?
       b.   I had a milkshake this afternoon.

By uttering (38a), the speaker makes the speech act of *asking*. Reply (38b) does not present a direct *yes* or *no* answer. However, according to the maxim of relation, (38b) must be relevant to the conversation. The speaker of (38a) might accordingly deduce that the speaker of (38b) is refusing the offer because she recently had eaten another dessert.

Conversely, communication breaks down when one participant purposely violates the cooperative principle. Consider sequence (39) from *Alice in Wonderland*.

(39)   King: Remove your hat!
       Mad Hatter: It isn't mine. (Carroll, 1960, p. 99)

Clearly, the thrust of the King's command was that the Hatter remove the hat that was on his head, regardless of who owned the hat. The Mad Hatter's reply is in violation of the maxim of relation.

To summarize, successful communication requires that the listener construct a situation model of the speaker's goals and intentions. The grammatical form of utterances, and knowledge of the usual form of a dialogue (e.g., Malt, 1985), guide the identification of speech acts. Frequently, however, the listener must deduce the intended speech act from the context, in the form of the mutual knowledge of the speaker and listener (Clark & Marshall, 1981; Sperber & Wilson, 1986).

Distinguishing Among Form, Text Base, and Situation Representations

An important test of the hypothesis that people construct multi-level representations of discourse is to show that phenomena of comprehension and retrieval cannot be accounted for with reference to only one level. Two principles capture the experimental approaches to this problem:

Principle 1. Sentence recognition should vary with the number of representations with which a test sentence is consistent. For example, recognition should be highest for test sentences consistent with all three of the form, text base, and situation representations.

Principle 2. It should be possible to identify understander and discourse factors that influence some of the levels but not others.

The approach expressed by Principle 1 is illustrated by a study in which people were asked to read brief computer-programming manuals, and then to make judgments about test items, such as the following (Schmalhofer & Galvanov, 1986):

(40)   PSY100 is a legal atom, that concludes with a number. (original)
(41)   PSY100 is a legal atom, that concludes with a numeral. (paraphrased)
(42)   PSY100 is a legal atom, that begins with a letter. (meaning-changed)
(43)   PSY.100 is a legal atom, that contains a dot. (correctness-changed)

Sentences (40) to (43) were consistent with three, two, one, and zero levels of representation, respectively. That is, sentence (40), which was identical to a sentence in the text, was consistent with the form, text base, and situation representations. Sentence (41) paraphrased an original sentence, and so was consistent with the text base and situation representations, but inconsistent with the form representation. Sentence (42) was consistent only with the situation model, and sentence (43) was consistent with none of the representations. As predicted, recognition accuracy increased systematically with the number of consistent levels: That is, it was highest for original test items and lowest for correctness-changed ones. Notice that, of course, no test item can be simultaneously consistent with the form representation and inconsistent with the situation model.

Principle 2 states that, if the three levels of discourse representation are qualitatively different, then certain understander and discourse variables ought to affect some of the representations without affecting all of them. For example, understanders differ from one another in their verbal ability, age, knowledge about the topic, and their reading goals. The effect of reading goals on the three representational levels was examined by Schmalhofer and Glavanov (1986) in their study of computer manual comprehension. One group read the manual with the goal of *summarizing* it, and another set out to *learn* the material in order to be able to write and verify computer statements. It was reasoned that an accurate summary requires a clear text base, whereas evaluating computer statements depends on a situation model that captures the main features of the computer language. Recognition judgment about sentences such as (40)–(43), examined earlier, bore this out: The *learners'* situation model affected their judgments more than either of their other two representations, whereas the *summarizers'* text base representation was about as influential as their situation model. This shows that the goals of the reader have qualitatively different effects on the form, text base, and situation representations.

Discourse variables also have differential effects on the three levels of representation. In one study, people read one of two descriptions of a town (Perrig & Kintsch, 1985). One version described a *route* for driving through the town, mentioning several landmarks. It included sentences like, **On your left, just after you cross the river, you see a gas station.** The second version identified the same landmarks in the form of a *survey*, with sentences such as **North of the highway just east of the river is a gas station.** It was predicted that understanding the *route* text would result in a "linear" situation model, emphasizing a sequence of places (e.g., Potts, 1972), whereas understanding the survey text would lead to the construction of a spatial model (e.g., Bransford et al., 1972).

Tests of surface, text base, and situation representation revealed different patterns of results. First, the surface memory performance of the route and survey groups were equivalent. Second, in free recall, the route group recalled more propositions than the survey group, indicative of a better-formed text base. This was attributed to the superior coherence of the route text. Finally, each group was better at verifying new *inference* statements written in the style that they had read. Because inference verification was proposed to be based on the situation representation, this outcome suggests that texts with the same content but different style (i.e., route vs. survey) can result in the construction of quite different situation models. Furthermore, the results show that the information in one representation level may be relatively useless for certain purposes. For example, neither the verbatim nor text base representations of the route text readers helped them to make judgments of relative spatial position.

In conclusion, there is growing evidence that a complete treatment of language understanding must include reference to the surface, text base, and situation representations of discourse. The multi-level representation of discourse is an important theme of this book. The remaining chapters provide many examples of how situation models are extracted from messages, and how the developing model in turn influences the interpretation of discourse.

SUMMARY

Understanding discourse results in several levels of representation, including the idea content and form of the discourse, and the situation to which it refers. Discourse content can be analyzed into a set of meaning units called *propositions*. Each proposition consists of a relation, or *predicate*, plus one or more arguments. For example, underlying the sentence, **The tailor cut the cloth with the scissors** is the proposition, (CUT, AGENT:TAILOR, OBJECT:CLOTH, INSTRUMENT:SCISSORS). The predicate of this proposition is CUT, and the arguments are TAILOR, CLOTH, and SCISSORS. The labels AGENT, OBJECT, and INSTRUMENT are *cases* that identify the semantic relations between an argument and its predicate. The predicate and arguments *refer* to particular entities in the world. For example, TAILOR refers to the particular tailor who cut the cloth.

The propositions extracted from a message are integrated by the understander into a hierarchical network called the *text base*. Higher propositions in the hierarchy are typically recalled better, a phenomenon called the *levels effect*. Active propositions send activation to other propositions that are nearby in the network.

Memory for the surface form of a message is weaker than memory for content. Memory for form declines dramatically immediately after comprehension, but is not entirely lost. Rather, people retain some information about the grammatical constructions, the choice of words, and the order of presentation used by a message. Memory for the form of conspicuous sentences in a message, such as jokes in a lecture, is particularly good. Memory for the form of a message cannot be entirely attributed to people's reconstructive guesses about the preferred form of the message.

Successful communication depends on the ability of the understander to extract a model of the situation that a message describes. Messages can refer to any situation, such as the spatial arrangement of objects, the elements of a problem to be solved, and the method for assembling a bookcase. Situation models are constructed by integrating the propositional content of a message with existing world knowledge.

To construct a model of the situation to which a conversation refers, the listener must determine the goals and intentions of the speaker. This is accomplished by identifying the *speech acts* of the utterances of the speaker, such as warning, ordering, promising, complaining, and declaring. Because speech acts are frequently expressed in an indirect fashion, speaker and listener must behave cooperatively with one another: They must be truthful, succinct, clear, and relevant.

3

Syntax and Parsing Processes

In order to understand a sentence, it is necessary to analyze it into its grammatical elements, called *constituents*. This analysis is known as *parsing*. Accomplishing this task requires knowledge of the grammar of one's native language. The fact that people are routinely in possession of this knowledge is reflected by their ability to discriminate between grammatical and ungrammatical sentences. In this regard, there is no doubt that (1a) is an acceptable English sentence, but (1b) is not.

(1) a. Wild beasts frighten little children.
     b. *Beasts children frighten wild little.

Likewise, (2a) and (2b) are acceptable ways of expressing Jane's thoughts about the crop, but (2c) is not.

(2) a. Jane thought the crop was not healthy.
     b. Jane did not think the crop was healthy.
     c. *Jane thought not the crop was healthy.

People's grammatical skills also permit them to recognize that the sentence, **Colorless green ideas sleep furiously,** complies with the rules of English, even though it is anomalous (Chomsky, 1957).

The ability to judge the grammaticality of a sentence reflects people's knowledge of the ideal form of their language, knowledge that is referred to as *linguistic competence* (Chomsky, 1957). Linguistic competence does not enable people to articulate the grammatical rules of their native tongue. Only instruction in linguistics provides this capability. There-fore, one's intuitive linguistic knowledge is procedural in nature (see chapter 1).

People's utterances, their language *performance* (Chomsky, 1957), frequently deviate from the ideal grammatical form. Consider the follow-ing fragment from the Watergate transcripts:

> President Nixon: Let me say with regard to Colson—and you can say that I'm way ahead of them on that—I've got the message on that and that he feels that Dean—but believe me I've been thinking about that all day yesterday—whether Dean should be given immunity. *(Watergate Tran-scripts, 1974).*

This sequence jumbles several streams of thought. For example, the first, third, and fifth portions express certain ideas about Colson. Yet, in spite of its grammatical violations, President Nixon's statement is neither very uncommon in its nature, nor is it completely incomprehen-sible.

The goal of the present chapter is to examine the psychology of parsing. The first section examines a procedure designed to identify the constituents of a sentence, called *immediate constituent analysis*. The psychological reality of the sentence constituent is also considered. The second section presents the syntactic and semantic factors that guide the parsing process. The third section describes general principles of parsing. In the final section, two distinct analyses of parsing, the inter-active and the modular, will be compared.

SYNTAX AND IMMEDIATE CONSTITUENT ANALYSIS

Syntactic Rules

A primary goal of linguistics is to specify the rules governing the form, or syntax, of sentences. Rules (3a)-(3c) identify the relations among several sentence constituents:

(3) a. S → NP VP
     b. NP → det Adj N
     c. VP → V NP

Each rule *rewrites* a sentence constituent into other constituents. A sentence (S) is analyzed to a noun phrase (NP) plus a verb phrase (VP). Noun phrases are rewritten as a determiner (det), an adjective (Adj), and a noun (N). Verb phrases are rewritten as a verb (V) and a noun phrase. The application of these rules *generates* grammatical English sentences.

Immediate constituent analysis is a linguistic technique that captures the hierarchical organization of sentences that is implicit in rules such as (3a)-(3c) (Bloomfield, 1933). Using this technique, the sentence is subdivided into its major parts, a noun phrase and a verb phrase. Each subpart is repeatedly subdivided until the level of individual words, or *terminal nodes*, has been reached. For example, Fig. 3.1 shows the analysis of the sentence, **The prince surprised the dragon.**

Figure 3.1 identifies several types of linguistic units. The top level of the tree represents the entire sentence. The second level shows the noun phrase and verb phrase constituents. At the third level, the phrases are decomposed into parts of speech, such as noun, verb, and adjective. Finally, Fig. 3.1 shows the particular words that appeared in the sentence. The complete tree is called the *phrase marker* of the sentence.

One feature of immediate constituent analysis is that it identifies the location of the boundaries between the constituents. The main constituent boundary of **The prince surprised the dragon** occurs between the noun phrase and the verb phrase, immediately after **prince.** Later, we will consider the role of major constituent boundaries in comprehension.

Immediate constituent analysis addresses a variety of linguistic phenomena. For example, it distinguishes among the interpretations of syntactically ambiguous sentences. The sentence, **They are fighting dragons** alternately means that those people are fighting some dragons, or those dragons are the fighting kind. This distinction is clearly drawn in the two immediate constituent analyses shown in Fig. 3.2. In the FIGHTING AGAINST DRAGONS interpretation, **fighting** is the main verb (Fig. 3.2a), and in the TYPE OF DRAGONS interpretation, *fighting* functions as an adjective (Fig. 3.2b).

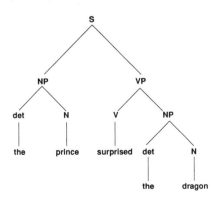

FIG. 3.1. Immediate constituent analysis of **The prince surprised the dragon.**

(A)

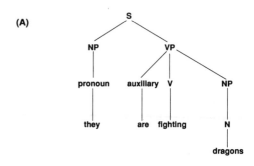

(B)

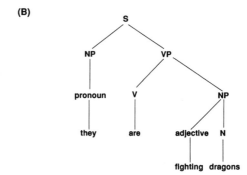

FIG. 3.2. Immediate constituent analyses of the alternative interpretations of **They are fighting dragons.**

Rules (3a)–(3c) do not illustrate some of the features of a complete syntax of a natural language. First, some constituents are optional. For example, the element, Adjective, in rule (3b) is optional. In fact, neither noun phrase of **The prince surprised the dragon** includes an adjective. Second, some constituents may occur several times. For example, a noun phrase can include several adjectives, as in **the large, purple, ugly dragon.**

Third, some syntactic rules are *recursive*: That is, they reintroduce higher level constituents. For example, the rule, NP → det N (S), reintroduces an optional sentence. This rule is needed for the parsing of the noun phrase, **the dragon that ate Chicago.** The relative clause of this phrase, **that ate Chicago,** stands for the sentence, **The dragon ate Chicago.** Recursive rules account for the infinity of possible sentences in any natural language. Fourth, transformational rules (Chomsky, 1957, 1965) transform the sentences generated by rules such as (3a)–(3c) into closely related forms, including passives, questions, and negatives.

Psychological Reality of Sentence Constituents

Numerous studies have addressed the question of whether the sentence constituent, a linguistic concept, functions as a psychological unit. This section considers the nature of the linguistic units that are retained in working memory, and the role of the sentence constituent in the perception of sentences. Then, the contribution of sentence constituents to the construction of propositions is examined.

Retention of Sentence Constituents in Working Memory. If sentence constituents function as psychological units, then sentence information ought to be accumulated in working memory in sets corresponding to constituents. Consider, for example, the sentence, **Tom was upset because he lost his job.** On the basis of this sentence, people should store words in groups such as **because he lost his job** rather than **was upset because he.** If the constituent indeed forms the unit of working memory analysis, it is also necessary to ask whether this analysis examines constituent units corresponding to words, phrases, clauses, or entire sentences.

Several studies of people's memory for sentence form, examined in chapter 2, bear on this issue. Recall, for example, the experiment of Caplan (1972). The participants read or heard sentences, and had to make a recognition judgment about a test word after each one. For example, the test word *freezing* followed both (4) and (5).

(4) Unless the temperature drops below *freezing*, rain will fall.
(5) Unless the storm center moves farther north, *freezing* rain will fall.

Recognition time was longer for *freezing* when it appeared before the last major clause boundary, as in (4), than when it followed the boundary, as in (5). This outcome suggests that sentence information is accumulated in working memory in constituents corresponding to the major clause. After the clause has been analyzed, it is deleted from working memory (see also Clark & Sengul, 1979; Jarvella, 1971).

Constituents as Perceptual Units of the Sentence. A second hypothesis states that the constituent is the *perceptual unit* of the sentence. This hypothesis was tested by presenting people with tape-recorded sentences, upon which were superimposed audible clicks (e.g., Fodor & Bever, 1965; Garrett, Bever, & Fodor, 1966). The subjects' task was to indicate where, in the sentence, the click had occurred. The reasoning was that, if the sentence constituent functions as a perceptual unit, it should be resistant to interruption by a click. As a result, people should report that the clicks occur closer to nearby constituent boundaries than is accurate.

The materials of the click studies are illustrated by sentences (6) and

(7), in which the parentheses designate major constituent boundaries: that is, boundaries between the clauses (Garrett et al., 1966).

(6) (In order to catch his train) *(George drove furiously to the station).*

(7) (The reporters assigned to George) *(drove furiously to the station).*

The clicks for (6) and (7) coincided either with *George* or *drove.* As predicted, people believed that the clicks had occurred systematically closer to the clause boundary in both versions of the sentence than was accurate. The result was not due to differences in intonation, because Garrett et al. spliced the same acoustic segment, **George drove furiously to the station,** into both tapes.

One shortcoming of these studies is that click placement is not an on-line measure: that is, measurement takes place after rather than during comprehension (see chapter 1). Therefore, the results may reflect people's judgments about sentence structure, rather than their perception of sentences. This argument is supported by the finding that, even when the test sentence includes no click at all (a *catch trial*), people who are listening for faint clicks claim to hear them near clause boundaries (Ladefoged, 1967; Reber & Anderson, 1970). However, even the catch trial findings indicate that people possess an intuitive knowledge of the location of constituent boundaries. The general convergence of the working memory and click investigations suggest that sentence constituents function as psychological units (see also Graf & Torrey, 1966).

Deriving Propositions From Sentence Constituents. The rapid deletion of sentence constituents from working memory requires that the understander rapidly identify the propositional content of each constituent. An outline of the processing of sentences was presented by Clark and Clark (1977, p. 49). First, the listener stores a phonological representation of the current sentence in working memory. Second, parsing processes are applied to this representation, resulting in the identification of the constituents of the sentence. Third, one or more propositions are extracted from the current constituent. For example, the second major constituent of **The reporters assigned to George drove furiously to the station** is the verb phrase, **drove furiously to the station.** From this constituent, the listener constructs the following propositions:

P1 (DRIVE, REPORTERS)
P2 (FURIOUSLY, P1)
P3 (LOCATION:TO, P1, STATION)

At the fourth stage of processing, the phonological representation is deleted from working memory to make room for the next sentence. This results in a marked reduction of memory for the surface form of the sentence. The propositions residing in working memory are, with some degree of probability, transferred to long-term memory (Kintsch & van Dijk, 1978).

Certain clause constructions convey complete propositions more clearly than others. One illustration is the tensed verb. A tensed verb, such as **revised,** must appear with its object. This is illustrated by the fact that sentence (8) is ungrammatical.

(8) *That John revised was acceptable.

When a tensed verb appears in a sentence such as **John revised the letter,** the understander is therefore likely to be able to extract a complete proposition.

In contrast, the nominalization, **revision,** does not require an object, as illustrated by the grammatical sentence, (9).

(9) John's revision was acceptable.

Therefore, nominalizations do not reliably signal complete propositions. These observations suggest the following hypothesis: Clause constructions that typically convey complete propositions are more likely to be purged from working memory after parsing than those that do not. Experimental evidence has supported this analysis (Carroll, 1978; Townsend & Bever, 1982). Of course, in the event that one or more complex clauses fail to clearly convey a proposition, there is the danger that the understander will accumulate too much information in working memory. In this event, comprehension will be difficult to achieve or will fail altogether.

In conclusion, identifying the immediate constituent structure of a sentence permits the understander to derive its propositional content. The remainder of this chapter examines the factors that influence parsing, as well as theoretical accounts of parsing processes.

FACTORS THAT AFFECT PARSING PROCESSES

The goal of parsing a sentence is the identification of its linguistic constituents. The course of parsing is influenced by the syntactic cues of a sentence. However, semantic characteristics of a sentence likewise contribute to parsing decisions. In this section, the impact of syntactic and semantic factors on parsing processes is considered in turn.

Syntactic Factors

The impact of syntactic cues on parsing decisions is exposed by sentence (10).

> (10)   In a glick with rup loxens and a cater, munk a loxen into the blump for a bim in the gratz.

Despite the fact that (10) is nonsensical, its structure permits the answering of questions, such as **Where is the cater?** (in the glick,) and **How do you get a bim?** (munk a loxen into the blump) (Lindsay & Norman, 1972). In this section, we examine the syntactic cues that convey this structure.

Parts of Speech.   Words belong to grammatical categories called *parts of speech.* Of these, nouns, verbs, and most adjectives and adverbs are *content words.* Each content word has a distinct sense, and there is no limit to the number of content words in a language. In contrast, prepositions, conjunctions, and certain adjectives, such as determiners, are *function words.* Many function words, such as the articles **the** and **a,** are difficult to define. The main role of function words is to identify the relationships among the entities described in a sentence.

The part of speech of each successive word guides parsing by generating expectations about the structure of the sentence. Consider the sentence, **The prince surprised the dragon.** The first article, *the,* signals the onset of a sentence, and, in particular, suggests that a noun phrase is being introduced. This preliminary analysis is represented by the partial phrase marker shown in Fig. 3.3a (Kimball, 1973). The syntactic rule, NP → det Adj N, indicates that the determiner of a noun phrase is typically followed by an adjective or a noun. Therefore, the understander can anticipate that the next word will come from one of these classes. The second word, *prince,* is recognized as a noun, and as a result, the current noun phrase is completed, as shown in Fig. 3.3b. The part of speech of each successive word suggests comparable hypotheses about the sentence structure, as illustrated by Figs. 3.3c to 3.3e.

Function words are particularly important in conveying sentence structure. Consider the telegraphic sequence, **student teacher tested,** from which all function words have been removed. The meaning of the words might suggest that a teacher tested a student. However, the origi-

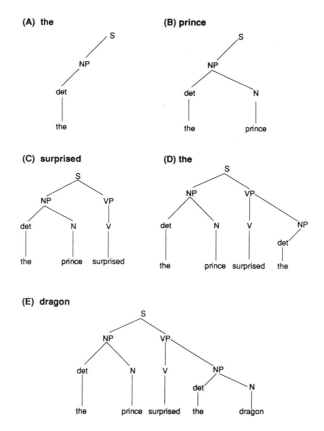

FIG. 3.3. Progressive immediate constituent analysis of **The prince surprised the dragon.**

nal sentence might have been, **The student teacher was tested,** which conveys quite a different idea.

Word Order.   In many languages, the subject, verb, and object have a typical order of arrangement. In English, this order is subject-verb-object (SVO), as in **The pilot painted the fence.** There are other languages that favor the orders SOV, VSO, and VOS (Greenberg, 1963). For example, Japanese is an SOV language. Latin, in contrast, does not have a typical order of subject, verb, and object.

The advantage of a typical order is illustrated by sentence (11).

(11)   Police book suspects.

Each of the words in sentence (11) could be a verb or a noun. The fact that the subject of English sentences typically appears first suggests that *police* introduces the subject noun phrase, and, in view of the absence of a determiner, is likely a noun. Because sentence (11) does not include any function words, order information is especially important in arriving at a satisfactory syntactic analysis.

Affixes.   The grammatical function of a word may be conveyed by meaningful subword units, called *bound morphemes*, that are affixed to the stem of the word. For example, in Latin, the ending of a noun systematically reflects its grammatical function. The **-us** ending of the Latin name, **Julius,** specifically indicates that the noun-stem **Juli-** is serving as the sentence object. In contrast, as the direct object of the verb, the name would be **Julium;** and to mean BELONGING TO JULIUS, it would be **Julii.**

Suffixes that do not change the part of speech of their stem words are called *inflections.* For example, the suffix **-ed** added to the verb **kick** results in a past tense verb, **kicked.** In contrast, the suffix, **-ly,** added to the adjective, **quick,** yields an adverb, **quickly.** Therefore, **-ly** is not an inflection.

English is a very slightly inflected language. The only inflection still added to nouns to identify a syntactic category is the possessive **'s,** as in **Jim's.** If English used inflections like Latin, then the sentence, **The rabbit chased the raccoon,** would take a form analogous to **The rabbitus chased the raccoonum.** English compensates for the absence of inflections with a relatively fixed word order.

Agreement.   One function of inflections is to show agreement among the words of a sentence. Certain sets of words are coordinated in their precise form to agree on language dimensions such as number, gender, and grammatical function. For example, the subject and verb of English sentences show number agreement. Therefore, we have the singular, **The babysitter eats,** as compared with the plural, **The babysitters eat.** Sentence (12) illustrates the benefit of agreement in parsing.

(12)   The kids the babysitter amuses.

Although peculiar, sentence (12) might occur in a context such as: A: We've been playing tennis on Sunday mornings. B: What about the kids? A: The kids the babysitter amuses. By the time that the verb, *amuses,* is encountered, there are ostensibly two candidate subjects, *kids* and *babysitter.* The number agreement between *babysitter* and *amuses* clearly establishes *babysitter* as the subject of the sentence.

TABLE 3.1
Agreement Between Personal Pronouns and Present Tense Verbs
in English and French

I give	Je donne
You *(sing.)* give	Tu donnes
He/she gives	Il/elle donne
We give	Nous donnons
You *(pl.)* give	Vous donnez
They give	Ils/elles donnent

English makes relatively little use of agreement. For example, Table 3.1 shows that there is little coordination of verb form with the number and *person* of English personal pronouns, whereas French shows systematic variation.

Importance of Syntactic Cues Across Languages.   The syntactic cues that guide parsing, such as word order, affixes, and agreement, provide redundant information. Perhaps as a result of this, these cues vary in their relative importance in different languages. A language with relatively fixed word order, such as English, does not need to show extensive inflection. Conversely, heavily inflected languages, such as Latin, can use free word order, because the word endings will reveal the syntactic relations. Finally, the presence of these cues in spoken and written sentences does not guarantee the success of parsing decisions. There still remain syntactically ambiguous sentences, such as **They are fighting dragons.**

Semantic Factors

Parsing decisions are influenced by semantic as well as syntactic factors. For example, although the scrambled fragment, **moose explorer photograph,** is entirely devoid of syntactic information, one is likely to guess that the explorer photographed the moose rather than the other way around. The understander knows that human agents can take photographs whereas animal agents cannot. Parsing is guided by several semantic factors.

Word Meaning.   The meaning of the words of a sentence has a measurable impact on syntactic analysis. This is reflected by people's comprehension of complex grammatical constructions. For example, children have difficulty understanding passive sentences. However, 6-year-old children are especially confused by reversible passives, such as (13).

(13)   The hunter was startled by the wolf.

Sentence (13) is reversible in the sense that wolves can also be startled by hunters. Irreversible passives, such as (14), also cause children difficulty, but not as much (Slobin, 1966; see also Strohner & Nelson, 1974).

(14)   The flowers were watered by the girl.

Thus, if the meanings of the words of a sentence permit only one interpretation, then the difficulty of a complex construction can be overcome.

Another construction that is notoriously difficult to understand is the *center-embedded* sentence, illustrated by (15) (Fodor & Garrett, 1967; Miller & Isard, 1963).

(15)   The artist the electrician the lawyer admired employed died.

What this sentence means, roughly, is that the lawyer admired the electrician who employed the artist who died. In contrast with (15), a different center-embedded sentence, (16), seems much easier to understand.

(16)   The bat the player the reporter interviewed swung broke.

In contrast with (15), the nouns and verbs of sentence (16) are inherently connected. Reporters conduct interviews, and players swing bats. This is another example of word meaning influencing parsing decisions.

These effects do not resolve the issue of whether word meaning is consulted during syntactic analysis, or only after a preliminary constituent analysis has been performed. The nature of the interactions between semantics and syntax is considered later in this chapter.

Word Order.   Word order functions as a semantic parsing cue as well as a syntactic cue. First, there is a systematic order of appearance of semantic cases in sentences (Fillmore, 1968; Braine & Wells, 1978; Segalowitz, 1982). For example, in English, agents tend to precede objects, which in turn precede locations, as exemplified by **The prince found the map in the forest.** Furthermore, semantic cases, such as the agent, do not always coincide with a particular grammatical relation, such as the subject. Therefore, the word order provides semantic as well as syntactic information that influences parsing processes.

Second, word order makes the semantic distinction between given and new sentence information. For example, in the sentence, **What the**

audience enjoyed was the music, it is given that the audience enjoyed something. The new concept is MUSIC. In general, given sentence information precedes new information. We see in chapter 5 that the given–new distinction is instrumental in the construction and integration of the propositions underlying sentences.

PRINCIPLES OF PARSING

This section presents several general parsing principles (e.g., Bever, 1970; Fodor, Bever, & Garrett, 1974; Kimball, 1973). Such principles need to satisfy at least three criteria. First, they must be consistent with the rules of grammar. Accordingly, applying these principles cannot result in ungrammatical sentences, such as *The girl the helped teacher and *Al ate very heartily spaghetti.

Second, these principles must reflect the characteristics of human information processing, such as memory constraints. Third, in combination, the principles must address familiar phenomena of comprehension, such as the fact that (17) is difficult to understand, and (18) misleads the reader.

(17)   The plumber thought the plan the woman proposed over.
(18)   Sam loaded the boxes on the cart onto the van.

The principles are grouped into three categories. First, there are *global principles* that describe general characteristics of human parsing, but do not identify specific parsing rules. Second, *construction strategies* specify how the words of a sentence are organized into constituents. Third, there are *cognitive parsing principles* that refer directly to human information processing characteristics. In several cases, alternative sets of principles are considered, such as the immediate versus delayed parsing of the words of a message.

Global Parsing Principles

Immediate Versus Delayed Parsing. Language messages consist of streams of words, encountered one by one. Spoken messages are particularly fleeting: Once a word has been spoken, it is gone. In reading, one may look back at an earlier part of a text, but only at the cost of interrupting ongoing processes. How, then, do people manage to process language messages at the necessary pace? This question is addressed by the *immediacy principle* (Just & Carpenter, 1980, 1987). According to this view, words are interpreted as soon as they are encountered. The proposal applies to parsing, and to other levels of analysis as well. That is, the identification of propositions, the assignment of referents, and the construction of the situation model are hypothesized to be carried forward as far as each word will permit.

Consider the sentence, **John bought the flower for Susan.** This sentence is syntactically ambiguous: It might mean that John bought something to give to Susan, or that John bought something that had been intended for Susan. This ambiguity is encountered upon the presentation of the word, **for.** Immediate parsing means that, when **for** is encountered, the understander will choose one of these interpretations and maintain it unless clearly contradictory evidence is presented.

The advantage of immediacy is that it prevents working memory from having to retain several words while the system looks ahead. Immediacy also avoids the danger of a *computational explosion* that is threatened if people need to retain two or more interpretations at each of several choice points. For example, in **John bought the flower for Susan,** the spoken word, **flower,** could be interpreted to mean either FLOWER or FLOUR. Coupling these two alternatives with the two syntactic interpretations of *for* yields four analyses to maintain. Maintaining an analysis for each distinct interpretation would soon overwhelm working memory.

One phenomenon that favors the immediacy of parsing is the *garden-pathing* that one experiences upon reading sentences such as (19) and (20).

(19)   The old train the young.
(20)   The florist sent the flowers was very pleased.

In sentence (19), the typical reader initially interprets *train* to be a noun rather than a verb, a decision that makes the sentence incomprehensible. Similarly, initially deciding that the florist in (20) was the sender rather than the recipient of the flowers results in a dead end. If understanders did not commit themselves to an immediate interpretation, then one should not experience the feeling of being garden-pathed.

Evidence for immediate parsing has also been provided by on-line measures of reading (Frazier & Rayner, 1982; Just & Carpenter, 1980; Rayner, Carlson, & Frazier, 1983). Frazier and Rayner (1982), for example, measured people's eye fixations for sentences such as (21) and (22).

(21)   Before the king rides his horse it's always groomed.
(22)   Before the king rides his horse is always groomed.

The word *horse* is the direct object in sentence (21) and the subject of the main clause in sentence (22). Therefore, upon reading *horse* in either sentence, there is a syntactic ambiguity. Immediacy of parsing states that the reader will immediately select one of these readings. Suppose that people interpreted *horse* as a direct object in both cases. This would be a correct decision for (21) and an incorrect one for (22). Therefore, the reader of (22) should run into difficulty upon encountering the phrase that solves the ambiguity, *is always* groomed. Eye fixation data reveal that people indeed take relatively longer to read **is always groomed** in (22) than **it's always groomed** in (21) (Frazier & Rayner, 1982). This supports the hypothesis that an immediate parsing decision is made about *horse* in both sentences.

The alternative to immediacy is the hypothesis of delayed processing. One form of this hypothesis states that the understander accumulates several words in working memory before interpreting them (Kimball, 1973; Marcus, 1980). A second analysis represents a compromise between immediacy and delay: It states that higher processing begins with the onset of a word, but may not be completed until the understander has progressed several words more through the discourse (Ehrlich & Rayner, 1983; Rayner, 1977). A third position is that syntactic and semantic analysis proceed continually, but that when two or more interpretations are possible, all are maintained until decisive evidence is encountered (e.g., Mitchell & Holmes, 1985). The advantage of delayed processing is that it would prevent premature and possibly incorrect parsing decisions. Experimental results favor the position of immediate rather than delayed parsing. However, there is evidence that, for other levels of linguistic analysis, such as the identification of referents of discourse (see chapter 2), processing lags slightly behind fixation (Ehrlich & Rayner, 1983).

Top-Down Versus Bottom-Up Parsing.   Cognitive theorists distinguish between bottom-up and top-down processing. *Bottom-up processing* begins with the sensory analysis of a stimulus, at the "bottom" of the nervous system, and proceeds toward higher levels of analysis. For example, reading an isolated word requires bottom-up processing. First, the written symbols have to be perceptually analyzed. Later, the representation of the word is accessed in lexical memory. Finally, the meaning of the word may be retrieved. In contrast, processing is *top-down* when analyses of higher systems influence lower ones. To illustrate, snow reflects mainly blue light toward sunset on a clear day. However, the knowledge that one is looking at snow results in the top-down effect that it appears white, not blue.

Top-down effects in parsing are suggested by the sequential nature

of both spoken and written messages, and by the principle of immediacy. That is, because the understander encounters one word at a time,
and because syntactic analysis is undertaken immediately, then parsing
decisions may be influenced in a top-down manner by the analysis of
the preceding words.

Top-down effects in syntactic analysis may be illustrated by reference
to Fig. 3.3, which was presented earlier. When the listener encounters
a sentence, such as **The prince surprised the dragon,** partial immediate
constituent analyses are performed on a word-by-word basis. Each partial analysis reflects the listener's expectations about what will follow,
and guides further parsing. For example, in Fig. 3.3b, the presence of
the NP node facilitates the recognition of **prince** as a noun.

Strictly bottom-up parsing would mean that higher nodes, such as
NP and VP, could be entered into the phrase marker only after all of
their constituents were identified. A determiner such as *the* would not
of itself signal the construction of a noun phrase. The S node would be
constructed last. In this case, the understander would not benefit from
expectations based on partial analyses (Frazier & Fodor, 1978).

In spite of the advantages of top-down processing, parsing must be
at least partly bottom-up. For example, if word recognition were strictly
top-down, one would not be able to read the word filling the blank in
a sentence such as **They thought it was the** _____ (Forster, 1979; van
Dijk & Kintsch, 1983). Excessive top-down processing would also result
in numerous inaccurate predictions, resulting in extensive backtracking. In spite of this, there is considerable evidence of top-down influences in syntactic analysis.

Figure 3.3 illustrated top-down effects within the syntactic level of
analysis. Semantic and situational analyses also influence syntactic
decisions in a top-down manner. These effects are addressed particularly by parallel, interactive models of parsing, which will be examined
later (e.g., Just & Carpenter, 1980, 1987; Waltz & Pollack, 1985). Conversely, strictly bottom-up parsing requires a serial progression from
lower to higher levels of analysis. Some drawbacks of serial processing
are inspected in the next section.

Parallel Versus Serial Parsing. A general issue in cognition is
whether different sorts of computations are executed serially or in parallel. In the context of parsing, a simple serial hypothesis is that syntactic
analysis precedes semantic analysis. According to this position, the
syntactic processor assembles constituent trees and passes them to the
semantic component of the grammar for interpretation. However, meaning frequently influences parsing. One phenomenon that is damaging
to the serial view is semantic garden-pathing, such as occurs in the

sentence, **The president of Timex watched the movie.** Many people notice the TIMEPIECE meaning of the morpheme **watch,** even though the verb **to watch** has nothing to do with timekeeping. If syntactic analysis strictly preceded semantic interpretation, then *watch* should be recognized as a verb, resulting in the retrieval of its LOOK meaning. In this event, no garden-pathing would be experienced.

The parallel-serial dimension of parsing is pertinent to the other principles that we have examined. Parallel operation of syntax and semantics is consistent with immediacy, according to which each word in a message receives immediate interpretation at every level of analysis. Parallel parsing is necessary for top-down effects of higher levels on lower ones: If parsing proceeded serially from lexical to syntactic to semantic analysis, then higher levels could not influence the lower ones.

Indeed, perhaps the only reason that serial parsing merits discussion is that syntactic analysis precedes semantic analysis in some computer understanding systems (e.g., Riesbeck, 1975; Winograd, 1972; Woods, 1968). However, even in the realm of artificial intelligence, this arrangement has largely been abandoned, as is illustrated by the interactive parsing models considered later in this chapter.

Lexical Effects in Parsing.   Information about words, or *lexical items,* forms a central part of syntactic rules. To cite a simple example, the syntactic rule, NP → det Adj N, is expressed in terms of word categories, such as det, Adj, and N. Both linguistically and psychologically, this is inevitable and uncontroversial. However, there is evidence that both the category and the meaning of a word guide parsing decisions. For example, sentences (23) and (24) have identical structure, and differ only in their verbs.

(23)   The groundsman chased the girl waving a stick.
(24)   The groundsman noticed the girl waving a stick.

Despite their identical structure, people tend to parse the two sentences differently. They associate the adverbial **stick** with the groundsman in (23), and with the girl in (24) (Mitchell & Holmes, 1985). One reason for this is that action verbs, such as **chased,** are more usually accompanied by adverbial phrases than are *stative* verbs, such as **noticed.**

This observation raises the question of whether lexical information is applied during syntactic analysis, or only after syntactic analysis has been completed. On-line measures of reading performance can distinguish between these two hypotheses. Consider sentences (25) and (26).

(25)   The groundsman chased the girl waving a stick *in his hand.*
(26)   The groundsman noticed the girl waving a stick *in his hand.*

Suppose that *chased* creates the expectation of an adverbial phrase but *noticed* does not. Then, the adverbial phrase **in his hand** should create a garden-path effect in sentence (26) but not (25). Similarly, if transitive verbs create an expectation of the appearance of a direct object and intransitive verbs do not, then readers should not expect a direct object in sentence (27).

(27)   After the musician had bowed the piano *was quickly taken* off the stage.

However, they should expect a direct object in sentence (28).

(28)   After the musician had played the piano *was quickly taken* off the stage.

In both sentences, the critical phrase, **was quickly taken,** disconfirms the appearance of a direct object. This ought to create difficulty only in sentence (28).

Phrase-by-phrase reading times for sentences such as (25)-(28) revealed that people needed more time to read the italicized phrase in sentence (26) than (25), and likewise in sentence (28) than (27) (Mitchell & Holmes, 1985; see also Clifton, Frazier, & Connine, 1984). These results support the hypothesis that lexical information is applied during syntactic analysis.

Construction Strategy Principles

Understanding a sentence requires the organization of its words into a complete constituent tree. Several strategies for constructing constituent trees have been identified (Bever, 1970; Clark & Clark, 1977; Kimball, 1973; van Dijk & Kintsch, 1983). These strategies are *heuristic* in nature. By this it is meant that they provide rules of thumb rather than a systematic procedure for parsing. They are generally effective but occasionally fail. This section presents two examples of heuristic construction strategies.

Strategy 1 concerns the initiation and completion of sentence constituents.

Construction Strategy 1:   Each function word in a sentence signals the construction of a new sentence constituent (Kimball, 1973).

Strategy 1 reflects the syntactic information provided by function words. In sentence (29), for example, the first word, *the*, signals the onset of a noun phrase.

(29)   The white of the glacier was blinding.

This signal operates in a top-down manner and results in the construction of the partial phrase marker shown in Fig. 3.4 (Frazier & Fodor, 1978). The phrase marker, in turn, makes it easier to analyze the next part of the message.

A corollary of Strategy 1 is that function words signal the end of earlier constituents (Clark & Clark, 1977). In sentence (29), one might make the preliminary analysis that *white* is an adjective. According to Strategy 1, however, the word **of** signals the onset of a new constituent, a prepositional phrase. Therefore, the preceding noun phrase must be complete, and **white,** accordingly, is recognized to be a noun. In a similar vein, Bever (1970, p. 323) introduced the strategy of closing a noun phrase upon encountering a second function word, a second noun, or morphemes such as the plural **s.**

Construction strategies such as Strategy 2 specify the manner of integrating each successive word into the sentence phrase marker.

Construction Strategy 2:   Each lexical item is to be attached into the phrase marker with the fewest possible number of nonterminal nodes linking it with nodes which are already present (Frazier & Fodor, 1978, p. 320).

In sentences (30) and (31), the phrase, **the mayor's position,** is ambiguous: It can function as the direct object of **argue,** as in (30), or as part of a sentence complement, as in (31).

(30)   The city council argued the mayor's position forcefully.
(31)   The city council argued the mayor's position was incorrect.

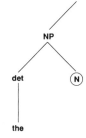

FIG. 3.4. Partial immediate constituent analysis of **The white of the glacier was blinding,** as signaled by the initial determiner, "the."

Following Strategy 2, known as *minimal attachment*, **the mayor's position** should be initially interpreted as a direct object, because the complement interpretation requires an extra sentence node between the verb phrase and the second noun phrase, as shown in Fig. 3.5 (Frazier & Rayner, 1982). Minimal attachment has at least two information processing advantages. First, the parser can immediately commit itself to the preferred analysis. Therefore, it does not have to wait for more sentence information, nor does it have to maintain two or more interpretations. Second, the construction of fewer nodes is hypothesized to be economical in processing terms.

Strategy 2 explains the sort of garden-pathing that one experiences upon reading (32).

(32)   The boat floated on the water sunk.

Minimal attachment causes **floated on the water** to be initially interpreted as the main verb phrase of the sentence, rather than as a *reduction* of the relative clause, **which floated on the water** (Rayner et al., 1983).

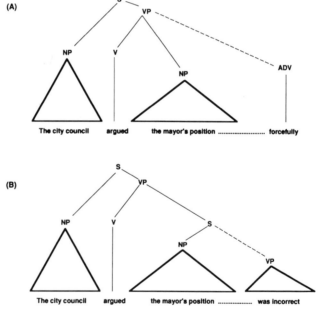

FIG. 3.5.   Immediate constituent analyses of **the mayor's position** as (A) a direct object (minimal attachment) and (B) a sentence complement (nonminimal attachment). *Source:* Frazier & Rayner, 1982, Figures 1 and 2, p. 181. Reprinted by permission.

As a result, the reader is garden-pathed when the word **sunk** is reached. The fact that minimal attachment results in this garden path stresses the heuristic nature of the parsing principles. They are generally effective, but do not guarantee a correct solution.

Cognitive Parsing Principles

Some parsing principles refer to human information processing characteristics. Consider Cognitive Principle 1:

Cognitive Principle 1: The constituents of no more than two sentences can be parsed at the same time (Kimball, 1973).

This principle expresses the number of sentence units that working memory can hold. One phenomenon that it addresses is the difficulty of understanding center-embedded sentences. For example, people generally have difficulty understanding sentence (33) but not (34) (e.g., Blumenthal, 1966; Miller & Isard, 1963).

(33)   The mouse the cat the dog hated saw escaped.
(34)   The mouse the cat saw escaped.

Although both (33) and (34) are center-embedded, only (33) requires that the understander maintain three sentence (S) nodes in working memory in order to complete the parse (see Fig. 3.6).

Cognitive Principle 2: Any Noun-Verb-Noun sequence within a potential internal unit in the surface structure corresponds to *actor-action-object* (Bever, 1970, p. 298).

Cognitive Principle 2 captures the relation between surface structure order and semantic case. If the understander is predisposed toward interpreting noun-verb-noun sequences in this fashion, then processing will be facilitated. This is because semantic cases are arranged in this typical way in many sentences. In those sentences in which surface and semantic cases do not conform to the usual arrangement, difficulties result. For example, passive sentences are sometimes more difficult to understand than their active counterparts. In this regard, children needed more time to verify passive sentences than active sentences with reference to accompanying pictures (Slobin, 1966; see also Herriot, 1969).

(A) The mouse the cat the dog hated saw escaped.

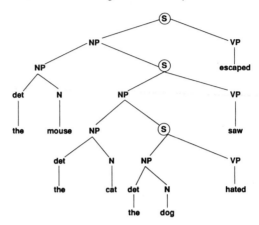

(B) The mouse the cat saw escaped.

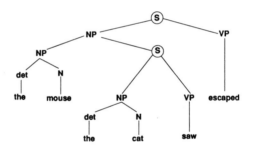

FIG. 3.6.   Immediate constituent analyses of center-embedded sentences. *Source:*   Kimball, 1973, p. 17. Adapted by permission.

Conclusions

Parsing principles can be classified as global characteristics, construction strategies, and cognitive constraints. The integration of the grammatical and information processing features of the parser, reflected
in these principles, represents a necessary step in understanding the
psychology of parsing. One qualification of a *principles* approach to
parsing is that the successful identification of parsing principles does
not in and of itself constitute a model of parsing. By the same token,
constructing a creature according to a list of characteristics such as
WEIGHS THREE TONS, HAS A FIVE-FOOT LONG NOSE, LIKES PEA-
NUTS, and HAS A GOOD MEMORY, by no means guarantees winding
up with an elephant. A second qualification is that many parsing princi-

ples are controversial, and more evidence will be needed in order to determine which ones are valid. When this is accomplished, parsing principles will provide a yardstick against which to measure comprehensive parsing models.

INTERACTION OF SYNTAX AND SEMANTICS: INTERACTIVE VERSUS MODULAR PARSING

The second section of this chapter identified several semantic factors that influence parsing. When the term *semantic* is broadly interpreted to include sense, reference, speech acts, and general knowledge (Crain & Steedman, 1985), the semantic influences on parsing are seen to be widespread.

Consider several examples. The sentence, ***The dentist eat the ice cream** is ungrammatical, because the noun and verb do not show number agreement. Any purely syntactic parser would be stymied by such a sentence, which might result from a typing error. In spite of this, most understanders would extract the intended interpretation of this sentence on the basis of word meaning.

Sentences (35) and (36) are identical in surface form, but are parsed differently.

(35)   John ate up the pie.
(36)   John ate up the street.

In (35), **up** is interpreted as a *verb particle*. In (36), after being garden-pathed by the JOHN ATE ASPHALT sense, the reader analyzes *up* as a preposition. The difference in the parsing of (35) and (36) is due to the meanings of **pie** and **street**.

A different sort of semantic impact on parsing is illustrated by the following examples (Clark, 1982).

(37)   Linda managed to PORCH the newspaper.
(38)   George set out to WAYNE GRETZKY down the ice.

Familiar terms such as **porch** and **Wayne Gretzky** are frequently used in novel ways, and post little difficulty for the understander. Such *contextual expressions* can foil a purely syntactic parser in two ways. Sentence (37) should not be parsed at all, because **porch** is not a verb. Sentence (38) should be misparsed: Because **Wayne Gretzky** is a noun, (38) ought to be interpreted in the same way as **George set out to**

McDonald's down the street (Clark, 1982). People's ability to understand (37) and (38) reflects the role of semantic information on parsing.

Observations of this sort indicate that syntactic and semantic cues collaborate closely in guiding parsing. This conclusion is addressed by two distinct cognitive hypotheses, the interactive and the modular. The *interactive* position states that syntactic and semantic analyses influence one another at every stage of parsing. The *modularity* view is that there exist dedicated cognitive analyzers, called modules, that compute their analyses without the influence of other levels. This distinction and debate merits careful consideration. This section examines the assumptions of the interactive and modular positions, outlines examples of each model, and compares the effectiveness of the two views in addressing parsing phenomena.

Interactive Parsing

The nature of interactive models is strikingly captured by the following example, which illustrates the interaction between people's lexical and orthographical analyzers (McClelland, Rumelhart, & Hinton, 1986). Figure 3.7 apparently shows the word, **RED.** Yet each letter in Fig. 3.7 is ambiguous: The first letter could be R or P, the second could be E or F, and the third could be D or B. One explanation of this effect is that the word context, **RED,** influences the recognition of the letters in a top-down manner. However, this presents a paradox: How does the reader know what the word context is, if all of the letters are ambiguous?

Suppose that, on the basis of the available evidence, the lexical level begins considering hypotheses about what word has been encountered. For the present example, the only possibilities are PED, PEB, PFD, PFB, RED, REB, RFD, and RFB. Because only one of these is an English word, the system "decides" that the current word is **RED.** This information is passed "down" to the orthographical level, and we see the letters as R, E, and D.

For theories of parsing, the interactive position particularly emphasizes the influence of semantic and contextual information on syntactic analysis. Of course, syntax likewise affects the semantic analysis of a sentence. The influence of syntax on semantic decisions is illustrated by sentences (39a) and (39b).

FIG. 3.7. Ambiguous display of letters. *Source:* Adapted from McClelland, Rumelhart, & Hinton, 1986, Figure 2, p. 8. Adapted by permission.

(39) a. The committee convinced the prime minister to table the purchase.
      b. The committee convinced the prime minister to purchase the table.

In sentence (39b), the appearance of *table* after the determiner *the* guides the retrieval of the FURNITURE interpretation of *table*. In (39a), **table** appears in the verb slot of the infinitive construction, **to . . .** This results in the retrieval of the LEGISLATIVE sense of **table.**

Much of the work on interactive parsing has been performed in the field of artificial intelligence, particularly in the realm of *connectionist* models of language processing. In connectionist parsing models, processors at each level of language analysis are "massively" interconnected to processors at other levels, particularly adjacent ones (McClelland & Kawamoto, 1986; Waltz & Pollack, 1985). As a result, the ongoing analysis at each level has the capability of influencing the course of events at every other level.

The mechanism that permits within-level and between-level influences in such models is spreading activation (see chapter 1). For example, Waltz and Pollack (1985) proposed that associated nodes at all levels send activation to one another, and dissociated nodes inhibit one another. Figure 3.8 shows an analysis of the sentence, **John shot some bucks** (Waltz & Pollack, 1985, Fig. 1b). In Fig. 3.8, the darker the outline of a node, the higher is its level of activation. In the connections between nodes, an arrowhead means that the node is receiving activation, and a circle means that it is receiving inhibition. Incompatible alternatives inhibit one another: For example, *shot* cannot simultaneously be a noun and a verb, and *bucks* cannot simultaneously mean DEER and DOLLARS. Most importantly for the present purposes, there are links between the levels. For example, the syntactic category, *verb*, and the lexical category, *verb*, mutually activate one another.

By expressing such models in the form of computer programs (see chapter 10), it has been shown that they are capable of arriving at the correct or preferred readings of syntactically ambiguous sentences, such as (40), and semantically ambiguous ones, such as (41).

(40) John ate up the street.
(41) The astronomer married the star.

Furthermore, the models reflect comprehension phenomena. For example, the CELESTIAL BODY interpretation of *star* receives a high level of activation at intermediate stages of the processing of (41) by the model. Then this activation diminishes. This reflects the semantic gar-

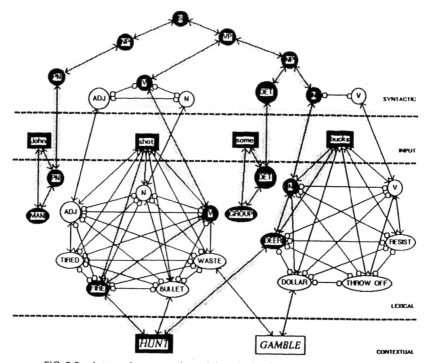

FIG. 3.8.   Interactive network model analysis of **John shot some bucks.**
Source: Waltz & Pollack, 1985, Figure 1b, p. 58. Reprinted by permission.

den-pathing that people experience when they read (41) (Waltz & Pollack, 1985).

Construction strategies, such as minimal attachment, appear as side effects of connectionist models, and do not have to be built explicitly into the programs (Waltz & Pollack, 1985). Freed from the influence of such rules, the system is more likely to successfully parse grammatically ill-formed sentences, such as **Linda managed to porch the newspaper.**

Modular Parsing

The *modularity* hypothesis states that there are cognitive analyzers, called modules, dedicated to specific tasks, such as word recognition and syntactic analysis. Modules are attributed with the following characteristics (Fodor, 1983):

1. The function of a module is obligatory. Once the module has received input, the analysis of the input cannot be inhibited.

For example, upon seeing the word, **bread,** one cannot avoid recognizing it as an English word and retrieving its meaning.

2. Modules operate at relatively high processing speeds.

3. Modules have limited access to central processes, such as people's conscious reasoning about a stimulus. As such, modules can neither benefit from nor be hindered by top-down influences.

4. Conversely, modules are informationally encapsulated. This means that the analysis performed by a module is shared with other systems only when processing is complete.

Properties 3 and 4 of the modularity hypothesis are in direct conflict with the interactive approach. The proposed merit of properties 3 and 4 is cognitive efficiency. Without the influence of other systems, a syntactic module could quickly analyze the current stimulus. For example, suppose that a syntactic module was equipped with the strategy of first treating *eat up* as a verb plus particle (i.e., *eat-up*) rather than a verb plus a preposition. Accordingly, this analysis would be applied both to (35) and 36).

(35) John ate up the pie.
(36) John ate up the street.

This analysis would succeed for (35). For (36), it would fail upon reaching the word **street,** requiring the reanalysis of **up** as a preposition. On the whole, the advantage of a fast and usually correct syntactic module would outweigh the costs of the occasional error (Fodor, 1983; Just & Carpenter, 1980).

A Sample Syntactic Module.   One computational module dedicated to syntactic analysis is the *augmented transition network* (ATN) (Kaplan, 1972; Wanner, 1980; Wanner & Maratsos, 1978; Woods, 1970, 1973). An ATN consists of grammatical rules in the form of networks. ATN analysis is performed in a sequential and top-down manner. Figure 3.9 presents the networks for the syntactic units, Sentence and Noun Phrase.

Each network consists of a series of circles, which represent states. The states are linked by arcs, which are "augmented" by conditions and corresponding actions. The transition from one state to the next can be made only if the corresponding condition is met. Furthermore, when a particular condition is met, then the corresponding action is executed.

Consider the application of the ATN of Fig. 3.9 to sentence (42).

Sentence Network:

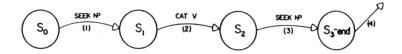

Noun Phrase Network:

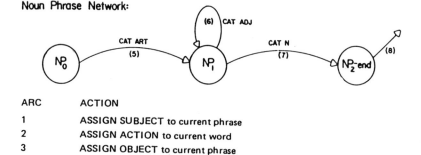

ARC	ACTION
1	ASSIGN SUBJECT to current phrase
2	ASSIGN ACTION to current word
3	ASSIGN OBJECT to current phrase
4	ASSEMBLE CLAUSE
	SEND current clause
5	ASSIGN DET to current word
6	ASSIGN MOD to current word
7	ASSIGN HEAD to current word
8	ASSEMBLE NOUN PHRASE
	SEND current phrase

FIG. 3.9. A simplified ATN grammar. *Source:* Wanner & Maratsos, 1978, Figure 3.1, p. 124. Reprinted by permission.

(42) The thoughtful aunt purchased the flowers.

The appearance of the first word indicates that a sentence is being presented. The parser therefore begins at the first state of the sentence network, S0. The condition between S0 and S1 is FIND NP. To find a noun phrase, the noun phrase network is entered at NP0. Its first condition is that the first word be categorized as an article. The first word of (42), **the,** is indeed on article. Therefore, following action 5, **the** is assigned the grammatical category, *determiner*. This permits the transition to NP1. The arcs emanating from NP1 demand that the next word be categorized as either an adjective or a noun. **Thoughtful** is discovered to be an adjective, and is assigned the category, *modifier*. The CAT ADJ arc returns the system to NP1, because no noun has yet been encountered. The next word, **aunt,** is categorized as a noun, and assigned the category, *subject*. Satisfying this arc sends the system to NP2, which unconditionally returns the system to the sentence network. Because a complete noun phrase has been analyzed, processing may ensue at S1. Processing continues until the entire sentence has been analyzed.

The ATN module has the merits of reflecting the speeded sequential nature of language processing, and of avoiding the need for redundant sets of rules, such as separate rules for noun phrases that appear before and after the verb (Wanner & Maratsos, 1978). One shortcoming of the ATN is that the hypothetical movement from network to network is expensive in processing terms. For example, while analyzing the first noun phrase of sentence (42), it is necessary to hold the incomplete sentence in working memory, with a marker indicating where the system must reenter upon completion of the noun phrase (Wanner & Maratsos, 1978). A second proposed drawback is that rigid rules such as ATN networks cannot account for people's ability to make sense of ungrammatical or scrambled sentences (Frazier & Fodor, 1978). With regard to the latter point, it is not clear whether the syntactic component of any type of parser can address this phenomenon.

Comparing Interactive and Modular Parsing

The differences between the interactive and modular views of parsing are surprisingly subtle. The central axiom of the modularity hypothesis is that processing modules are dedicated to particular tasks. However, many interactive parsers likewise separate lexical, syntactic, and semantic analysis into different systems (Crain & Steedman, 1985; Just & Carpenter, 1980, 1987; McClelland & Kawamoto, 1986; Waltz & Pollack, 1985). This is not an inevitable position: For example, we have already seen that certain lexical information is probably integrated with syntactic analysis. Similarly, it is possible to conceive of an interwoven module responsible for syntactic and semantic analysis. However, the fact that people can parse completely anomalous sentences, such as **Colorless green ideas sleep furiously,** and sentences with unanticipated meanings, such as **The patient was by the cured doctor** (please read it carefully), justifies proposing a separate syntactic processor.

Conversely, modularity theorists agree that the different modules must eventually interact with one another (e.g., Fodor, 1983; Rayner et al., 1983). Without interaction, one would never reject the ASPHALT interpretation of **John ate up the street.** Therefore, a crucial difference between interactive and modular parsing is that the processors of interactive parsers exchange information at every stage of analysis, whereas parsing modules share only complete or semi-complete analyses.

One line of psychological investigation has provided support for the modular view of parsing. If syntax is modular, then the application of syntactic principles should not be influenced by sentence meaning. Recall, for example, the minimal attachment principle (Construction Strategy 2). According to minimal attachment, the phrase, **sent the flowers,** should initially be incorrectly interpreted as the verb phrase of a simple active sentence in both (43a) and (43b)

    (43)   a.   The florist sent the flowers WAS VERY PLEASED.
            b.   The performer sent the flowers WAS VERY PLEASED.

This is because interpreting it as a reduced relative clause (i.e., **The performer who was sent the flowers)** yields a nonminimal phrase marker.

If **sent the flowers** is always initially interpreted as a verb phrase, then both (43a) and (43b) will be misparsed. In this event, the disambiguating phrase, **WAS VERY PLEASED,** would signal the recomputation of the syntax of both (43a) and (43b). In contrast, the interactive hypothesis states that semantic information influences parsing. If this were true, then the reader of (43b) would interpret the performer to be the recipient of the flowers, the nonminimal reading. As a result, no recomputation would be necessary for (43b).

People needed more time to read the phrase **was very pleased** in *both versions* of sentence (43), than when it appeared in control sentences in which the minimal attachment interpretation was correct (Rayner et al., 1983). Ferreira and Clifton (1986) presented a similar finding using semantic contexts consisting of complete sentences, rather than single words such as **florist** and **performer.** These results suggest that semantic information does not influence syntactic analysis at an early stage. In turn, this outcome supports the modular view of the parser. In order to generalize this conclusion to natural reading tasks, future studies along these lines will need to examine additional parsing principles, and extend the quantity and variety of discourse context (van Dijk & Kintsch, 1983, p. 26).

Support for the interactive view of parsing is provided by computational models of the sort examined earlier (e.g., Waltz & Pollack, 1985). These models arrive at the correct interpretation of ambiguous sentences, such as **John shot some bucks,** and reflect the garden-pathing that the human understander experiences. Another benefit of these computational models is that they provide the opportunity to parse sentences that include contextual expressions, such as **Linda managed to porch the newspaper** (Clark, 1982). This is because these models generate an interpretation of each sentence, even when the best interpretation is not completely satisfactory. In contrast, syntactic modules, such as the ATN, cannot parse contextual expressions.

If the syntactic processor is not freely interactive, then it is necessary to determine the stage at which it shares its products with other systems. Because there is evidence that working memory accumulates sentence information in clause units (Caplan, 1972; Carroll, 1978; Clark & Sengul, 1979; Jarvella, 1971, 1979), a tentative hypothesis is that the syntactic processor communicates the structure of complete clauses with semantic systems. A variation of this hypothesis is that communication occurs when the syntactic system has analyzed a clause conveying at least one complete proposition (Carroll, 1978; Townsend & Bever, 1982; but see Crain & Steedman, 1985, pp. 322-325 for a critique of such an analysis).

Conclusions

Theorists are in agreement that a final interpretation of a message requires the coordination of syntactic and semantic information. Furthermore, proponents of both modular and interactive parsing have proposed the existence of distinct syntactic and semantic levels of analysis (e.g., Just & Carpenter, 1987; McClelland et al., 1986; Rayner, et al., 1983). The crux of the debate concerns whether the levels interact freely, or whether syntactic analysis is partially independent of semantic influence.

Both positions carry processing benefits. In an interactive parser, semantic influence can theoretically identify the correct syntactic analysis of syntactically ambiguous sentences, and so prevent unnecessary backtracking. An autonomous syntactic module, on the other hand, can ignore evidence of other levels of analysis, and therefore can operate at a fast speed.

Empirical support for modular parsing stems from the demonstration that certain parsing strategies appear to be immune from semantic influence (Ferreira & Clifton, 1986; Rayner et al., 1983). Modular parsing also receives indirect support from demonstrations of the modularity of the processes of the retrieval of word meaning (Seidenberg & Tanenhaus, in press; Swinney, 1979). Interactive parsing is supported by the observations of garden-pathing effects and of people's ability to understand ungrammatical sentences. Both viewponts have provided the basis for computational models of parsing. Much more research will be needed to resolve this debate.

SUMMARY

The linguistic analysis of a sentence into its underlying constituents is accomplished by the application of syntactic rewrite rules. Each rule analyzes a sentence constituent into other constituents. The sentence constituent has been shown to have psychological validity. In particular, there is evidence that sentence information is accumulated in working memory in constituent units corresponding to the clause. After the propositional content of these constituents has been extracted, working memory is cleared in order to accommodate new information.

Parsing processes are guided by the syntactic characteristics of sentences. These characteristics include parts of speech, word order, affixes, and agreement. Parsing is also influenced by the semantic characteristics of word meaning, and by the semantic implications of word order.

Parsing principles can be classified as global characteristics, construction strategies, and cognitive constraints. The global approach addresses parsing dimensions, such as its immediate versus delayed nature, and whether it proceeds in a top-down or bottom-up fashion. Construction strategies identify the manner of the construction of the constituent tree of a sentence. Cognitive constraints show how human information processing characteristics affect parsing.

According to the interactive view of parsing, information is freely shared among all levels of linguistic analysis. In contrast, the modularity position states that an independent syntactic processor analyzes sentences before interacting with other levels. Both viewpoints provide the basis for computational models of parsing. Experimental evidence has been provided for the modularity hypothesis, but interactive parsing is supported by phenomena such as garden-pathing and the parsing of contextual expressions. Further research will be needed to resolve this controversy.

4

The Role of Knowledge
in Language Comprehension

Knowledge and Understanding

What does it mean to say that a complex message has been understood? Certainly, it is necessary that the reader identify the meanings of the individual words. Furthermore, the principles of chapters 2 and 3 suggest that understanding requires the parsing of the sentences underlying the message, and the construction and integration of its propositions. However, there is considerably more to understanding than is captured by these factors. Another dimension of language comprehension is illustrated by the following passage.

> The procedure is actually quite simple. First you arrange things into different groups depending on their makeup. Of course, one pile may be sufficient depending on how much there is to do. If you have to go somewhere else due to lack of facilities that is the next step, otherwise you are pretty well set. It is important not to overdo any particular endeavor. That is, it is better to do too few things at once than too many. In the short run this may not seem important, but complications from doing too many can easily arise. A mistake can be expensive as well. The manipulation of the appropriate mechanisms should be self-explanatory, and we need not dwell on it here. At first the whole procedure will seem complicated. Soon, however, it will become just another facet of life. (Bransford & Johnson, 1972, p. 722)

This passage strikes the typical adult listener as virtual gibberish. This is noteworthy, because the passage presents familiar words and ordinary grammatical constructions. In spite of this, the understander has a very hard time making any sense of this passage. Why is this the case? The general answer to this question is that, barring a clever guess, it is difficult to determine what the passage refers to. As a result, the understander cannot determine what the words *things* and *facilities* denote. It is also difficult to identify the connection among the ideas, such as *why* overdoing things may lead to complications. The impact of pertinent knowledge is revealed when we are informed that the passage is about washing clothes. Take a moment to reread the passage, making this substitution.

Suddenly, the passage is no longer incomprehensible. **Things** obviously refers to clothes, and **facilities** means a washer and dryer. **Overdoing things,** such as overloading the washer, may lead to **complications,** such as the machine breaking down. These clarifications arise from the fact that most people in our culture possess reasonably detailed knowledge about washing clothes.

One might argue that, because messages do not usually mask their theme, the clothes-washing passage overemphasizes the role of knowledge in comprehension. Consider then the next passage:

> Spike slowly got up from the mat, planning his escape. He hesitated a moment and thought. Things were not going well. What bothered him most was being held, especially since the charge against him had been weak. He considered his present situation. The lock that held him was strong but he thought he could break it. He knew, however, that his timing would have to be perfect. Spike was aware that it was because of his early roughness that he had been penalized so severely—much too severely from his point of view. The situation was becoming frustrating; the pressure had been grinding on him for too long. He was being ridden unmercifully. Spike was getting angry now. He felt he was ready to make his move. He knew that his success or failure would depend on what he did in the next few seconds. (Anderson, Reynolds, Schallert, & Goetz, 1976, p. 10)

It is easy to imagine that this passage comes from a drugstore novel about a convict. It addresses Spike's frustration with prison life, and his dreams for escape. Consider, then, the proposal that Spike is not a prisoner but a wrestler. Suddenly, the whole meaning of the passage has changed. **Lock** now refers to a wrestling hold rather than a cell door, and **charge** refers to the opponent's rush rather than a legal accusation. Once again, it is readily seen that understanding depends on knowledge that underlies a passage.

The dependence of understanding on relevant knowledge is a pervasive phenomenon. Even the single sentence, **The haystack was important because the cloth ripped,** appears nonsensical until we are informed about the plight of a parachutist above a field. Similarly, **George thinks vanilla** is an incomprehensible fragment, except as an answer to, **What flavor ice cream does Carol want?** (Clark & Clark, 1977). Understanding cannot succeed until a language message can be related to some realm of familiar knowledge (Anderson & Pichert, 1978; Auble & Franks, 1983).

People's knowledge of the world is hypothesized to be stored in organized structures called *schemata*. As discussed in chapter 1, theorists have proposed the existence of schemata for ordinary concepts, such as CHAIR; for stereotypical situations, such as going to the beach; for familiar text types, such as the story; and numerous other knowledge realms. Language understanding requires that the sentences of a discourse be examined in the context of the appropriate schema. In the examination of the role of knowledge in understanding, this chapter places considerable emphasis on the interpretation of messages with reference to relevant schemata.

Encoding Versus Retrieval Effects of Knowledge

An important principle of this chapter is that knowledge can exert its effects both when one understands, or *encodes*, a message, and also during the later retrieval of the message from memory. This principle was suggested by a well-known study of people's understanding of passages such as the obscure laundry passage that was presented at the outset of this chapter (Bransford & Johnson, 1972). In the experiment, some of the participants were informed that the passage would concern washing clothes, and others were not. The participants listened to the passage, rated their comprehension of the passage, and then attempted to recall it. Those individuals who were told what the passage was about rated it easier to understand and remembered more of its propositions than those who were not given this information.

On the basis of these results, Bransford and Johnson (1972) made an important distinction: They emphasized that relevant knowledge can affect both the encoding and the retrieval of a message. For example, during encoding, access to one's clothes-washing schema can help the understander determine that *things* refers to clothes. During retrieval, the schema can suggest useful guesses about what the passage stated (Bartlett, 1932; Dooling & Lachman, 1971). For example, because clothes are usually washed with detergent, the understander might guess that the passage included a sentence about adding detergent to the wash.

The next section of this chapter examines the encoding effects of knowledge on understanding, and the following section inspects the retrieval effects of knowledge. Then, the final section considers several characteristics of schemata that affect the impact of stored knowledge on language processes.

THE ROLE OF KNOWLEDGE DURING ENCODING

This section focuses on the encoding functions of knowledge. For the present purposes, it is useful to make reference to the following passage:

> Last night, Fred was washing some shirts at his apartment building laundromat. While reading his magazine, he realized that he had no coins left for the dryer. It took Fred twenty minutes to get some change from a building acquaintance. When he got back, Fred found that his washer had overflowed. The place was a mess and the janitor was furious.

This passage concerns washing clothes, and therefore refers to the schema representing the corresponding knowledge: namely, the clothes-washing script. This script is outlined in Table 4.1 Like the restaurant

TABLE 4.1
Outline of Clothes Washing Script

Name:	Washing clothes
Props:	Clothes
	Laundry basket
	Washing machine
	Water
	Detergent
	Clothes dryer
Role:	Person washing the clothes
Entry condition:	Clothes dirty
	Have access to facilities
Result:	Clothes clean

Event chain:	remove clothes from hamper
	sort clothes
	place clothes in laundry basket
	go to laundry facility
	place clothes in washing machine
	choose desired setting
	start washing machine
	wait$_1$
	remove clothes from washing machine
	place clothes in dryer
	wait$_2$
	remove clothes from dryer
	return clothes to proper places

script that was examined in chapter 1, the clothes-washing script consists of props, roles, entry conditions, results, and a causal chain of events. Notice that the main point of the passage, the flood, is a deviation from the clothes-washing script: That is, one does not expect the washing machine to overflow on a regular basis. On the other hand, unlike the obscure laundry passage, this one mentions relatively few of the components of the script. There is no reference to certain props, such as detergent and a laundry basket, nor to many clothes-washing events, such as sorting clothes and going to the laundromat.

This passage is, in fact, quite typical. It is unlikely that one person would tell another about doing one's laundry unless something unusual occurred (Graesser, Gordon, & Sawyer, 1979; Spiro & Esposito, 1981). It is the unusual element that has the potential of making the message interesting. Conversely, one would seldom recite all of the components of a script. To do so would bore the listener, and so would violate the maxims of quantity and relation (Grice, 1975).

Knowledge influences the encoding of a message in at least three ways. First, the propositions of the message can be *integrated* with the understander's knowledge. For example, the ideas underlying the sentence, **He had no coins left for the dryer,** may be linked to the script knowledge that the operation of laundromat machines requires change. Second, knowledge permits the understander to select the correct sense of a word. For example, when reading a wrestling story, the reader would more likely interpret **lock** to refer to a hold than a device to secure a door. Third, knowledge provides the understander with *expectations* about what the message might state. These expectations might facilitate understanding. In this section, these three encoding functions of knowledge are considered in turn.

Integration and Instantiation

One of the main functions of scripts during encoding is to provide a frame of reference for integrating the contents of a message. What this means is that statements in a message become linked to elements of the script. Consider the phrase from the "flooded laundry" story, **in his apartment building laundromat.** This phrase identifies the type of laundry facilities that are being used. Integrating this idea with the clothes-washing script means that it becomes linked with the script event GO TO LAUNDRY FACILITY. Likewise, the statement, **While reading his magazine,** is integrated with the script statement, $WAIT_1$. Table 4.2 lists the parts of the "flooded laundry" episode that are likely to be integrated with components of the clothes-washing script. The integration of dis-

TABLE 4.2
Integration of Elements of Flooded Laundry Episode
with the Clothes Washing Script

Script Component	Script Concept		Story Concept
Props	CLOTHES	→	"shirts"
	CLOTHES DRYER	→	"dryer"
Role	PERSON WASHING THE CLOTHES	→	"Fred"
Events	GO TO LAUNDRY FACILITY	→	"at his apartment building laundromat"
	WAIT$_1$	→	"while reading his magazine"

course statements with script components increases the likelihood that the discourse statements will be reliably stored in memory.

Another facet of integration is referred to as *script instantiation* (Anderson et al., 1978). Instantiation refers to specifying a script component in terms of a particular discourse idea. For example, the clothes-washing script includes the prop, CLOTHES. However, the particular clothes to be washed vary from situation to situation. Therefore, CLOTHES becomes instantiated as SHIRTS when the story statement **Fred was washing some SHIRTS** is encountered. Similarly, the script component, LAUNDRY FACILITY is instantiated as HIS APARTMENT BUILDING LAUNDROMAT.

The principle of script integration provides a possible explanation of people's recall of the obscure laundry passage (Bransford & Johnson, 1972). Those individuals who were told the topic before listening could activate their clothes-washing script, and integrate the discourse ideas with the script components during encoding. This could account for the outcome that the "topic" participants recalled about twice as many idea units as participants who were not told the topic.

Activating the wrong schema during comprehension can prevent the integration of discourse ideas. Consider the following passage, "Watching a Peace March from the 40th Floor."

The view was breathtaking. From the window one could see the crowd below. Everything looked extremely small from such a distance, but the colorful costumes could still be seen. Everyone seemed to be moving in one direction in an orderly fashion and there seemed to be little children as well as adults. The landing was gentle, and luckily the atmosphere was such that no special suits had to be worn. At first there was a great deal of activity. Later, when the speeches started, the crowd quieted down. The man with the television camera took many shots of the setting and the crowd. Everyone was very friendly and seemed glad the music had started. (Bransford & Johnson, 1973, p. 412)

In an experiment, half of the participants were given the "Peace March" title, whereas the others were equipped with the title, "A Space Trip to an Inhabited Planet." (Please take a moment to reread the passage from "Space Trip" perspective.) The entire passage is consistent with the space trip context. In the peace march interpretation, however, the *landing* sentence makes no sense. Fifty-three percent of the "Space Trip" subjects recalled at least part of the *landing* sentence, as compared with only 18% of the "Peace March" subjects. A likely cause of this outcome is the failure to integrate the *landing* sentence with the peace march script.

Selection of Word Sense

A glance at any dictionary will reveal that most common English words are ambiguous. For example, **deck** can refer to a ship's floor or to playing cards, and **table** can refer to an item of furniture or to a mathematical chart. In order to select the correct meaning for each word, one needs to take the current context into account. Accessing knowledge relevant to the message can contribute to these decisions. For example, in the "flooded laundry" story, the clothes-washing script suggests that *washer* should be interpreted as referring to a washing machine rather than to a rubber or metal ring.

To study the impact of knowledge on word-sense selection, passages, such as the 'Spike' prison/wrestling passage, were presented to different groups of students (Anderson, Reynolds, et al., 1976; see also Anderson, Pichert, Goetz, Schallert, Stevens, & Trollip, 1976). (Please take a moment to reread the Spike passage.) Most people who read the Spike story make the PRISON interpretation rather than the WRESTLING interpretation. However, it was anticipated that students on the college weight-lifting team would make the WRESTLING interpretation. A second passage included statements such as, *Lets hear the score.* It was usually interpreted as a card game, but was expected to be interpreted as a concert by music students.

The passages were presented to a group of weight-lifters and a group of music students. The students attempted to recall the stories, and then performed a multiple-choice answering task. Both memory tasks provided evidence of the students' decisions about word sense. In recall, the students wrote down material that clearly reflected one sense or the other. For example, the music students wrote recall statements such as, **Spike was angry that he had been . . . arrested,** revealing that the ARRESTED sense of *held* had been chosen. In contrast, the wrestlers produced statements such as, **Spike was penalized . . . for a dangerous hold.** This indicates that they interpreted *penalty* as a match assessment rather than a criminal sentence. The multiple-choice data likewise revealed that each group interpreted the passages according to their special backgrounds.

Prediction and Expectation

As one encodes a message, one develops a notion of what the message is about. Relevant knowledge may be activated, and in turn generate expectations of what may follow. The creation of such expectations is the third role of knowledge during discourse encoding. In the event that parts of the message match these expectations, the encoding of the message may be made easier.

Consider, for example, the following passage.

> John was in a great hurry to get to work because of an important meeting with his boss. As he was about to leave the house, he slipped on his son's roller skate, fell down the stairs, and . . . (Miller, 1980, pp. 4-5)

The phrase **broke his leg** is a reasonable continuation of this passage. This is because one's knowledge about falling down a flight of stairs includes the possibility of an injury. In contrast, **made some coffee** would be a peculiar continuation at best. It is important to note that falling down a flight of stairs by no means guarantees a broken leg. However, reading that someone fell down the stairs limits the possible outcomes of the message.

Miller (1980) studied the role of people's expectations during reading. In one experiment, people read passages one segment at a time. An example is shown in Table 4.3 After each segment, the participant tried to predict what would follow in the passage. The experimenter classified the segments as occupying one of five locations in the message: paragraph start, sentence start, within sentence, sentence end, and paragraph end. For example, statement 1 is a paragraph-start segment. Across these five locations, there was a systematic increase in people's ability to anticipate what would come next. The scores were especially high for the segments at the end of the paragraph. This suggested that, as the paragraph proceeded, it constrained more and more what was likely to follow.

Inspecting Table 4.3, it is quite easy to understand this result. After

TABLE 4.3
Segments of a Text

1:	It may be the greatest show on earth—
2:	A fantastic fireworks of music and color,
3:	of snappy marching bands and stately floral floats
4:	of beautiful girls and brightly outfitted horses.
5:	It's the annual Tournament of Roses in Pasadena, California,
6:	which begins with a five-and-one-half mile parade
7:	and ends with the spirited competition
8:	of the Rose Bowl football game.

Source: Miller, 1980. Reprinted by permission.

statement 1, the paragraph-start segment, one is likely to generate all sorts of incorrect continuations, including references to rock concerts and circuses. After statement 7, however, almost anyone with some knowledge of the Tournament of Roses will generate an answer that refers to the football game.

If expectations facilitate comprehension, one would also predict that reading rate would be fastest for those passage locations with the most accurate expectations. Reading rate data for passages such as the one shown in Table 4.3 partly supported this prediction (Miller, 1980). From paragraph start to sentence end, reading rate became slightly *slower.* As predicted, however, the rate was by far fastest at the end of the paragraph. This confirms that reading generally proceeds most quickly at those locations in a passage for which the expectations are the most accurate.

How, then, might accurate expectations facilitate comprehension? One hypothesis is that *knowledge-based expectations speed up sense selection for individual words.* In a test of this hypothesis, people read sentences such as (1):

(1) The child's birthday party was going quite well. They all sat round the table prepared to sing.

Immediately afterwards, the subjects had to judge whether test strings of letters formed words (a lexical decision; see chapter 1). They took less time to judge that a test string such as CANDLES was a word when it was preceded by relevant-script material, such as (1), than after reading irrelevant-script sentences, such as (2) (Sharkey & Mitchell, 1985).

(2) The restaurant was quite empty when we got there. We sat down at a vacant table.

In a comparable study, people were more successful in identifying barely audible words when the words were related to the script knowledge suggested by a preceding sentence (Auble & Franks, 1983). These results support the hypothesis that knowledge-based expectations speed up the selection of word sense.

Understanders may be more consciously aware of some types of expectation than others. When one reads, **John fell down the stairs and . . .** one may have a conscious expectation that reference will be made to an injury. In contrast, when the birthday party script is activated by the sentence, **The child's birthday party was going quite well,** it is unlikely that one will consciously expect all of the reasonable continuations, including ones concerning the concepts CANDLES, CAKE, PRESENTS, and MESS. Nonetheless, people's judgments about words in different script contexts (Auble & Franks, 1983; Sharkey & Mitchell, 1985) suggest that the increased activation of script-related concepts contribute to expectations about the words that will appear in a message.

Conclusions

Knowledge affects discourse encoding by permitting the integration of discourse ideas with schema components, by facilitating the selection word sense, and by generating expectations about the remainder of the message. These functions are not completely independent of one another. For example, knowledge-based *expectations* speed up people's selection of word sense. We next turn our attention to the retrieval functions of knowledge.

THE ROLE OF KNOWLEDGE DURING RETRIEVAL

Knowledge Structures as Retrieval Plans

Perhaps the most significant role of prior knowledge during the retrieval of a message is that it provides a *plan for retrieving the needed information* (Anderson & Pichert, 1978; Anderson et al., 1978). For example, if you wished to recall the "flooded laundry" episode, it would be useful to consider your general knowledge about doing laundry. The elements of the clothes-washing script are likely to remind you of story components that have been integrated with them. For example, according to Table 4.2, the script prop CLOTHES would provide access to SHIRTS; and the event, WAIT$_1$ would remind you of WHILE READING A MAGAZINE.

Memory Aids as Retrieval Plans.   Memory aids, such as the peg-word method (Bulgeski, 1968), provide a clear illustration of knowledge providing a retrieval plan. To use the peg-word method, one first memorizes a simple rhyme, such as **One is a bun, two is a shoe, three is a tree, four is a door, five is a hive, six is sticks, seven is heaven, eight is a gate, nine is a pine, ten is a hen.** The rhyme then provides a springboard for learning new material.

For example, suppose one wished to learn the random-word list, **skirt, trout, house, store, crow, fan, pole, snail, suit, knee.** To do so, one would link each successive word in the list with the corresponding word in the peg-word rhyme. That is, because the first word is **skirt, skirt** would be associated with **bun.** The most effective way to relate **skirt** and **bun** is to construct a striking mental image that combines them. For example, you might imagine a cartoon-like burger bun wearing a skirt, such as one might encounter in a TV commercial. Next, **trout** is linked to **shoe:** One might visualize a trout (with legs) wearing shoes, or a trout peeking out of a shoe filled with water. The whole list may be learned in this fashion.

One clear function of the peg-word method is to provide a plan for the retrieval of the new list. Because the rhyme is simple and highly familiar, all of its lines will be recalled, and their order will be preserved. Upon retrieving the first line, **One is a bun, bun** is very likely to remind the learner of its associated word, **skirt.** In other words, **One is a bun** signals the word **bun,** which evokes the image of the bun wearing the skirt, and hence the answer, **skirt.** Because each successive line of the rhyme is easy to retrieve, most of the new words are recalled.

To summarize, the core of the memory aid is an organized knowledge structure, which may be used to integrate new material. Instead of storing numerous unrelated items in memory, the learner integrates each one with part of a familiar knowledge structure. Because of the familiarity and simplicity of the structure, such as the peg-word rhyme, there is little difficulty in retrieving the newly learned information. Analogously, the familiarity and organization of a script provides a plan for retrieving discourse statements that have been integrated with script components during encoding.

Retrieval Plans for Discourse.   Anderson and Pichert (1978) used an ingenious design to provide evidence for the retrieval-plan function of relevant knowledge. In the study, people read a story about two boys who played hooky from school and who visited the home of one of the boys. The story described the characteristics of the large house, such as its leaky roof and damp basement, and its contents, including ten-speed bicycles and a coin collection.

The participants were asked to read the passage from the perspective either of a burglar or of a home buyer. This caused the two groups to apply different knowledge to the passage. Clearly, a coin collection would interest a burglar and a leaky roof would interest a home buyer.

A recall test followed shortly after reading. Not surprisingly, the participants recalled 64% of the idea units relevant to their perspective, and only 50% of the ideas relevant to the other perspective. Of particular interest, however, was a second recall trial. On this trial, some participants were instructed to switch their perspective, such as from home buyer to burglar. Across two experiments, people who switched perspectives recalled 9% more of the ideas relevant to the new perspective than they had on the first recall trial, and 13% fewer of the idea units relevant to the old perspective.

These results indicated that relevant knowledge was influencing people's retrieval (Anderson & Pichert, 1978). Consider a person who, after switching from the homebuyer to the burglar perspective on recall trial 2, suddenly remembers the ten-speed bikes for the first time. Because the passage was read only once, TEN-SPEED BIKES must have been encoded originally. For the participant to recall this unit only after changing perspectives, it must be that the relevant knowledge has exerted its influence at retrieval time.

The authors concluded, in particular, that the knowledge corresponding to the new perspective was used as a retrieval plan. A burglar, for example, would need to know the ways to enter and exit a house, the layout of the rooms, and the location of valuables. By considering these elements one by one, a person might be reminded of relevant ideas. Interviews with the subjects supported this view. For example, one individual said:

> —You say "OK, I'm a burglar, now what do I want to get out of this house," and then you write it down . . . I knew that there were a lot of things, like furs and stuff, that had been described, but I couldn't remember them because I wasn't programmed that way the first time. (Anderson & Pichert, 1978, p. 9)

Reconstruction

Reconstructing the Content of Discourse. In chapter 2, it was proposed that people can reconstruct features of the surface form of messages. Likewise, when retrieving a message, it is possible to reconstruct the content. This refers to generating reasonable guesses about the message, on the basis of pertinent knowledge (e.g., Bartlett, 1932; Frederiksen, 1975; Kintsch & van Dijk, 1978; Spiro, 1980).

Consider the understander who is trying to recall the "flooded laundry" story. Because the story concerned doing laundry, the understander may access the laundry script (Table 4.1). This script includes the event-chain statement, PLACE CLOTHES IN WASHING MACHINE. Although the "flooded laundry" story included no statement about Fred loading the washing machine, this script statement might induce the understander to guess that the sentence, **Fred put his shirts in the washer,** appeared in the story. In making this guess, one would be using relevant knowledge to reconstruct part of the message.

This example reveals that the reconstruction function of knowledge interacts with its role as a retrieval plan. That is, in considering the form of the laundry script, the understander is using it as a retrieval plan. The appearance in the script of the statement, PLACE CLOTHES IN WASHING MACHINE, permits a corresponding reconstruction.

People do not reconstruct messages in a blind fashion. For example, no one trying to recall the "flooded laundry" story would write down **Fred's arm muscles contracted,** even though that might be a true statement (Kintsch & van Dijk, 1978). Furthermore, the reader is likely to have some notion of the length and general sense of the original passage, and will therefore not write down innumerable statements about washing clothes.

Reconstruction in Recall.   It is important to distinguish between *reconstruction* and *reproduction* in recall. Reproduction refers to the recall of ideas that actually appeared in the message, whereas reconstruction involves guessing ideas that are consistent with the message but that did not actually appear (e.g., Bartlett, 1932; Hasher & Griffin, 1978; Kintsch & van Dijk, 1978). Recall becomes gradually less reproductive and more reconstructive as the time interval between comprehension and recall increases. Figure 4.1 shows that, in one study (Kintsch & van Dijk, 1978; see also Singer, 1982), people reproduced about three times as many ideas as they reconstructed immediately after reading. Three months later, the number of reproductions and reconstructions were approximately equal.

The convergence of reproduction and reconstruction over test delay is likely due to the gradual decay of the memory for the details of the message, including its surface form. When faced with a delayed recall task, people understand that they are expected to write down a certain amount of information. To the extent that the precise details are no longer available in memory, they may engage in the reconstruction of the message.

In one study which emphasized the role of reconstruction in discourse recall, Hasher and Griffin (1978) used a method reminiscent of the perspective-change technique examined earlier (Anderson & Pich-ert, 1978). People read ambiguous passages, with the expectation that they would receive a memory test. They were equipped with one of two titles. For example the following passage was titled either "Going Hunting" or "An Escaped Convict."

> The man walked carefully through the forest. Several times he looked over his shoulder and scrutinized the woods behind him. He trod care-fully, trying to avoid snapping the twigs and small branches that lay in his path, for he did not want to create excess noise. The gay chirping of the birds in the trees almost annoyed him, their loud calls serving to distract him. He did not want to confuse those sounds with the type he was listening for. (Hasher & Griffin, 1978, p. 322)

Of greatest importance for the present purposes is a recall test admin-istered one week after reading. Just before the recall test, some of the participants were given the same title that they had originally received and were asked to recall the passage. Other individuals were informed that they had inadvertently been given the incorrect title one week earlier. They were provided with the alternate title. The impact of this

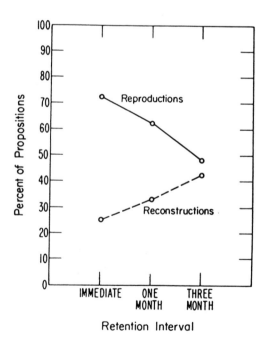

Retention Interval

FIG. 4.1.   Percent of reproductions and reconstructions in text recall as a function of retention interval. *Source:* Adapted from Kintsch & van Dijk, 1978, Figure 5, p. 385. Adapted by permission.

manipulation was striking. The Same-Title participants *reconstructed* an average of 3.0 ideas that were consistent with the original title. For example, with the "Convict" same title, a person might have written down, **He smashed his handcuffs on the rock,** even though the original passage made no reference to such an action. In contrast, the Alternate-Title subjects reconstructed only 0.5 ideas consistent with the original title: that is, only one-sixth as many as the Same-Title group. Equally interesting, the Alternate-Title subjects *reproduced* more ideas from the passage than the Same-Title subjects.

The presentation of an alternate title appears to have discouraged people from using their knowledge to reconstruct the story. For example, having been provided with the alternate title about going hunting, it would no longer have made sense to refer to handcuffs. The Alternate-Title participants appear to have compensated for the inability to reconstruct the message by making a greater effort to retrieve ideas from the text base. This may have resulted from a desire to write down an acceptable number of ideas. Consequently, they reproduced more ideas from the original message than did the Same-Title subjects. To summarize, to recall a message, people appear to be able to consult both the text base, yielding recall reproductions; and related schemata, resulting in reconstructions.

It is possible for an understander to reconstruct an idea that actually appeared in the message. This is a subtle but important feature of the reproduction–reconstruction distinction. Suppose that a person who read the "flooded laundry" passage either failed to integrate **at Fred's apartment building laundromat** with the script event GO TO LAUNDRY FACILITY; or integrated it, but subsequently forgot it. During retrieval, the reader would discover that the script event, GO TO LAUNDRY FACILITY, was not linked with a discourse statement. This might prompt the understander to reconstruct a statement about the laundry facility. Of course, in this event, it would be difficult for an experimenter to detect that the understander had reconstructed this idea, rather than having reproduced it.

Reconstruction in Recognition.   An interesting parallel of recall reconstruction is observed in recognition memory tests. In one study, people read brief narrative passages, equipped with one of two titles. For example, people were told that the following passage concerned either Helen Keller, or the fictional character, "Carol Harris."

HELEN KELLER'S (CAROL HARRIS') NEED
FOR PROFESSIONAL HELP
Helen Keller (Carol Harris) was a problem child from birth. She was wild, stubborn, and violent. By the time Helen (Carol) turned eight, she was

still unmanageable. Her parents were very concerned about her mental health. There was no good institution for her problem in her state. Her parents finally decided to take some action. They hired a private teacher for Helen (Carol). (Sulin & Dooling, 1974, p. 256)

A recognition test was administered either immediately after reading, or one week later. Of particular interest was the following test sentence.

(3)   She was deaf, dumb, and blind.

Although sentence (3) did not appear in the passage, it is consistent with what most people know about Helen Keller. Table 4.4 shows the percentage of times that people recognized test sentences such as (3). In immediate testing, more people in the Helen Keller group reported recognizing sentence (3) than Carol Harris participants. More dramatic was the difference after one week: 50% in the Helen Keller condition, and 5% for Carol Harris participants.

Two aspects of these results should be emphasized. First, the tendency of the Helen Keller subjects to recognize sentence (3) can be attributed to the fact that they consulted their knowledge about Helen Keller. Second, as time elapses, people shift their reliance from the text base to the knowledge underlying a message. In the Helen Keller condition, it is difficult, after one week, to determine that the consistent sentence, (3), did not appear in the passage. In contrast, the Carol Harris participants, who had no pertinent knowledge to examine, virtually never reported recognizing sentence (3).

Output Editing

In addition to its retrieval plan and reconstruction functions, relevant knowledge may permit the understander to engage in *output editing* during discourse retrieval. This refers to the hypothesis that people may

TABLE 4.4
Reported Recognition of Crucial Test Sentence,
"She was Deaf, Dumb, and Blind"

Title	Test Delay	
	Immediate	*One Week*
Helen Keller	20%	50%
Carol Harris	0%	5%

Source: Sulin & Dooling, 1974.

decide not to report ideas that they seem to remember, but which are inconsistent with the relevant knowledge. Suppose that a person read the Burglar–Homebuyer passage, using the burglar perspective during both encoding and retrieval. During recall, the idea about the basement being damp might come to mind. However, the reader might choose to omit this idea, because it does not fit the burglar script. This would constitute output editing.

It is difficult to determine whether the failure to report an idea during recall is a result of output editing or of the retrieval plan function of knowledge. However, interviews with readers of the Burglar-Homebuyer passage (Anderson & Pichert, 1978) suggest that they did not engage in output editing. For example, one person said, "No, I tried to write everything down, even if it seemed stupid" (Anderson & Pichert, 1978, p. 9).

Similarly, Bransford and Johnson (1973) considered the possibility that people who read the Peace March–Space Trip passage from the peach march perspective edited their recall of the sentence, **The landing was gentle, and luckily the atmosphere was such that no special suits had to be worn.** To see whether those individuals remembered that sentence, the experimenters asked them to fill in the blanks in the fragment, **Luckily the landing was _____ and the atmosphere _____.** However, this increased recall only from 18% to 29%. Thus, there is little direct evidence to date of output editing. In spite of this, it is quite conceivable that people edit inconsistent ideas out of their recall reports.

CHARACTERISTICS OF SCHEMATA

Careful scrutiny of the role of knowledge in discourse comprehension began only around 1970. Research since that time has refined our understanding of the characteristics of knowledge schemata. This section examines the way in which those characteristics affect language processes. Five particular issues are examined: differences among scripts, individual differences in knowledge, the acquisition of schemata, the activation of schemata during encoding, and the role of knowledge in summarization and discourse production.

Differences Among Scripts

As we have discussed, scripts represent stereotypical situations in terms of their props, roles, entry conditions, results, and an event chain (Schank & Abelson, 1977). However, there are also interesting differences in the organization of scripts. For example, scripts differ in the extent to which they are associated with a fixed arrangement of places or a fixed sequence of events. In this regard, both the airport script and the amusement park script refer to numerous places. At the airport, the relative locations of the check-in counter, the departure lounge, the shops, and the baggage claim are generally predictable, at least in large North American cities. In contrast, at the amusement park, the physical layout of the funhouse, the roller coaster, and the ferris wheel is relatively arbitrary.

To study the organizational differences among scripts, Anderson et al. (1978) compared people's memory for a restaurant story that mentioned 18 foods, and for a parallel grocery shopping story, which mentioned the same 18 foods in the same order (see also Bower et al., 1979). One would expect the restaurant script to specify the usual sequence in which foods are eaten. In contrast, the grocery script does not prescribe a comparable sequence for purchasing foods. Two of the experimental results were of particular interest. First, the foods were remembered better in the restaurant story than the grocery story. This outcome was attributed to the fact that foods mentioned in the restaurant story are likely to be *integrated* with the food categories that appear in the restaurant script, such as appetizer, soup, entree, and dessert. In contrast, the grocery script does not include comparable food categories with which to integrate story ideas.

Second, people attributed foods to characters more accurately in the restaurant story than the grocery story. The assignment of foods to characters is important in a restaurant meal. It is unlikely, for example, that a person would order three salads and no main course. In grocery shopping, the connection of foods to characters is arbitrary.

Individual Differences in Knowledge

If knowledge is essential for understanding, then the particular knowledge of the understander is likely to influence the course of comprehension. For example, whereas most people who read the "Spike" passage (considered earlier) make the prison interpretation, weight-lifters predominantly see the wrestling sense (Anderson, Reynolds, et al., 1976). The natural appearance of a completely ambiguous passage, such as the "Spike" passage, is highly unlikely. However, most ordinary messages are likely to carry quite different meanings to those familiar and unfamiliar with the theme. It is easy to imagine that a recipe for a multilayered cake will have special meaning for a chef, the account of a world-championship chess match for a chess expert, and a chapter from a graduate-level text in economics for an economics graduate student.

Knowledgeable understanders can apply sophisticated schemata to the understanding of a message. This point was emphasized in a study of people who were either high or low in baseball knowledge (Spilich, Vesonder, Chiesi, & Voss, 1979). The investigators proposed that the baseball schema includes setting information, such as which teams are playing; the goal structure of the game, such as scoring runs; and game actions, such as the shortstop throwing the ball to first base.

The participants listened to an account of a baseball half-inning. Although most of the statements were relevant to the baseball schema, others referred to nongame actions, such as the weather and the behavior of the crowd. In 15 minutes of recalling the passage, people high in baseball knowledge performed better. However, their advantage was confined to statements relevant to the baseball schema. There was no difference in the recall of nongame actions by high-knowledge and low-knowledge individuals. The experimental design did not identify which particular encoding and retrieval functions of relevant knowledge accounted for the outcome. However, one may speculate that the high-knowledge individuals were able to integrate game-relevant statements with their baseball schema.

The particular knowledge that readers bring to bear on language messages has become an important concern in the study of language comprehension. It is clear that, with insufficient knowledge about the content of a message, the understander will be as badly off as the individual who reads the obscure laundry passage (Bransford & Johnson, 1972) without the benefit of a title.

Acquisition of Schemata

Throughout this chapter, it has been assumed that the knowledge that the understander applies to incoming messages is always available in its complete form. However, theorists have acknowledged that a person's knowledge schemata develop gradually from infancy, and throughout adulthood. The young child does not come equipped with a restaurant schema, or knowledge of Helen Keller. However, we may be sure that a general EATING schema quickly becomes available. As experience with restaurants grows, the child presumably refines the eating schema, picking out those aspects of eating that are characteristic of the restaurant setting.

Schema specialization and *schema generalization* are two processes that contribute to the development of schemata (Rumelhart & Ortony, 1977). Schema specialization is exemplified by the evolution of the restaurant schema from the eating schema. Like the more general eating schema, eating in a restaurant involves sitting at a table, using knives and forks, and the consumption of a meal. However, there are numerous special aspects of eating in a restaurant. One usually is approached by the waiter, gives an order, and ultimately pays for the meal.

Schema generalization refers to a process opposite to specialization: namely, extending a schema to a wider range of circumstances. For example, a child might initially possess a BREAK schema that involves the physical destruction of an object, such as a plate. Later, it might be observed that destroying the function of an object, such as a radio, does not require that it be broken into numerous pieces. The result might be the evolution of a more general BREAK schema, according to which an object may be broken either by physical destruction or by disruption of its function (Rumelhart & Ortony, 1977).

Activation of Schemata

The main theme of this chapter is that complex messages are interpreted with reference to relevant knowledge. This raises the question of how one accesses and activates the appropriate knowledge. For example, the first segment of the Tournament of Roses passage, **It may be the greatest show on earth—** (see Table 4.3), is consistent with many topics, such as the circus and an important auto race. However, information processing limitations (e.g., Newell & Simon, 1972; Posner & Snyder, 1975) are likely to prevent the simultaneous use of all of these schemata.

One obvious way in which the correct schema might become active is if a message is accompanied by an appropriate title or topic sentence. A magazine headline, such as **The Drug Crisis,** leaves little doubt as to which knowledge schema to invoke. Similarly, a topic sentence, such as **Washing clothes is actually quite simple,** permits the understander to activate the relevant script (see chapter 6).

Without such clues, the problem is more complicated. Sentences such as **It may be the greatest show on earth–** can refer to many contexts. However, it clearly does not refer to grocery shopping or to typing a letter. Thus, the information from such a text can be used to narrow down schema selection, until a reasonable hypothesis is generated. On occasion, the wrong schema may be accessed, which can have surprising consequences. In this vein, the present author once tuned into a radio news report to hear the announcer state that soldiers in a foreign country were searching the countryside. Because a major earthquake had occurred recently, I activated my AFTERMATH OF AN EARTHQUAKE script. I was then startled when the announcer stated that soldiers, who I had assumed were digging out survivors, had arrested some villagers. The news item in fact referred to a guerilla conflict.

It might appear circular to propose that a knowledge schema is necessary for understanding, and that, at the same time, discourse information must be used to identify the relevant schema. However, this observation provides another illustration of the role of both top-down and bottom-up processes in comprehension. In particular, using discourse ideas to select the appropriate schema is a bottom-up function. The influence of an active schema upon the interpretation of a discourse statement is top-down in nature.

The principles of script activation were inspected in Sharkey and Mitchell's (1985) study of the influence of script information on lexical decisions (see earlier discussion). To review, the presentation of the sequence, **The child's birthday party was going quite well. They all sat round the table prepared to sing** sped up people's subsequent judgment that CANDLES is a word. This outcome was interpreted to show that the sequence activated the birthday party script, which in turn raised the activation of the concept, CANDLES. Using similar manipulations, Sharkey and Mitchell found that a script can be activated by even a single script-relevant statement. However, it takes several statements pertinent to a new script to deactivate an already active script. In addition, neutral statements do not deactivate current scripts. For example, in the sequence, **The child's birthday party was going quite well. Al looked out the window,** the sentence **Al looked out the window** does not deactivate the birthday party script. More experimentation of this sort is needed to further clarify the mechanisms of knowledge activation.

The Role of Knowledge in Other Language Tasks

Although this chapter has emphasized the role of knowledge in comprehension, knowledge exerts comparable influences on other language functions. For example, after understanding a complex message, people have the ability to summarize it (Brown & Day, 1983; Kintsch & van Dijk, 1978). One reason that knowledge structures, such as scripts, contribute to summarization is that script components vary in their importance (Bower et al., 1979; Schank & Abelson, 1977). For example, the restaurant script has been proposed to consist of important *scene headers,* such as ENTERING, ORDERING, EATING, and EXITING. These categories may be further broken down to less important details, called *scene actions* (Abbott, Black, & Smith, 1985). When asked to summarize a restaurant story, it is more likely that one would choose to report the ideas that were integrated with scene headers during encoding than those associated with scene actions.

Likewise, schemata have been proposed to guide the production of new messages (Bracewell, Frederiksen, & Frederiksen, 1982; Kintsch & van Dijk, 1978). For example, to create a story about fighting a forest fire, one would almost certainly have to activate one's forest fire script. The presence, in the script, of components such as the goal of extinguishing the fire, the need for volunteers and equipment, and the effect of the weather conditions, would likely influence the creation of the story. This by no means implies that a sentence would be derived from each component of the script. However, the structure and content of the script would likely exert an impact on the form of the message.

SUMMARY

There is considerable evidence that language understanding can proceed only with reference to one's knowledge about the world. Even a single sentence, such as **The haystack was important because the cloth ripped,** makes sense only when one is informed about the plight of a parachutist. Complex messages are understood with reference to schemata that represent the understander's organized knowledge of the world.

World knowledge influences both the encoding and the retrieval of a message. During encoding, knowledge serves several functions. First, discourse ideas may be integrated with the components of a schema. Second, relevant knowledge contributes to the selection of word sense. For example, when one encounters the word *fork* in a passage describing a car chase, the car chase script favors the ROAD DIVISION sense of *fork* over the EATING UTENSIL sense. Third, knowledge provides the basis of expectations about what the message is likely to say next. These expectations facilitate comprehension.

During retrieval, relevant knowledge acts as a plan for efficiently retrieving the message components. It plays a role analogous to that of familiar memory aids, such as the peg-word method. Second, knowledge permits the understander to reconstruct parts of the message. For example, having read a message about a restaurant meal, it would be reasonable to propose that the message stated that a waiter took the order, even if one did not distinctly recall such a statement. Third, knowledge may prompt the understander to edit the memory report, so as to exclude ideas that do not seem to fit.

The characteristics of schemata influence language processes. First, schemata that are associated with a usual sequence of events or arrangement of locations provide certain advantages in organizing discourse ideas, as compared with more loosely organized schemata. Second, people exhibit extensive differences in their knowledge. These differences influence the interpretation of messages. Third, knowledge schemata are not static: Rather, they are constantly being generalized to broader circumstances, or refined to narrower ones. Fourth, a schema can be activated by one or more of its component statements, and deactivated by a sequence of statements relevant to a different schema. Fifth, schemata contribute to language tasks other than comprehension and retrieval. For example, pertinent knowledge guides the understander's summarization of a message, and the speaker's production of new messages.

5

Understanding Coherent Discourse

Language messages consist of units of many levels of complexity, including words, phrases, clauses, and sentences. However, people seldom need to make judgments about isolated linguistic units. Rather, they typically manipulate spoken or written discourses that convey sensible meanings in appropriate contexts. Later, they need to retrieve the discourse to report it to others, to answer questions, and to make judgments of accuracy.

Consider the following brief excerpt from the beginning of a chapter in a novel:

(1) "Flight 108 to Paris. Air France. This way please."
(2) The persons in the lounge at Heath Row Airport rose to their feet.
(3) Hilary Craven picked up her small lizard-skin travelling case and moved in the wake of the others, out on to the tarmac. (4) The wind blew sharply cold after the heated air of the lounge. (5) Hilary shivered and drew her furs a little closer round her. (Christie, 1967, pp. 24–25)

This passage appears clear and sensible, and few would object to its appearance in a mystery novel. A central feature of this paragraph is that it is *coherent*. This means that the parts of the message are related or connected to one another. Because the reader can identify these connections, the message can be understood.

What are these connections, and how does the understander identify them? Many of them are straightforward and easy to pick out. The repetition of the term *lounge* in sentence (4) obviously refers to the

113

Heath Row lounge introduced in sentence (2). Likewise, the possessive pronoun *her* in sentence (3) refers to Hilary Craven, and *others* is a shorthand phrase referring to the other persons.

Consistent with the ideas of chapter 4, other connections in the passage depend on the reader's knowledge of the usual relations among its concepts. This is readily illustrated by making a few substitutions in the passage:

> (1') "Flight 108 to Paris. *British Rail.* This way please."
> (2') The persons in the lounge at Heath Row Airport rose to their feet.
> (3') Hilary Craven picked up her small *electric toaster* and moved in the wake of the others, out on to the tarmac. (4') The *air conditioning* blew sharply cold after the heated air of the lounge. (5') Hilary shivered and drew her furs a little closer round her.

The phrase **British Rail,** is puzzling because it is not obvious what a railway has to do with Flight 108. It is not impossible for a traveler to carry a toaster, but it is certainly less likely than a suitcase. Finally, it is hard to understand the appearance of **air conditioning** in sentence (4'), because sentence (3') suggested that the passengers went outside. The disruption caused by these substitutions suggests that the coherence of a sequence such as **Flight 108 to Paris. Air France.** depends on the consistency of the underlying ideas with our world knowledge.

This chapter addresses the problem of how people discover and make use of the coherence relations underlying discourse. The first section proposes that, to maintain coherence, the understander needs to distinguish between given and new information in each sentence. Given information refers to those ideas with which the speaker assumes that the listener is already familiar. Coherence is enhanced if the understander can find a referent for given sentence ideas.

The second section examines differences in the processing of given and new sentence information. The third section inspects the impact on coherence of discovering referents for given information. The fourth section considers how understanders overcome impediments to coherence. The last section examines the factors that affect the speed of reading coherent text.

COHERENCE AND THE GIVEN-NEW ANALYSIS

Defining Given and New Sentence Information

Most sentences in a discourse permit the understander to distinguish between *given* and *new* information. Given ideas are those that the speaker assumes are already familiar to the listener. In contrast, new assertions about the given information form the new component (Halliday, 1967; Haviland & Clark, 1974). For example, in the sentence, **What the crowd enjoyed was the music,** it is given that the crowd enjoyed something. The speaker supplies the new information that what was enjoyed was the music. Given information is frequently referred to as being *presupposed* (e.g., Hornby, 1974). The given–new distinction is also similar to one made between the *topic* and the *comment* of a sentence: "The speaker announces a topic and then says something about it" (Hockett, 1958, p. 201).

It has been hypothesized that identifying the given and new segments of a sentence permits the understander to encode corresponding given and new propositions. For example, the sentence, **What the crowd enjoyed was the music** conveys the proposition, (ENJOY, CROWD, MUSIC). This proposition can be further decomposed into a given and a new proposition. The given proposition is (ENJOY, CROWD, X). The argument X represents an unknown entity. The new proposition is (MUSIC, X), in which the characteristic of being music is predicated of the entity, X (Clark & Clark, 1977). For most of the purposes of this book, it is not necessary to show the decomposition of propositions into their given and new components.

If the given proposition of a sentence is not true, then the entire sentence is inappropriate (Strawson, 1952). For example, it makes no sense to ask whether the sentence **What the crowd enjoyed was the music** is true or false unless the given proposition, THE CROWD ENJOYED SOMETHING, is true.

In the treatment of the given–new analysis of sentences, investigators have sometimes distinguished primarily between the *nouns* associated with the given and new components. In our example sentence, **crowd** is the given noun and **music** is the new noun. However, the given and new components of sentences are propositions, and not simply nouns.

The Given–New Strategy

It has been proposed that a strategy based on the given–new distinction plays a central role is discourse comprehension (Clark & Haviland, 1977; Haviland & Clark, 1974). Following the principle of cooperation between speakers and understanders (Grice, 1975), the speaker should mark as given just those ideas that the understander is believed to already know. Assuming that this has been done, the *understander* executes the given–new strategy in three states, as follows:

Stage 1:   The understander divides the sentence content into given and new propositions. For example, the sentence, **It is the sailor who**

is holding the cat, yields the given proposition (HOLD, X, CAT) and the new proposition (SAILOR, X).

Stage 2:   The understander searches memory for a referent idea that matches the given proposition, which in the present example is (HOLD, X, CAT). This means that the understander must have previously learned, either from the current discourse or another source, that someone held the cat.

Stage 3:   The new information is integrated with the referent of the given component. As a result, the referent proposition is updated to the form (HOLD, SAILOR, CAT).

Factors Distinguishing Given and New Sentence Information

To use the given–new strategy, the understander must be able to distinguish given and new information. People's judgments about given sentence information are influenced by syntactic, lexical, intonational, and semantic factors. These four categories will be examined in turn. The role of *syntax* is illustrated by grammatical constructions called *clefts*. For example, the cleft-agent sentence, **It is the dog that chased the squirrel,** makes a reasonably clear distinction between the given information, SOMETHING CHASED THE SQUIRREL, and the new information, THE DOG DID IT. Likewise, in the pseudocleft-agent sentence, **What chased the squirrel was the dog,** it is given that something chased the squirrel. The new information again refers to the agent, DOG.

Simpler syntactic constructions also distinguish given and new ideas. In the passive sentence, **The squirrel was chased by the dog,** the given information is that the squirrel was chased, and the new information is that the dog did the chasing. The simple active, **The dog chased the squirrel,** makes only a weak, though non-negligible distinction between the given concept, DOG, and the new concept, SQUIRREL (Hornby, 1972; Lehnert, 1978; Lyons, 1977).

The syntactic form of individual phrases also signals givenness. For example, both the descriptive relative clause (sentence 6) and adjectival modification (sentence 7) present given information.

(6)   The cup *that was dropped* broke.
       Given: THE CUP WAS DROPPED
(7)   The *green* cup broke.
       Given: THE CUP WAS GREEN

The definite article, **the,** carries the suggestion that the modified noun is part of the given information.

(8)   A doctor visited *the* lawyer.
      Given: SOMEONE VISITED THE LAWYER

Finally, sentence (9) illustrates that information referred to by a pronoun must be given rather than new.

(9)   *He* visited the lawyer.
      Given: A referent exists for *he*

Like syntax, the *lexical* features of discourse identify given ideas. For example, adjectives such as **more,** adverbs such as **again, too,** and **still,** and verbs, such as **stop** and **forget,** can convey the fact that a particular idea is given (Haviland & Clark, 1974). This is illustrated by examples (10) and (11).

(10)   "Take some *more* tea," the March Hare said to Alice, very earnestly.
       "I've had nothing yet," Alice replied in an offended tone; "so I can't take more" (Carroll, 1960, p. 65).
(11)   Gene *forgot* to cancel the newspaper.
       Given: GENE WAS SUPPOSED TO CANCEL THE NEWS-PAPER

Strong *intontational stress* in spoken utterances conveys that the stressed information is new (Cutler & Fodor, 1979; Hornby, 1972). If one emphasizes **lawyer** in the pronunciation of sentence (12), then it is given that someone visited the doctor.

(12)   The lawyer visited the doctor.
       Given: SOMEONE VISITED THE DOCTOR

If the stress were instead placed on **doctor,** then the given idea would be that the lawyer visited someone.
   Finally, *semantic* characteristics of sentences help to distinguish given and new information. As discussed in chapter 3, sentence information is usually interpreted as given if it appears in the initial sentence position (sentence 13) (Clark & Clark, 1977, p. 32; Lehnert, 1978; Lyons, 1977, p. 503).

(13)   The lawyer visited the doctor.
       Given: THE LAWYER DID SOMETHING or THE LAWYER VISITED SOMEONE

Another semantic cue of given information is quantification. If a noun phrase is quantified, it is very difficult to interpret the idea it conveys as given (sentence 14).

(14)   Four turtles devoured the lettuce.
        Given: SOMETHING DEVOURED THE LETTUCE

PROCESSING GIVEN AND NEW INFORMATION

A significant component of the task of language comprehension is the discovery of coherence connections. Many hypotheses concerning the comprehension of coherent discourse are based on the distinction between given and new sentence information, and the given–new strategy (Clark & Haviland, 1977). The present section examines people's ability to distinguish between given and new sentence information, and the relative amount of processing of given versus new information. The following section considers the role of retrieving referents of given information in maintaining coherence.

Distinguishing Given and New Sentence Information

At Stage 1 of the given–new strategy (Clark & Haviland, 1977), described earlier, the listener divides a sentence into given and new components. This subsection examines evidence that (a) people are sensitive to the difference between given and new sentence information, and (b) people identify the given component as the sentence topic.

Sensitivity to Given Versus New Information.   The distinction between given and new sentence information suggests that two sentences with the same propositional content but different given–new structure have somewhat different meanings. If this is true, then people's judgments about a sentence should vary as a function of its given–new structure. This hypothesis was tested by embedding sentences such as (15a)–(15d) in brief paragraphs (Offir, 1973).

(15)   a.   That Sioux Indian he befriended represented the Chief.
        b.   He befriended that Sioux Indian who represented the Chief.
        c.   A Sioux Indian he befriended represented the Chief.
        d.   He befriended a Sioux Indian who represented the Chief.

Sentences (15a) and (15b) have different given–new structures. The use of the demonstrative adjective *that* to modify **Sioux Indian** designates one of the propositions in each sentence as given. In (15a), the juxtaposition of **that Sioux Indian** and the reduced relative clause, **(who) be befriended,** signals that HE BEFRIENDED THAT SIOUX-IN-DIAN is given and THAT SIOUX-INDIAN REPRESENTED THE CHIEF is new. Just the opposite is true in (15b). In contrast, because both sentences (15c) and (15d) use the indefinite article *a* to modify **Sioux Indian,** their given–new structures are similar. That is, in both (15c) and (15d), both of the propositions, HE BEFRIENDED A SIOUX-INDIAN and A SIOUX-INDIAN REPRESENTED THE CHIEF, are new.

People read paragraphs that included sentences such as (15a)–(15d). A subsequent recognition test showed that they could distinguish between (15a) and (15b) much more easily than between (15c) and (15d) (Offir, 1973). This outcome revealed that people are sensitive to the given–new structure of sentences, and that the distinction is encoded in the course of sentence comprehension.

Identification of Given Sentence Information as the Topic.   The topic of a sentence is generally defined as "what the sentence is about" (e.g., Hockett, 1958; Reinhart, 1982). The distinction between given and new sentence information suggested the hypothesis that people identify the given component of a sentence as the topic. In a test of this proposal, people were presented with sentences that were accompanied by a pair of pictures (Hornby, 1972). For example, **The one who is hitting the bag is the carpenter** was accompanied by pictures of a carpenter hitting a nail, and of a boxer hitting a (punching) bag (see Fig. 5.1). The participants were informed that, although the sentence accurately described neither of the pictures, they were to identify the picture that the sentence was about.

If people identify the given noun of the sentence as the topic, then they should choose the picture that portrays the given noun in this task. The study inspected seven constructions hypothesized to distinguish given and new information: active, passive, cleft-agent, cleft-object, pseudocleft-agent, pseudocleft-object, and the intonationally stressed agent. The prediction was strongly supported: For all seven constructions, people selected the picture showing the given noun more often than the picture showing the new noun. In the example sentence, **The one who is hitting the bag is the carpenter,** *bag* is the given noun. For this sentence, people predominantly selected the picture showing the bag being hit by the boxer (see Fig. 5.1) (Hornby, 1972).

Priority of Processing Given and New Information

People's ability to distinguish given and new sentence information raises the possibility that it is more important to check the accuracy and truth of new information than given information. After all, given

FIG. 5.1. Participants were asked whether **The one who is hitting the bag is the carpenter** was "about" the left or right picture, even though it was incorrect. They predominantly selected the picture showing the given sentence noun, *bag*.

information is likely to have been previously evaluated. To test this hypothesis, Hornby (1974) presented people with tape-recorded cleft and pseudocleft sentences, such as (16).

(16)   It is the girl that is holding the cat.

Each sentence was followed one second later by a corresponding picture. The picture was displayed for only ¹⁄₂₀ second. The task was to indicate whether or not the sentence accurately described the picture. In fact, most of the sentences did not match their pictures. The discrepancy could lie either in the given or the new component of the sentence. For example, in (16), **cat** is part of the given component. If this sentence is followed by a picture of a girl holding a dog, then the discrepancy resides in the given sentence component. If the same sentence is followed by a picture of a boy holding a cat, then the discrepancy appears in the new component of the sentence.

The data supported the proposal that new information is scrutinized more closely than given information. People overlooked 72% of discrepancies between the picture and given sentence information, as compared with 39% of the discrepancies between the picture and new information (Hornby, 1974; see also Erickson & Mattson, 1981; Loftus, 1975; Loftus & Palmer, 1974). In terms of our example, people more frequently stated that sentence (16) accurately described a picture of a girl holding a dog than one of a boy holding a cat.

If people inspect new information more closely than given information, then the new information should be *remembered* better. To test this hypothesis, I presented people with lists of cleft and pseudocleft sentences. Subsequent memory tests revealed, as predicted, that new nouns were recognized more often than given nouns, that new nouns were more effective recall prompts for their sentences than given nouns, and that the adjectives modifying new nouns are recalled more often than those modifying given nouns (Singer, 1976).

It is interesting to note that, in these studies (Hornby, 1972, 1974; Singer, 1976), the sentences were presented without prior linguistic context. The given component of a sentence is truly given only if the corresponding concepts have been mentioned earlier in a discourse, or are available in the context of the discourse. Therefore, these findings particularly attest to the power of given–new sentence structure in guiding comprehension.

The fact that people noticed more discrepancies in new than in given information (Hornby, 1974) might be interpreted to suggest that people process new sentence information *before* they process given information. This proposal directly contradicts the given–new strategy (Clark & Haviland, 1977). However, it has been shown that, although given information is processed more superficially than new information, it is processed before the new information (Conrad & Rips, 1986).

COHERENCE AND THE IDENTIFICATION
OF THE REFERENTS OF GIVEN INFORMATION

Stage 2 of the given–new strategy requires that the understander find, in memory, a referent idea that matches the given information of the current sentence. Psychologists and linguists have identified many linguistic devices that signal that two expressions refer to the same entity, a phenomenon called *coreference* (e.g., Clark & Haviland, 1977; Halliday & Hasan, 1976). These devices guide the retrieval of the referents of sentence information.

In this section, we first examine the constructions that provide access to the referents of sentences, and review pertinent experimental evidence. Second, special attention is devoted to the role of pronouns in the retrieval of referents. Third, some general principles of the retrieval of referents are considered.

Coherence and Coreference

Syntactic Coherence Cues.   Many sentences describe either a concept or an action that was directly mentioned earlier in the discourse. In this event, it is usually possible for the understander to detect this coreference. Frequently, the given component of a sentence consists of a noun phrase that makes *direct reference* to a concept introduced earlier. For example, in sentence (17b), the definite article, *the,* marks *beer* as given.

> (17)   a.   We got some beer out of the car.
>   b.   The beer was warm.

The reader of (17b) should have no difficulty identifying a referent for **beer,** because (17a) specified the existence of the beer, using the exact same word.

Only slightly more demanding is the use of a pronoun to refer to an earlier entity of a message. For example, one can readily determine that the pronoun **she,** in sentence (18b), refers to Hilary.

> (18)   a.   Hilary Craven picked up her small lizard-skin travelling case and moved in the wake of the others, out on to the tarmac.
>   b.   She shivered and drew her furs a little closer round her.

Other syntactic devices that signal a connection between the current sentence and prior discourse are illustrated by (19) and (20) (Halliday & Hasan, 1976).

> (19)   Jill has a red kite and Bill has a green one.
> (20)   Frank's grades were good but Fred's were terrible.

In sentence (19), the word *one* functions as an article that is *substituted* for the noun, **kite.** In sentence (20), **but Fred's were terrible** is called an *elliptical* clause, in which the term **grades** is omitted entirely.

Coherence and Semantic Relations.   In many messages, coherence is signaled not by grammatical devices but rather by semantic relations. Sequences (21)–(24) provide several cases in point.

> (21)   a.   The victim called the lawyer.
>   b.   The attorney accepted the case.

(22) a. The author painted the fence.
      b. The brush was too small.

(23) a. The lightning struck suddenly.
      b. The hut collapsed in a pile of splinters.

(24) a. Anne chased the fly.
      b. The insect flew out the window.

In sequence (21), the referent of **attorney** in (21b) is the individual to whom **lawyer** referred in (22a). Coreference is signaled by the substitution in (21b) of the synonym, **attorney.** In (22), there is no explicit connection between sentence (22a) and sentence (22b). On the basis of general knowledge, however, it is apparent that **brush** in (22b) functions as the instrument used to accomplish the action described in (22a). Similarly, (23b) is agreeable in the context of (23a) because the understander can detect that the lightning strike *caused* the hut to collapse (Black & Bern, 1981; Keenan et al., 1984). Sequence (24) uses both coreference and meaning relations to maintain coherence: In particular, the reader's knowledge of category relations makes it a simple matter to decide that the term **insect** in (24b) refers to the same entity as **fly** in (24a). There are a great many meaning relations that have the capacity of linking the sentences of a discourse in this fashion.

Coherence and Situation Models.   It was proposed in chapter 2 that comprehension results in the representation of the surface form, text base, and situation of a discourse. The situation model captures any context to which a message refers. It may represent the spatial arrangements of objects, the procedure for performing a task, or the goals and intentions of the participants in a conversation. Coherence can be maintained with reference to the situation model underlying a discourse. This is referred to as *global coherence.* In contrast, coherence signaled by the coreference of the propositions and arguments of the text base is *local coherence* (van Dijk & Kintsch, 1983).
    Consider the following example.

(25) a. Carl heated the oven to 425 degrees.
      b. He took some butter out of the refrigerator.
      c. Carl went outside and picked some raspberries in the garden.

At a superficial level, sentences (25a)–(25c) might be viewed as describing a disjoint set of activities on the part of Carl. However, if the reader recognizes those activities as contributing to the *plan* of baking a raspberry pie, the sequence is satisfactorily coherent.

Sequence (26) presents a narrative dialogue of a sort that might appear in a novel.

(26)   a.   Bob's first solo was to be on Saturday.
       b.   "Does Bob think that his performance will go well?" Jane asked.
       c.   "It should be an enthusiastic audience."
       d.   "He certainly does," Bill said.

Sentence (26d) might be expected to pose some difficulty for the reader. This is because it includes the pronoun, *he*, for which there is no referent in the immediately preceding sentence, (26c). However, the structure of the discourse provides an important clue about the role of (26d): Namely, it answers a question posed in (26b). In fact, people have little difficulty understanding sentences such as (26d), suggesting that their situation model of the discourse contributes to the sense that sequences such as (26) are coherent (Malt, 1985).

Conclusion.   In order to comprehend discourse, the understander must integrate the content of the current sentence with what has preceded. According to the given–new strategy, the understander seeks referents for the given information of discourse sentences. This is achieved by the detection of coreference among the elements of the text base. Referents for given information are also signaled by semantic relations, relevant world knowledge, and the situation model of the discourse.

Resolution of Pronouns

> Mouse: "I proceed. 'Edwin and Morcar, the earls of Mercia and Northumbria, declared for him; and even Stigand, the patriotic bishop of Canterbury, found it advisable—' "
> "Found what?" said the Duck.
> "Found it," the Mouse replied rather crossly: "of course you know what 'it' means."
> "I know what 'it' means well enough. When I find a thing," said the Duck, "it's generally a frog or a worm . . ." (Carroll, 1960, p. 21)

Pronouns identify given sentence information. The substitution of pronouns for nouns is a pervasive shorthand device for referring to previously mentioned concepts. For example, in sequence (27), the possessive pronoun **his** and the personal pronoun **he** both refer to Bob.

(27) a. "Does Bob think that his performance will go well?" Jane
          asked.
      b. "He certainly does," Bill said.

Furthermore, the use of pronouns is not merely an optional shortcut.
The repetition of *Bob* in sequence (28) seems either to be ungrammatical,
or to refer to two different Bobs (Halliday & Hasan, 1976, p. 8).

(28) a. "Does Bob think that Bob's performance will go well?" Jane
          asked.
      b. "Bob certainly does," Bill said.

This section examines the cognitive principles of *pronominal resolution:* that is, of identifying the correct referents of pronouns. The linguistic function of referring back is called *anaphoric reference.* There are,
in fact, many different anaphoric constructions. For example, sentence
(29b) refers back to the concept PLUM with the *definite noun phrase,*
the sweet fruit.

(29) a. Sam ate the plum.
      b. The sweet fruit was delicious.

Sentence (30) refers to PLUM using the nominal substitution, **one.**

(30) Sam ate a sweet plum and Pam ate a sour one.

Finally, sentence (31b) refers to PLUM using the pronoun, *it.*

(31) a. Sam ate the plum.
      b. It was delicious.

Pronominal reference in particular has been studied so extensively that
it has provided some important clues about the principles of anaphoric
reference.

Local and Syntactic Factors of Pronoun Resolution.   To facilitate
comprehension, the appearance of a pronoun must permit the quick
retrieval of its referent. What guides this retrieval? There are several
factors that intuitively appear to play an important role in this regard.
For example, it should be easier to resolve a pronoun *with only one
possible referent* than several, and easier to resolve pronouns with
recent referents in the message than distant ones. In addition, the fact
that pronouns vary on dimensions such as *person, number,* and *gender*

suggests that these features guide pronominal resolution. These factors have been the object of psychological investigations.

Sequences (32)–(37) typify the sorts of materials that have been inspected in the study of the factors that guide pronominal resolution. For example, the pronoun *it* in sentence (32b) has only a single possible antecedent, **education,** whereas in (33b), *it* has two possible antecedents, **education** and **well-trained mind.**

(32) a.   Education is, above all, supposed to enlighten.
      b.   *It* should concern itself with developing the high ability to read, learn, and understand.

(33) a.   Education is, above all, supposed to produce a well-trained mind.
      b.   *It* should concern itself with developing the high ability to read, learn, and understand.

In both (34c) and (35c), the antecedent of **it** is **a book.** In sequence (34), this antecedent appears in the immediately preceding sentence, and in (35), it appears two sentences earlier. This difference makes it slightly harder to understand sentence (35c) than (34c).

(34) a.   Yesterday I met a woman who was an expert on viruses.
      b.   She had written a book on the topic.
      c.   *It* was selling very well.

(35) a.   Yesterday I met a woman who had written a book on viruses.
      b.   She had studied them for years and years.
      c.   *It* was selling very well.

Finally, gender agreement reveals only one possible antecedent for **he** in (36), as compared to two in (37).

(36)   Sal scolded Ron because he was annoying.
(37)   Tom scolded Ron because he was annoying.

The experimental study of these factors has borne out their impact on pronominal resolution. Typically, investigators have measured the time that people need to read all or part of a sentence that includes a pronoun. Sentences including pronouns with only a single referent indeed take less time to read than ones with several candidates (Ehrlich, 1980; Frederiksen, 1981; Springston, 1975). Similarly, pronoun understanding proceeds faster when the gender of the pronoun rules out all but one antecedent (Caramazza, Grober, Garvey, & Yates, 1977; Vonk, 1985). Finally, it takes less time to read sentences whose pronouns have recent referents than distant ones. The reason that recency affects pronoun resolution is that, as the understander proceeds through a discourse, earlier propositions are deleted from working memory. Restoring a proposition to working memory from long-term memory, a process called reinstatement, is a time-consuming mental activity. Because of this, it takes a relatively long time to read a sentence that includes a pronoun that demands such a reinstatement (Carpenter & Just, 1977; Clark & Sengul, 1979; Frederiksen, 1981; Kintsch & van Dijk, 1978; Lesgold, Roth, & Curtis, 1979; McKoon & Ratcliff, 1980b; O'Brien, Duffy, & Myers, 1986).

Semantic Factors of Pronoun Resolution.   Pronoun resolution is also guided by semantic factors. The role of these factors becomes apparent particularly when grammatical factors do not provide a satisfactory solution. One semantic relation that has received considerable attention is the implicit causality of verbs, illustrated by sequences (38) and (39).

(38)   Donna punished Alice because she confessed to shoplifting.
(39)   Donna phoned Alice because she needed money.

In both sentences, the pronoun she has two possible antecedents. In spite of this, most people agree that she refers to Alice in sentence (38) and to Donna in sentence (39) (Caramazza et al., 1977). This judgment appears to be based on which character's qualities "caused" the action: For example, Alice's committing shoplifting might prompt someone to punish her. It is interesting to note that, in sentence (39), the impact of causality overcomes the recency variable, resulting in the assignment of she to the less recent noun.

To assess the impact of implicit causality, Caramazza et al. (1977) created sentences such as (40) and (41), in which the subordinate clause (i.e., **because he . . .**) expressed an idea that was either consistent or inconsistent with the causal sense of the main clause.

(40)   John telephoned Pete because he needed some information. (consistent)
(41)   John telephoned Pete because he withheld some information. (inconsistent)

The participants' task was to read each sentence and judge whether the pronoun referred to the first or second noun phrase in the main clause.

As predicted, this took longer for inconsistent than consistent test items (see also Au, 1986; Ehrlich, 1980; Matthews & Chodorow, 1988; Springston, 1975). Other semantic factors, such as category relations, have likewise been demonstrated to affect the resolution of anaphoric phrases, although some of the studies in question have inspected definite noun phrases rather than pronouns (see sentence 29 in this chapter) (Corbett, 1984; Garrod & Sanford, 1977).

Global Factors of Pronoun Resolution. As discussed earlier, discourse coherence may be maintained by linking the current sentence with any level of the evolving discourse representation, including the situation model. The situation model has been shown to exert a measurable impact on pronominal resolution.

The situation model of narratives includes the function of the *main character*. It has been proposed that the special status of the main character might make it a preferred referent for pronouns. In a test of this hypothesis, people were asked to read brief narrative texts (Morrow, 1985). Different groups viewed one of the following three sequences: (42a)-(42b)-(42c), (42a)-(42b')-(42c), or (42a)-(42b'')-(42c).

(42)　a.　Paul caught the flu and was feeling pretty awful. He told his eldest son Ben to keep the house quiet. He got up from bed to go to the bathroom, irritated by the noise. Traffic was rushing by the house. The kids were arguing in the den.

　　　b.　That noisy Ben was messing up the kitchen.

　　　b'.　Noisy Ben was tramping around in the kitchen.

　　　b''.　Ben was wondering when his father would feel better as he ate in the kitchen.

　　　c.　The floor felt cold on *his* feet.

Each text consisted of a five-sentence section, such as (42a); one of the alternatives, (42b), (42b'), or (42b''); and sentence (42c). The last sentence, (42c), included a pronoun with more than one possible referent.

The reader's task was to select the referent for the pronoun *his* in sentence (42c). For all three sequences, another character, Ben, was mentioned more recently in the text than the main character. Furthermore, sequence (42a)-(42b')-(42c) presented the other character in a motion event, and sequence (42a)-(42b'')-(42c) changed the perspective of the text to that of the other character.

People predominantly reported that *his* referred to Paul, the father, except when the text switched to Ben's perspective, as in sequence

(42a)-(42b'')-(42c). This reveals that the narrative function of main character exerts a considerable impact on pronominal resolution, strong enough to overcome the more local factor of recency (Morrow, 1985).

Situation models of typical discourse structure have likewise been shown to influence the resolution of pronouns. Sequence (43), considered earlier, illustrates this point (Malt, 1985).

(43)   a.   Bob's first solo was to be on Saturday.
       b.   "Does Bob think that his performance will go well?" Jane
            asked.
       c.   "It should be an enthusiastic audience."
       d.   "He certainly does," Bill said.

Because readers expect that questions asked in a dialogue will receive answers, it is relatively easy to resolve he in (43d) as referring to Bob. Similarly, the elliptical verb, **does,** in (43d) is interpreted as referring to **think that his performance will go well.**

To examine the impact of discourse structure on pronominal resolution, Malt (1985) compared people's reading time for test sentence (43d) when sequence (43) included either (43b) or the alternative, (43b').

(43)   b'.   "Bob thinks that his performance will go well," Jane said.

Because (43b') is not a question, it does not raise the expectation of encountering an answer. People needed less time to read (43d) when sequence (43) included sentence (43b) than (43b'), indicating that discourse structure guides pronominal resolution. To summarize, there is considerable evidence that the representation of discourse models influences fine-grained language functions such as pronominal resolution (Frederiksen, 1981; Hobbs, 1979; Murphy, 1985; Sag & Hankamer, 1984).

Cognitive Principles of Anaphoric Reference

The studies examined in the previous section indicate that pronoun resolution is guided by the syntactic and semantic characteristics of a message and by the situation model of the discourse. These studies have also suggested several general principles of discovering the coherence connections among sentences. There is evidence that these principles apply both to the resolution of pronouns and also to other types of anaphoric expressions, such as definite noun phrases. We next examine these principles.

Immediacy. The principle of immediacy, considered in chapter 3, states that the words of a discourse are fully analyzed as soon as they are presented (Just & Carpenter, 1980, 1987). According to this principle, pronouns will be resolved as soon as they are encountered. Immediate pronoun resolution can be explained with reference to sequence (44) (Sanford, 1985).

(44)   a.   Fred got his kite tangled in a tree.
       b.   It had cost him $20.
       b'.   It was 20 feet tall.
       b''. It was a silly thing to do.

In the sequence, **Fred got his kite tangled in a tree. It . . .**, the word **it** can refer to the kite, as in (44b), the tree, as in (44b'), or the entire action, as in (44b''). Immediate pronominal resolution states that the understander will immediately select one of these interpretations, even though this will occasionally result in an error and require backtracking.

Several eye fixation studies have supported the immediate resolution of anaphoric expressions. For example, Carpenter and Just (1977) presented people with sequences such as (45), in which a pronoun had more than one possible referent.

(45)   a.   The guard mocked one of the prisoners in the machine shop.
       b.   He had been at the prison for only one week.

Upon encountering ambiguous pronouns, such as *he* in (45b), the readers frequently looked back in the text. Over 50% of these *regressive fixations* were to one of the two nouns in the text preceding the pronoun. This suggests that the readers attempted to resolve the pronoun immediately.

In a comparable study, the time spent fixating pronouns in sentences such as (46) and (47) was measured.

(46)   Harry lied to Pete because he smelled trouble.
(47)   Harry lied to Mary because he smelled trouble.

In sentence (47), the gender of *he* unambiguously identifies the referent, whereas in (46) it does not. The readers spent 50 msec less fixating those pronouns resolved by gender (Vonk, 1985). This again indicates that the pronouns were resolved immediately (see also Ehrlich & Rayner, 1983).

Anaphors Access Several Candidate Referents.   In many sentences, anaphoric expressions have several possible referents. For example, in (48), examined earlier, the pronoun *he* might refer to either John or Pete.

(48)   John telephoned Pete because he needed some information.

This raises two alternative hypotheses: Namely, either anaphoric expressions provide access only to the correct referent, under the guidance of syntactic and semantic factors; or they access all candidate referents.

There is evidence that anaphoric expressions access all reasonable referents, and that the understander then chooses among them. One line of reasoning is that if an anaphoric expression accessed only the single correct referent, then the time needed to process an anaphoric expression should not vary with the number of candidate referents. In this regard, we saw earlier that it takes longer to understand a pronoun if it has two possible referents than if it has only one (Frederiksen, 1981). That is, people needed more time to understand the pronoun **it** in sentence (49b) than in (50b).

(49)   a.   Education is, above all, supposed to enlighten.
       b.   *It* should concern itself with developing the high ability to read, learn, and understand.

(50)   a.   Education is, above all, supposed to produce a well-trained mind.
       b.   *It* should concern itself with developing the high ability to read, learn, and understand.

Similarly, Corbett (1984) measured reading times for anaphoric parts of sentences, such as the noun phrase, **frozen vegetable.** Reading time was shorter when the anaphor had only one possible referent, such as **frozen asparagus,** than when there also existed a distractor referent, such as **canned corn.** These results support the view that several candidate referents are accessed (see also Corbett & Chang, 1983).

A second approach to this problem is the following. If an anaphoric expression accesses a particular referent, then that referent should be activated. In that event, people should need less time to make judgments about referents that have been accessed than those that have not (Corbett, 1984; Corbett & Chang, 1983; McKoon & Ratcliff, 1980b). In one study that used this approach, people read sentences such as (51) and (52) (Corbett, 1984).

(51)   Gary gave Kevin a lot of money and *Kevin* spent it foolishly.

(52)   Gary gave Kevin a lot of money and *he* spent it foolishly.

Immediately after each sentence, the reader viewed a recognition probe name, such as **Gary.** People needed less time to recognize the nonreferent, **Gary,** when the sentence used a pronoun, as in (52), than when it used a proper name, such as **Kevin** in (51). This suggests that the pronoun *he* in (52) provided access to the nonreferent, GARY. This outcome provides further evidence that anaphoric expressions activate all of their reasonable referents.

Strategies of Anaphoric Resolution.   The influence of a wide variety of factors on anaphoric resolution raises the problem of how these factors are coordinated. The following quote illustrates the complexity of this issue:

> The binoculars settle again—they have found their mark, straddled between a windowsill and a drainpipe.
> *It* is a dark figure, splayed against the wall, looking down, looking for a new foothold, looking upwards. (Adams, 1987)

There are numerous possible referents for the pronoun *it* in this quote, including BINOCULARS, MARK, WINDOWSILL, DRAINPIPE, as well as several complex events, such as the SETTING OF THE BINOC-ULARS. The understander must eventually decide that **it** refers to MARK. One proposal about the necessary processing is that there are hard and fast rules for anaphoric resolution. However, it is difficult to find rules that apply in all circumstances. Consider the hypothetical rule, *Link a personal pronoun to the most recent antecedent of the same gender.* It is apparent that this rule fails for a sentence such as (53).

(53)   Muriel won the money from Helen because she was a skillful player.

It is likely that almost any specific rule of this sort would frequently fail, and so impede comprehension.

An alternative hypothesis is that anaphoric resolution is strategic in nature (Fletcher, 1984; van Dijk & Kintsch, 1983). According to this position, anaphoric expressions are resolved by the application of heuristic strategies, which do not guarantee the correct solution but which are satisfactory in most circumstances (see chapter 3). The strategies correspond to local and global factors of anaphoric resolution, such as the ones that we have considered.

There are certain reasons to be cautious about the strategic approach to anaphoric resolution. One of the characteristics of a cognitive strategy is that it is intentional in nature (van Dijk & Kintsch, 1983, p. 62). However, it is questionable that language understanders are consciously aware of the many local and global factors that contribute to discourse coherence (Bever, 1970). Therefore, it is unlikely that these factors could be manipulated in an intentional, strategic fashion.

The concept of a strategy should particularly come into play when the understander engages in active reasoning about a message. In the realm of anaphoric resolution, there is preliminary evidence that understanders resort to such reasoning when the referent of the anaphor is not currently held in working memory (Murphy, 1985). In this event, the topic structure and the situation model of the discourse appear to play a greater role in the identification of the referent. It may be that strategies of anaphoric resolution are used when local syntactic and semantic factors fail to access a referent.

OVERCOMING IMPEDIMENTS TO COHERENCE

For a discourse to appear coherent, the understander must discover the connections among its parts. This requires that the referents of the given components of the sentences be accessed. There are, however, a variety of circumstances in which this is difficult to achieve. All of these situations arise when an initial scan of working memory reveals no referent for the given component. This may be due to the fact that either (a) the referent has been stored in long-term memory and must be reinstated to working memory, (b) the given–new structure of the current sentence is incongruent with previous parts of the message, or (c) there is a complete absence of a referent. In each of these circumstances, additional mental processes are needed to locate the proper referent. These three circumstances will be considered in turn.

Reinstatement From Long-Term Memory

When a referent for given information cannot be located in working memory, the understander may proceed to search for one in long-term memory. If this search is successful, the referent must be reinstated to working memory (Lesgold et al., 1979), a time-consuming process. Sequence (35) previously demonstrated that it is relatively difficult to resolve a pronoun whose referent does not reside in working memory. A similar phenomenon is illustrated by sequences (54) and (55).

(54) a. A thick cloud of smoke hung over the forest.
      b. Glancing to the side, Carol could see a bee flying around the back seat. Both of the kids were jumping around, but made no attempt to free the insect.
      c. The forest was on fire.

(55) a. A thick cloud of smoke hung over the forest.
      b. The smoke was thick and black, and began to fill the clear sky. Up ahead Carol could see a ranger directing traffic to slow down.
      c. The forest was on fire.

Both sequences make sense, but the final sentence appears more awkward in sequence (54). In sentences (54c) and (55c), the use of the definite article, **the,** signals that fire is given information. Therefore, the understander must find a referent for this noun. This is more difficult to achieve in sequence (54) than (55): This is because sentence (54b) removes the referent, FIRE, from working memory, whereas (55b) does not. For (54c) to be linked with the preceding text, the concept, FIRE, must be reinstated to working memory.

Lesgold et al. (1979) tested the hypothesis that it takes longer to understand a sentence that requires the reinstatement of its given information than one that does not. The experimental participants viewed sequences such as (54) and (55), or sequence (56).

(56) a. A thick cloud of smoke hung over the forest.
      b. Glancing to the side, Carol could see a bee flying around the back seat. Both of the kids were jumping around, but made no attempt to free the insect.
      b'. Carol continued to be distressed as she drove through the forest.
      c. The forest was on fire.

Sequence (56) is identical to sequence (54), except that sentence (56b') ought to return FOREST to working memory before the target sentence (56c) is encountered. The main prediction was that reading time would be greater for target (54c) than either (55c) or (56c), because only (54c) depends on a memory reinstatement for comprehension to result. The data clearly supported this prediction.

In a similar study (McKoon & Ratcliff, 1980b), people read four-sentence passages, the first sentence of which introduced a crucial concept, such as BURGLAR. It was assumed that this concept would be removed from working memory by the time the fourth sentence was encountered. Three different versions of the fourth sentence were used, as follows: Sentences (57a) and (57b) were intended to reinstate BURGLAR by direct and indirect reference, respectively. In contrast, sentence (57c) was not expected to reinstate BURGLAR.

(57) a. The burglar slipped away from the streetlamp.
      b. The criminal slipped away from the streetlamp.
      c. The cat slipped away from the streetlamp.

The passages were read one sentence at a time. Immediately after reading the last sentence, the participant had to indicate whether a test word, such as **burglar,** had appeared in the passage. It was predicted that it would take less time to correctly recognize test words that have been reinstated to working memory. Consistent with the prediction, recognition time was faster both for the direct-reference and the indirect-reference conditions than for the condition not expected to reinstate the crucial concept (McKoon & Ratcliff, 1980b; see also O'Brien et al., 1986). This finding supported the contention that the reinstatement of discourse ideas influences the course of comprehension.

Incongruence of Given–New Structure

The second situation in which it is difficult to access a referent for the given component of a sentence arises when the given–new structure of the current sentence is incongruent with the preceding text. In this regard, sentence (58b) is *congruent* with (58a).

(58) a. The banker was charged with the crime.
      b. The one who charged the banker was the district attorney.

This is because the given proposition of (58b) is SOMEONE CHARGED THE BANKER, and (58a) includes a referent for that proposition.
    In contrast, (59b) is incongruent with (59a).

(59) a. The banker was charged with the crime.
      b. The one who the district attorney charged was the banker.

This is because (59a) includes no referent for the given proposition of (59b), THE DISTRICT ATTORNEY CHARGED SOMEONE.
    Sentences such as (59b) may be understood by reorganizing the given and new information. That is, if readers realize that the new noun of (59b), **banker,** has appeared in (59a), then they can proceed to treat **banker** as given (Clark & Haviland, 1977). However, this reorganization

is likely to be time-consuming. In a test of this hypothesis (Carpenter & Just, 1977), people were presented with line drawings of a single character walking toward the left or the right: either of a female, **Barb,** or a male, **John.** Each picture was followed by a cleft or pseudocleft sentence, such as (60).

(60)   The one who is following John is Barb.

The participants had to judge whether, according to the sentence, the person *not* shown in the picture would be to the left or the right of the one shown.

In this study, the congruence of the given–new structure of the sentence, with reference to the picture, was varied. For example, in sentence (60), *John* is part of the given information. Therefore, this sentence is congruent with a preceding picture of John, and incongruent with a preceding picture of Barb. As predicted, correct left–right decision time was almost ⅕ second faster for congruent sentences than incongruent ones.

Similar effects have been detected when people understand sentences in the context of preceding sentences. Consider sequences (61) and (62).

(61)   a.   The vandals started *the fire* in the basement with kerosene.
       b.   *The fire* filled *the room* with smoke.

(62)   a.   In the hotel, the vandals doused *the room* with kerosene.
       b.   *The fire* filled *the room* with smoke.

In both sequences, word order marks *fire* as given and *room* as new in **The fire filled the room with smoke.** In sequence (61), the second sentence is linked to the first by the coreference of *fire,* the given noun of (61b). In sequence (62), in contrast, (62a) has no direct antecedent for **fire.** Rather, (62b) is linked to (62a) by the new noun, **room.** Thus, (61b) is congruent with the given–new structure of (61a), whereas (62b) is incongruent with (62a). Consistent with this analysis, people needed 165 msec longer to read **The fire filled the room with smoke** in sequence (62) than sequence (61) (Yekovich, Walker, & Blackman, 1979).

In ordinary discourse, the apparent incongruence of the given–new structure of the current sentence may signal a *topic shift.* Lorch, Lorch, and Matthews (1985) predicted that people would need more time to read topic sentences that introduced major topic shifts than ones introducing minor shifts. As an example, one of Lorch et al.'s stories discussed attributes, such as geography and economy, of two fictional countries. In the *organized* version of the story, the paragraph examining an attribute of one country was followed by a paragraph examining the *same* attribute of the other country. In this version, paragraph transitions that changed both country and attribute were called *major topic shifts*, and transitions that changed only the country were called *minor topic shifts*. In a *disorganized* version of the story, every paragraph transition altered both country and attribute. Accordingly, every topic shift was a major one.

In agreement with their prediction, Lorch et al. (1985, Experiment 1) found that reading time was greater for topic sentences that introduced major topic shifts than ones presenting minor topic shifts. This finding is consistent with other results indicating that comprehension time is greater if a sentence has an incongruent given–new structure. It also suggests that such incongruence may be a typical feature of sentences introducing topic changes.

Absence of a Referent for the Given Component, I: Indirect Referents and Bridging

Sometimes, neither the reinstatement of an idea to working memory, nor the reorganization of an incongruent sentence, produces a referent for the given component of the current sentence. When this occurs, it is sometimes possible to identify an indirect referent for the given. In other situations, the only option is to create a new mental representation of the concept designated by the given information. These two alternatives are inspected in this and the following subsection.

In a classic study, Haviland and Clark (1974) proposed that sequence (63) can be understood only by discovering an indirect connection, or *bridge*, between (63b) and its antecedent, (63a).

(63) a. We checked the picnic supplies.
      b. The beer was warm.

The connection might take the form of the proposition, THE PICNIC SUPPLIES INCLUDED BEER. It was hypothesized that bridging is a time-consuming mental process.

To test this hypothesis, Haviland and Clark presented sequences like (63) and (64) to their participants.

(64) a. We got some beer out of the trunk.
      b. The beer was warm.

Unlike sequence (63), coherence is maintained in sequence (64) by the direct reference of the word, **beer.** If bridging is time-consuming, then it should take longer to read **The beer was warm** in sequence (63) than in sequence (64). The results of several experiments supported this prediction (Haviland & Clark, 1974).

Because sentence (64a) mentions *beer* and (63a) does not, one might argue that the comprehension time advantage of (64b) resulted from this repetition, rather than from the extra bridging processes needed to understand (63b). To discount this explanation, Haviland and Clark (1974) also examined sequences such as (65).

(65)   a.   John was particularly fond of beer.
      b.   The beer was warm.

Although sentence (65a) mentions *beer*, it does not specify the existence of a particular glass or bottle of beer. Therefore, the reader should still need to construct a bridge between (65b) and (65a). Comprehension time was indeed longer for **The beer was warm** in sequence (65) than (64). This difference must be due to extra bridging processes rather than a repetition advantage.

Text sequences that require bridging have sometimes been used as control conditions in the study of other factors that influence the linking of the given component with its referent. These studies have shown that sentences requiring bridging to preserve coherence take even longer to comprehend than sentences requiring memory reinstatement (Lesgold et al., 1979, Experiment 4) and sentences exhibiting given–new incongruence (Yekovich et al., 1979). These findings confirm that identifying an indirect referent for the given component of a sentence places high demands on the understander's cognitive resources.

Absence of a Referent for the Given Component, II: Creating a New Representation of the Given Referent

Intuitively, it seems apparent that the greatest difficulty in linking given information to prior discourse will result when neither a direct nor an indirect referent exists. Consider a novel that begins with the sentence, **She was dead** (Auel, 1982). The use of the pronoun *she* suggests that the existence of a particular female is given information. Because no appropriate referent for the given component can be retrieved, the understander must construct new propositions to represent the referent of **she.** These propositions might take the form, (EXIST, E_{770}) and (FEMALE, E_{770}), where E_{770} means AN ENTITY WITH THE (ARBITRARY) NUMBER 770 (Clark & Clark, 1977; Winograd, 1972; see chapter 2).

Only after the construction of these propositions may comprehension proceed. The addition of these new propositions has been posited to be very time-consuming (e.g., Graesser, Hoffman, & Clark, 1980; Kintsch et al., 1975).

Experimental evidence supports this analysis. For example, Ehrlich and Johnson-Laird (1982) studied their participants' ability to extract, from simple texts, the representation of the relative spatial arrangements of three objects. In sequences such as (66), the second sentence was *continuous* with the first, because the word **pot** made a direct reference to the first sentence.

(66) The knife is in front of the pot. The pot is on the left of the glass. The glass is behind the dish.

In contrast, the second sentence in sequence (67) was discontinuous with the first sentence.

(67) The knife is in front of the pot. The glass is behind the dish. The pot is on the left of the glass.

After reading a sequence, the participant drew a diagram of the position of the objects. As predicted, accuracy was greater for the continuous texts. This is presumably because, in discontinuous sequences, information from the second sentence could not be integrated with the first. Instead, upon reading the second sentence of discontinuous sequences, the reader had to construct propositions specifying the existence of the given element, such as **glass.** These additional mental operations apparently made it more difficult to extract a correct representation of the arrangement of the objects described in discontinuous sequences.

In a comparable study, it was predicted that referential discontinuities in discourse would hamper comprehension. People were presented with passages such as those shown in Fig. 5.2a (Kieras, 1978, Experiments 2 and 3). Figure 5.2b shows that the two passages have identical propositional organization. However, one passage used a depth-first order, in the sense that the passage addressed first the entire left branch of the propositional graph, and then the right branch. The other passage used a breadth-first order. There are more referentially discontinuous sentences in the breadth-first passage.

After reading 20 passages, the participants received a cued recall test. For each passage, the agent of P1, such as *ants,* was the cue. Recall performance was better for the depth-first passages, supporting the prediction. However, it should be noted that, in both passages, the sentence, **The ants ate the jelly,** was presented last. In two other conditions, in which this sentence was presented first, referential continuity did not affect cued recall.

Conclusions

Discourse coherence is threatened whenever a search of working memory reveals no referent for the given component of the current sentence. In this event, the understander must engage in a variety of remedial actions. The options include the reinstatement of a referent to working memory, the reorganization of the given–new structure of the current sentence, discovering an indirect referent by the process of bridging, and constructing a new representation of the given component. There is evidence that these options vary systematically in the demands they place on cognitive resources, ranging from reinstatement at the low end of the continuum, to constructing new representations at the high end. Messages that require extensive processing of this sort are harder to understand than those that do not (Miller & Kintsch, 1980).

FACTORS INFLUENCING THE SPEED OF READING COHERENT TEXT

The processes of understanding discourse are time-consuming, and the reading time of a message provides an excellent on-line reflection of these processes. The rate of acquiring information from a message is not uniform. Rather, examples throughout this chapter have illustrated that comprehension time varies with the coherence of messages. Many other sorts of factors likewise influence reading speed. For example, people take longer to read long words than short ones, and infrequent words than frequent ones. Likewise, the complexity of a grammatical construction can influence reading speed.

Reading time has emerged as a central measure of comprehension. The study of reading time has two thrusts. First, reading time is a phenomenon worthy of study in its own right. Determining why some texts take longer to read than others, and why there are individual differences in reading speed among people, are interesting and important issues. Accordingly, it would be useful to determine which characteristics of texts and readers regulate reading speed. Second, the identification of the determinants of reading speed bears on the evaluation of theories of comprehension. For example, if it is true that comprehension involves the representation of the form, text base, and situation underly-

A

Depth-First

The kitchen was spotless.
The ants were in the kitchen.
The ants were hungry.
The table was wooden.
The jelly was on the table.
The jelly was grape.
The ants ate the jelly.

Breadth-First

The kitchen was spotless.
The table was wooden.
The ants were hungry.
The ants were in the kitchen.
The jelly was grape.
The jelly was on the table.
The ants ate the jelly.

B

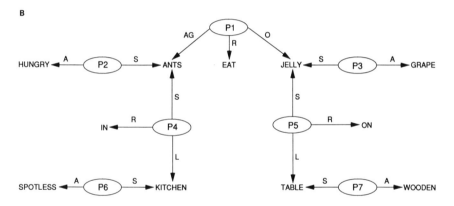

Key : A - attribute
       AG - agent
       L - location
       O - object
       R - relation
       S - subject

FIG. 5.2.   Depth-first and breadth-first passages (A) and their propositional organization (B). *Source:* Adapted from Kieras, 1978, Figure 1
and Table 1, p. 16. Adapted by permission.

ing a text, then variables bearing on each of these levels should influence
reading time.

The central assumption of reading-time studies of comprehension is
that reading time increases with the demands on the reader's cognitive

resources. These demands are high when the reader has to maintain a lot of information in working memory. Likewise, controlled processes are more demanding of cognitive resources than automatic ones (see chapter 1).

Regression Analysis of Reading Time

To assess the impact of a factor on reading time, it is possible to vary that factor systematically in experimental messages. To cite one example, Kintsch et al. (1975) created passages that included either *few* or *many* different arguments. Reading time was greater for passages with many arguments (see chapter 2). However, varying two or more text factors simultaneously is difficult, and frequently produces awkward texts (Kieras, 1981a). Because of this, an alternative technique for studying the factors affecting reading speed is to measure reading time for natural texts, and to use a quantitative method called *regression analysis* to analyze the data.

Regression analysis identifies the factors that affect a variable, behavioral or otherwise. Consider a variable such as the grade achieved in a college course. The grade may be influenced by factors such as the number of previous courses that the student has taken in the same subject, the number of hours spent studying during the semester, one's aptitude for the subject, and the student's interest in the material. To perform the regression analysis, each student's grade is entered, along with that individual's score on each of the plausible factors. The regression analysis reveals which factors, if any, systematically predicts the student's grade. Analogously, regression analysis applied to reading times helps to identify the factors that influence those times.

What sort of reading times are inspected using this technique? As discussed in chapter 1, reading times can be measured for single words, phrases of different sizes, and for whole sentences. Of these alternatives, sentence reading times have the disadvantage of masking the influence of the individual words. Researchers accordingly favor, although not exclusively, methods that yield reading times for smaller sentences units. For example, the measurement of eye fixations reveals word-by-word reading times. Another method for measuring reading times is the *moving window* technique (Just, Carpenter, & Woolley, 1982). Following this procedure, the reader views a screen that is either blank or filled with dashes. A button is pressed to view each successive unit of a text, such as a word or phrase. It is as though the reader were advancing a small window across the text. The intervals between button-presses provide the reading times.

Sets of Reading Time Factors

In the study of the factors influencing reading time, investigators have examined sets of variables that are related to word-, sentence-, and text-level processing. It is reasonable to expect that factors relevant to each level of analysis will influence reading speed.

A difficulty in this sort of analysis is that there is no limit to the factors that one might examine. To take some farfetched examples, one might decide to measure the impact of the number of curved letters (e.g., **s**) on word reading time, or the number of adverbs in a sentence on sentence reading time. Therefore, it is important that researchers constrain their study to variables that are based on theories of comprehension (Carrithers & Bever, 1984; Danks, 1986). Table 5.1 lists several sets of variables that have been hypothesized to affect reading time. It is useful to briefly examine these sets.

Word Level Factors.   It is plausible that word reading time will increase directly with its length. This hypothesis has received support, both when word length is measured in terms of the number of syllables (Just & Carpenter, 1980) and the number of letters (Carpenter & Just, 1983; Haberlandt & Graesser, 1985).

Words also vary in their frequency of appearance in the language.

TABLE 5.1
Some Factors That Affect Reading Time

Level of Analysis	Factors
Word	Word length
	Word frequency
Sentence	
Within clause	Sentence length
	Beginning of sentence
	Case Assignment
	Number of new arguments
Between clause	Theme
	Causal connections
	End of clause
	End of sentence
	End of paragraph
Text	Beginning of new episode
	End of episode
	Narrativity
	Familiarity
	Serial position of sentence
Layout	Beginning of line
	End of line

(Kucera & Francis, 1967, provided a widely used set of word-frequency norms). The time needed to make judgments about isolated words increases as the word-frequency decreases (Glanzer & Erhrenreich, 1979; Morton, 1969; Thibadeau, Just, & Carpenter, 1982). Likewise, text reading time is influenced by the frequency of its words (Haberlandt & Graesser, 1985; Just & Carpenter, 1980; Rayner, 1983b). This *word frequency effect* may be due to the fact that infrequent words are lower in their levels of resting activation than frequent words. In this event, retrieving an infrequent word would demand more cognitive resources than retrieving a frequent word (Thibadeau et al., 1982). Novel words, for which the reader has no meaning representation at all, and whose frequency is effectively zero, are examined for a very long period of time (Haberlandt & Graesser, 1985; Just & Carpenter, 1980).

Sentence Level Effects.   The time needed to read sentences is influenced by sentence length (Graesser, Hoffman, et al., 1980; Haberlandt, Berian, & Sandson, 1980), and by factors that guide the integration of information within and between clauses (Haberlandt & Graesser, 1985; Just & Carpenter, 1980). At the sentence level, text coherence is affected primarily by between-clause integration.

Within-clause integration refers to the organization of the concepts conveyed by the clause into one or more propositions (see chapter 3). This process affects reading time in several ways. First, reading the beginning of a sentence consumes a disproportionate amount of time. This is likely because the reader must create a memory node to represent the current proposition (Haberlandt & Graesser, 1985; Miller, 1980). Second, reading time data indicate that the assignment of case roles to arguments, particularly agents, objects, and instruments, is time-consuming (Just & Carpenter, 1980). Third, the time needed to encode new arguments, whose referents do not currently reside in working memory, is longer than that of arguments previously encountered in the text (Graesser, Hoffman, et al., 1980; Haberlandt et al., 1980; Haberlandt & Graesser, 1985; Haberlandt, Graesser, Schneider, & Kiely, 1986; Kintsch et al., 1975; Singer, 1982).

Integration *between* clauses requires that the reader determine the meaning relations among the clauses. One requirement for constructing a coherent representation is the detection of the theme of a message (see chapter 6). It is not surprising, therefore, that reading sentences that convey thematic clauses is more time-consuming than nonthematic ones (Just & Carpenter, 1980; Kieras, 1981a). Also essential for maintaining coherence is the analysis of the causal connections among the sentences of a text. For example, most readers would agree that there is a causal connection between the two sentences of sequence (68), even though this connection is not explicit.

(68)   He lowered the flames and walked over to the refrigerator, bumping a bowl he had left on the table. Suddenly it fell off the edge and broke.

Consistent with this observation, sentences conveying causal connections consume more reading time than ones that do not (Black & Bern, 1981; Just & Carpenter, 1980; Kieras, 1981a).

Finally, reading time is relatively high at the ends of clauses, sentences, and paragraphs (e.g., Haberlandt & Graesser, 1985; Just & Carpenter, 1980). These effects likely bear on the integration of information both within and between clauses. As discussed in chapter 3, people accumulate individual clauses in working memory until their propositional content has been extracted. The purging of working memory at the end of this process is likely to raise the cognitive load, and so affect reading time. Reaching the end of a sentence also affords the opportunity to resolve remaining ambiguities. For example, only at the end of sentence (69) can the reader identify THE LITTLE BOY as the referent of the pronoun, he (Just & Carpenter, 1980).

(69)   Although he spoke softly, yesterday's speaker could hear the little boy's question.

Text Level Effects.   The construction of the situation model underlying a text is guided by people's knowledge about the usual form of texts, and about the content of the text. Both of these factors have a measurable impact on reading time. Story structure has been shown to influence reading time in several ways. In particular, people take more time to encode the beginning and end of story episodes than the middle of an episode (Gee & Grosjean, 1984; Haberlandt et al., 1980). At the beginning of the episode, the reader must identify the topical structure, particularly with reference to the goals of the characters. In addition, it is necessary to establish referents for new arguments, especially for central ideas such as the main character. Reading time is high at the end of an episode because the reader must complete the construction of the situation model, and purge working memory of text information that is no longer needed (Haberlandt et al., 1980).

Most stories focus on the actions that the main character executes to achieve his or her goals. As a result, stories are high in their degree of causal coherence, a characteristic called narrativity (Graesser et al., 1980). Texts high in narrativity take relatively less time to read than texts low on this dimension, such as expository texts. This may be due to the ease of discovering meaning connections among the propositions of narratives.

Prior knowledge about the content of a text is an index of the text's familiarity to the reader. Familiarity with the subject of a text ought to save the reader the time of constructing new propositions, because some of the text propositions ought to be retrievable from long-term memory. Familiarity produces measurable, though not powerful, effects on reading time (Graesser et al., 1980; Haberlandt & Graesser, 1985; Johnson & Kieras, 1983).

Finally, reading time diminishes systematically as a reader proceeds through a text (Haberlandt et al., 1980; Haberlandt & Graesser, 1985; Singer, 1982). This is because the need to identify the theme of a message, retrieve the referents of new arguments, and create new representations of unfamiliar entities diminishes as the text is read. There is a notable exception to the trend of speeding up through a text: Reading the final sentence of a message is very time-consuming.

Layout Variables. Texts have physical arrangements: That is, they appear in many styles and sizes of print, with paragraphs indented or not, and lines that are usually left-adjusted but not always right-adjusted. It is to be expected that these layout characteristics affect reading time. For example, reading time for the beginning of a line of text ought to be disproportionately high, because the reader needs to sweep the eyes from the end of the preceding line and locate the beginning of the new one. Consistent with these hypotheses, people need extra time to encode information at the beginning and ends of text lines, whether they appear on printed pages or on computer screens (Haberlandt & Graesser, 1985; Just & Carpenter, 1980; Just et al., 1982).

Reading Time and Reading Tasks. As discussed previously, people approach texts with goals such as learning, memorizing, or entertainment. It is reasonable to expect the processes of comprehension to be influenced by the reader's task. To explore this hypothesis, researchers have compared the reading times of people who have read in anticipation of either a recall, comprehension, or topic-identification test; or who have performed free reading (Haberlandt et al., 1986; Kieras, 1981a). Reading times differed systematically among these tasks. To cite one example, people read more slowly when they anticipate a recall task than in a free reading situation (Haberlandt et al., 1986; Kieras, 1981a). This is presumably because the recallers dwell at greater length on the fine detail of a text.

Furthermore, different reading tasks yield different *patterns* of reading times. Recallers spend a disproportionate amount of time on the last word of a sentence (Haberlandt et al., 1986), and spend more time processing each connection among the arguments of the text (Kieras, 1981a). Those who read in order to identify the theme of a text have especially high reading times for the first sentence of a text (Kieras, 1981a). These findings indicate that the reader's goals influence reading processes and the reading times that reflect them.

Conclusions.   To understand a passage, readers must perform analyses at the level of letters, words, clauses, sentences, and the text as a whole. As a result, variables at each of these levels influence reading time. This influence is mediated by the reader's cognitive load: Those text features that elevate the load of working memory or require the execution of controlled processes raise the reading time of a segment of text.

There is a reciprocal relationship between the analysis of reading time and theories of comprehension. On one hand, detailed comprehension theories predict the reading time for different sections of a text. For example, the *coherence graph model* (Kintsch & van Dijk, 1978) specifies the understander's cognitive load in terms of the contents of working memory, and the number of memory reinstatements and bridging inferences needed to identify the referent of text arguments. Specific predictions about reading time can be generated by computer simulations of these models (e.g., Kieras, 1981a; Miller & Kintsch, 1980; Thibadeau et al., 1982; see also chapter 10). On the other hand, the empirical study of text reading time provides a source of new insights about comprehension, and a method for evaluating theories of comprehension.

SUMMARY

The coherence of a discourse requires the discovery of connections among its underlying ideas. The execution of the given–new strategy contributes to discourse coherence. The strategy requires that the understander analyze propositions into already familiar, or given, components, and new components. Next, a referent is retrieved for the given idea. Finally, the new information is integrated with the retrieved referent.

Given and new information is distinguished by syntactic, lexical, intonational, and semantic characteristics of a message. Given information is treated by the understander as the sentence topic. Experimental evidence indicates that, consistent with the given–new analysis, given information is processed first, but new information is scrutinized more carefully.

The retrieval of a referent for given information is guided by many factors. Syntactic devices, such as the repetition of phrases and the appearance of synonyms, facilitates the retrieval of the correct referent. In addition, the retrieval of referents is guided by semantic factors and on the basis of the situation model underlying the discourse. Because of their pervasive use in language, pronouns constitute an important shorthand device for signaling referents. As is true of the retrieval of referents in general, pronoun resolution is guided by syntactic, semantic, and situational factors.

Expressions, such as pronouns, that refer to previous concepts in a discourse are called *anaphoric expressions*. There is experimental evidence that the resolution of anaphors occurs as soon as the anaphor is encountered, and accesses all of the reasonable referents for each anaphor. Anaphoric resolution may be strategic, because no one rule applies in all situations.

Discourse coherence is threatened by the failure to discover a referent for given ideas in working memory. This can be overcome if the correct referent can be reinstated from long-term memory, if the given–new structure of an incongruent sentence can be reorganized, if an indirect referent can be identified by bridging, or if new representations of the given information can be constructed. All of these remedial operations are time-consuming and retard comprehension.

Understanding coherent discourse requires the analysis of numerous levels of linguistic units. Reading time is influenced by factors relevant to the levels of the word, sentence, and text, and to the layout of a text. Those factors that add to the load of working memory or require the execution of controlled processes raise reading time. The relative impact of the different factors is assessed by applying regression analysis to text reading times. Reading time is affected by the goals that the understander brings to the reading situation.

6

Theme

The theme of a discourse has been alternately defined as the idea that functions as the focus or topic of a discourse (Eamon, 1978–79; Thorndyke, 1977), that unifies a discourse (Bisanz, Laporte, Vesonder, & Voss, 1978), and that constitutes the general idea of the discourse (Pompi & Lachman, 1967). The problem of discourse theme is distinct from that of sentence topic: that is, of what individual sentences are about (e.g., van Dijk & Kintsch, 1983; see also chapter 5). The theme of a discourse plays two important roles: First, the theme serves as a pointer to the relevant world knowledge of the understander. Second, the theme serves as an anchor for the integration of the ideas conveyed by the message (e.g., Kozminsky, 1977). As such, theme contributes to the organization of discourse ideas.

Evidence that the theme of a message points to relevant world knowledge was examined in detail in chapter 4. The present chapter concentrates on the second role of theme, namely, its contribution to the organization of the representation of discourse. The first section examines the features of discourse that signal the theme. The second section describes the representational structures and the processes associated with thematic propositions. In the last section, we consider a mental representation that particularly captures the theme of a message, called the *macrostructure*.

DISCOURSE FACTORS THAT SIGNAL THEME

A person's ability to understand and recall a message depends on the successful identification of the theme. Researchers have examined many factors that signal theme: title, initial mention, frequency of mention, grammatical role, content of ideas, structural quality of a discourse, and explicit markers, such as "the important thing is." For several of these factors, pertinent experimental evidence is available.

Title

Explicit titles are typically provided for many types of communications, including newspaper articles, recipes, book chapters, and stories. By identifying the theme of the message, the title permits the understander to retrieve knowledge relevant to the message. In chapter 4, it was seen that manipulating the title of a message has profound effects on encoding and retrieval. Consider the following passage, alternately titled "Columbus Discovers a New World" or "First Trip to the Moon" (Hasher & Griffin, 1978).

> The voyage was long and the crew was full of anticipation. No one really knew what lay beyond the new land that they were heading for. There were, of course, speculations concerning the nature of the new place, but this small group of men would be the only ones who would know the real truth. These men were participating in an event that would change the shape of history.

Discourse ideas are integrated with the thematic knowledge signaled by the title. The precise form of this integration depends on what one believes the theme to be. In the present example, **The voyage was long** might be equated with an ocean voyage taking months for the "Columbus" title, and a week-long voyage in a space-craft for the "Moon" title. A misunderstanding about theme can prevent the integration of discourse statements (Bransford & Johnson, 1973). The complete absence of a theme results in poor comprehension and recall of the message (Bransford & Johnson, 1972; Dooling & Lachman, 1971). At the time of retrieval, reactivating the relevant knowledge provides the understander with a plan for retrieving the discourse ideas (Anderson & Pichert, 1978), and suggests plausible reconstructions of the message content (Hasher & Griffin, 1978; Kintsch & van Dijk, 1978).

The Columbus/Moon passage is unusual in its vagueness. However, titles have a similar impact on more typical messages. In one study, for example, people read an ordinary but unfamiliar brief fairy tale, either with or without a title. The participants recalled over 50% more story ideas in the presence of a title (Schwarz & Flammer, 1981, Experiment 1).

In two other studies, people read texts with two underlying themes, but which bore a title conveying one theme or the other. In one of these studies, people recalled more text ideas pertinent to the theme conveyed by the title, although this difference was small (Kozminsky, 1977). In the other study, the participants received the 18 sentences of a text on a scrambled deck of cards. They were asked to arrange the sentences into the most meaningful order. The participants tended to place those sentences pertinent to the title earlier in their constructed stories (Bock, 1980). These findings indicate that the ideas conveyed by a title acquire a special status in the representation of a message.

Initial Mention

It has been proposed that the theme of a message may be derived from the initial sentences, particularly when the message has no title. To test this hypothesis, investigators have used the measures of thematic judgments, free recall, and cued recall.

In one study, people read passages that included two themes, such as SEA URCHINS and BIOCRYSTALS (Kieras, 1980, Experiment 2). One version of the passage mentioned **sea urchins** first and another mentioned **biocrystals** first. The two versions, presented in Table 6.1, were shown to different individuals.

The participants' task was to identify the main idea of the passage: that is, to make a thematic judgment. The concept that was mentioned first was selected as the main idea more often than the one that was mentioned second. This was true whether or not there was a bias to prefer sea urchins or biocrystals to be the theme, all other things being equal (see also Kozminsky, 1977).

In a comparable cued recall study, people read eight brief passages, such as the ones shown in Table 6.1 (Kieras, 1981b). Afterwards, they were prompted for recall of the passages using cues that corresponded either to the theme that was mentioned first or second. The pattern of results was asymmetrical: When the cue corresponded to the first theme, people recalled more about the first theme than the second theme. However, when the cue corresponded to the second theme, the recall of the two themes was equal. Kieras suggested that, during comprehension, readers store information pertinent to the second theme. However, it is difficult to retrieve this information when the cue corresponds to the first theme.

An analogous effect is detected in free recall. For example, even for messages without titles, readers reproduce initial ideas more often than later ideas (Kintsch et al., 1975). This finding was just one feature of the general pattern called the levels effect (see chapter 2): Namely, propositions high in the discourse text base are recalled better than low

TABLE 6.1
Two-Theme Passages with either Sea Urchins
or Biocrystals Mentioned First

Sea Urchins First

The development of the sea urchin begins when millions of microscopic eggs are ejected into the sea through pores in the spiny shell of the adult. The tiny embryonic sea urchin, which swims about freely and feeds on plankton, is so transparent that its internal structure is clearly visible. The skeleton of the sea urchin develops from two spicules which are made of biocrystals that eventually fuse to form a spherical shell. Structures such as bone, tooth, and shell are made up of biocrystals which are three-dimensional arrays of calcium, silicon and phosphate and carbonate. These biocrystals are chemically indistinguishable from crystals found in the inanimate world.

Biocrystals First

Structures such as bone, tooth, and shell are made up of biocrystals which are three-dimensional arrays of calcium, silicon and phosphate and carbonate. These biocrystals are chemically indistinguishable from crystals found in the inanimate world. The skeleton of the sea urchin develops from two spicules which are made of biocrystals that eventually fuse to form a spherical shell. The development of the sea urchin begins when millions of microscopic eggs are ejected into the sea through pores in the spiny shell of the adult. The tiny embryonic sea urchin, which swims about freely and feeds on plankton, is so transparent that its internal structure is clearly visible.

Source: Kieras, 1980. Reprinted by permission.

propositions. The relationship between theme and hierarchical level is considered later in this chapter.

Frequency of Mention

The selection of theme is influenced by the frequency with which a concept or proposition is mentioned. For example, in one study, people read a story that ordered four animals on dimensions such as friendliness and age (Eamon, 1977). Four versions of the story were identical, except that the name of one animal, such as the deer, was mentioned four extra times, in contexts such as **Now the _____ was a very peculiar looking animal.** The participants rated the frequently mentioned animal as more important, a judgment comparable to theme selection. They also judged statements about the frequently mentioned animal more accurately and more quickly than statements about the other animals. The frequency with which the animals were mentioned was independent of the order of their initial mention (see also Bisanz et al., 1978; Perfetti & Goldman, 1974).

Grammatical Role

It has been hypothesized that the subject of a sentence signals the theme of a discourse. To test this proposal, Kieras (1981a, 1981c) created passages that included two candidate themes, such as VACCINE and VIRUS. Two versions of each passage were created: In each version, one of the themes appeared as the subject of each sentence. Sentences (1) and (2) appeared in the vaccine-theme and virus-theme versions respectively.

(1)   Vaccines require for their preparation the keeping of a large supply of virus that is usually grown in systems such as egg or cell cultures.
(2)   Viruses must be kept in large supply in order to prepare vaccines and are usually grown in systems such as egg or cell cultures.

People who read these passages were asked to produce a noun phrase that expressed the theme of each passage. These noun phrases included the sentence-subject theme 68% of the time and the alternate theme only 21% of the time (Kieras, 1981c). Similarly, the sentence-subject theme is a more effective cue for the recall of a passage than is the alternate theme (Kieras, 1981a; Perfetti & Goldman, 1974).

Content

The selection of the theme of a discourse is influenced by the properties of its content, such as its abstractness, distinctiveness, importance, and interest value. In this regard, people tend to prefer abstract concepts, such as BIOLUMINESCENCE, over concrete concepts, such as FLASH-LIGHT FISH, as the theme of a discourse (Kieras, 1980). The distinctiveness of discourse ideas forms the basis of the theme judgments of approximately 25% of people, and others can be instructed to use this criterion (Waters, 1983). The importance of text ideas likewise affects thematic status. Goetz (1977) manipulated the importance of a text idea by coupling it with different consequences. For example, missing a plane could result either in being late for a business meeting, or avoiding death in an air crash. Goetz found that the implications of important ideas were verified more accurately, and rated as "closer" to the story, than the implications of unimportant ideas. Finally, certain ideas, such as power, romance, sex, money, and death are inherently interesting (Schank, 1979). The interestingness of ideas might affect the identification of theme (Hidi & Baird, 1986; Kintsch, 1980; Schank, 1979). However, there is little direct evidence about this hypothesis.

The subtlety of the impact of content on theme was illustrated in a study by Revlin, Bromage, and Van Ness (1981). By changing one sentence in a lengthy passage to assert **Some senators formed a pro-canal association** rather than **Some farmers formed a pro-canal association,** the investigators altered a complex pattern of judgments on the part of readers. This was apparently due to the fact that the change removed an underlying theme of conflict between the senators and the farmers.

Conclusion

Empirical evidence has supported researchers' intuitions that theme is signaled by discourse title, initial mention, frequency of mention, grammatical role, and content. It is also likely that discourse structure and the use of explicit markers contribute to the identification of a theme. The ideas that are signaled by these factors are recalled better and are judged more thematic than are other ideas. In the next section, we consider structural and processing explanations of these effects.

DISCOURSE THEME: STRUCTURE AND PROCESS

The effectiveness of factors such as title, initial mention, and grammatical role in signaling theme does not explain *how* the signaled propositions acquire their privileged status. For example, to explain the high recall level of the first concept of a discourse by asserting that "it is the theme" would be to engage in circular reasoning. For discourse ideas to be judged to be thematic or to be remembered best, they must be distinct in terms of the structures and processes of comprehension.

This section identifies three structural features of discourse representations that distinguish themes from nonthemes: namely, hierarchical level, connectivity, and causal chain membership. For each feature, we consider the empirical evidence, the pertinent thematic signals, and the associated processing explanations.

Hierarchical Level

Structural Analysis. As discussed in chapter 2, the text base representation of a message is hierarchical. Propositions high in the hierarchy are considered to be privileged as compared with low ones (e.g., Britton, Meyer, Hodge & Glynn, 1980; Kintsch et al., 1975; McKoon, 1977), and some investigators explicitly view the top, or superordinate, node of the text base as the theme of the message (Kieras, 1978, 1981a; Kozminsky,

1977; Waters, 1983). As an illustration, Table 6.2 presents again the text that was examined in Table 2.1

The top level proposition of this text is (LOVE, GREEKS, ART). Therefore, according to the present analysis, it is viewed as the theme.

Empirical Evidence. The contention that the superordinate node of a discourse representation constitutes the theme is supported by measures of free recall, theme judgments, and reading time. Evidence that people *recall* propositions high in the text base of a message better than low level ones has been presented by many investigators (e.g., Britton et al., 1980; Britton, Meyer, Simpson, Holdredge, & Curry, 1979; Kintsch et al., 1975; McKoon, 1977; Thorndyke, 1977; Waters, 1983). This result is known as the levels effect (see Fig. 2.4 in chapter 2). It is useful to note that the levels effect in free recall appears for several systems of text analysis, including propositional text bases (Kintsch et al., 1975), story schema analysis (e.g., Thorndyke, 1977), and causal chain analysis (e.g., Graesser, Robertson, Lovelace, & Swinehart, 1980).

The relationship between hierarchical level and people's *judgments about the importance* of discourse propositions was studied by Waters (1983). Her subjects read and recalled descriptive passages whose text bases included four hierarchical levels. After recalling each text, the participants were asked to rate the importance of all of its propositions. Half of them chose the superordinate proposition as most important. There was also an interesting difference among the participants: In particular, 25% of the participants made their importance ratings on the basis of the distinctiveness of the text ideas, rather than hierarchical level. However, regardless of which importance criterion the participants adopted, their *recall* data revealed the usual levels effect.

TABLE 6.2
Hierarchical Text Base of a Brief Passage

The Greeks loved beautiful art. When the Romans conquered the Greeks, they copied them, and thus, learned to create beautiful art.

P1	(LOVE, GREEKS, ART)
P2	(BEAUTIFUL, ART)
P3	(CONQUER, ROMANS, GREEKS)
P4	(COPY, ROMANS, GREEKS)
P5	(WHEN, P3, P4)
P6	(LEARN, ROMANS, P8)
P7	(CONSEQUENCE, P3, P6)
P8	(CREATE, ROMANS, P2)

Source: Adapted from Kintsch et al., 1975, Table 2, p. 198. Adapted by permission.

The third measure that reflects the relation between theme and hierarchical level is *sentence reading time*. Cirilo and Foss (1980) proposed that it might take people longer to read high level sentences than low ones. This is because sentences conveying high level propositions are detected as important, and because they introduce a lot of new information. Using Thorndyke's (1977) story grammar analysis, Cirilo and Foss classified story sentences as high or low level. As predicted, they found that people took almost $3/10$ of a second longer to read high sentences than low ones.

Signals.   Researchers have been very explicit about the factors that identify the superordinate proposition of a message. It has been proposed that the proposition expressed by title (Kintsch & van Dijk, 1978; Kozminsky, 1977) and initial mention (Kieras, 1978, 1981a) are assigned to the superordinate position of the discourse representation.

Processes.   The special role of the superordinate proposition in organizing the representation of a message has been explained in terms of Clark and Haviland's (1977) given–new analysis (Bock, 1980; Kieras, 1978). Because the superordinate proposition is provided toward the outset of the message, it constitutes given information with reference to subsequent parts of the message. As a result, later propositions are integrated into the text base by connecting them with the concepts of the superordinate.

Two accounts of why the superordinate and other high level propositions are recalled better than low level ideas have been distinguished (Britton et al., 1980). The *encoding* view states that, because people devote more attention to the superordinate proposition, it is encoded more effectively. In contrast, according to the *retrieval* hypothesis, one can use the text base of a message as a retrieval plan. In particular, one begins with the text base superordinate node, and proceeds to retrieve the message. According to this position, low level ideas are recalled poorly because high level propositions do not reliably provide access to them. The loss of any one of the links between the superordinate propositions and a low level idea would result in the failure to recall that idea. Recall failure would also occur if the low level proposition has been stored in relative isolation, rather than being properly integrated in the representation.

To distinguish the encoding and retrieval hypotheses, Britton et al. (1980) compared people's free and cued recall of text ideas. In free recall, they detected the usual levels effect. However, in cued recall, there were no differences between high and low propositions. This outcome indicates that low level propositions are, in fact, encoded, and are retrievable given the appropriate cue. This indicates that the levels effect in free-recall is predominantly a retrieval phenomenon. This conclusion is consistent with the findings of Anderson and Pichert (1978), and Alba, Alexander, Hasher, and Caniglia (1981). However, a slight *encoding* advantage of text ideas relevant to a theme was measured by Borland and Flammer (1985).

Connectivity

Structural Analysis.   The quantity of connections between a proposition and other propositions in the text base is called its *connectivity*. It has been proposed that the greater the connectivity of a proposition, the more thematic it is (Graesser et al., 1980; Omanson, 1982; Trabasso, Secco, & van den Broek, 1984; Trabasso & Sperry, 1985). Connectivity can be computed for hierarchical text base representations, for story schema analyses, and for hierarchical and nonhierarchical causal analyses.

To illustrate, a thematic analysis based on connectivity was performed for the story fragment, **A thirsty ant went to a river and became carried away by the rush of the stream** (Graesser, Robertson, & Anderson, 1981). Table 6.3 lists 21 idea units of one or more propositions that are either directly expressed or implied by the text. Figure 6.1 organizes those units into a network. For example, unit 17, which represents the implied idea, THE STREAM OVERPOWERED THE ANT, is connected to six other ideas. Unit 1, THE ANT WAS THIRSTY, is connected to only one idea.

Empirical Evidence.   Trabasso and Sperry (1985) examined the relationship between connectivity and discourse theme. In view of the importance of causal relations in discourse meaning (e.g., Schank & Abelson, 1977), Trabasso and Sperry (1985) used causal analysis to construct the representations of stories. They then made a comparison of the causal connectivity of the story propositions and of the importance ratings that had been collected for those stories by Brown and Smiley (1977). It was found that the more causal connections that a story idea has, the more important it is rated. Similarly, ideas with more connections are more likely to be recalled (Graesser et al., 1980). Thus, connectivity has been shown to predict people's scores on two behavioral indices of theme: namely, importance ratings and recall.

Signals.   The thematic signal that is most distinctly associated with connectivity is frequency of mention. It seems apparent that, the more

TABLE 6.3
Idea Units of "Ant" Fragment

Number	Unit
1	Ant was thirsty
2	Ant satisfy thirst
3	Ant get (ingest) water
4	Ant liked fresh water
5	River was closest place for water
6	Ant drink river water
7	Ant go to river
8	Ant crawl
9	Ant walk
10	Ant's crawling was slow
11	Ant go into river
12	Ant became too close to stream
13	Ant fell into stream
14	Stream was rushing hard
15	An accident occurred
16	Ant slipped
17	Stream overpowered ant
18	Ant was small
19	Ant was light
20	Ant was unable to swim
21	Stream carried ant away

Source: Adapted from Graesser, Robertson, & Anderson, 1981, Table 1. Adapted by permission.

often a concept or proposition is mentioned, the greater the number of discourse ideas with which it will be connected.

Processes.   The superior recall of richly connected propositions may be due to both encoding and retrieval processes (Trabasso et al., 1984). During encoding, there is little likelihood that richly connected propositions will fail to be integrated into the representation. With regard to retrieval, Graesser et al. (1980) invoked the mechanism of spreading activation in propositional representations (McKoon & Ratcliff, 1980a). Graesser et al. argued that, independent of their hierarchical level, propositions with numerous connections are more likely to receive activation during the course of free recall than propositions with only one or two links.

Causal Chain Membership

Structural Analysis.   Investigators have distinguished between propositions on the main causal chain of events underlying a message, and propositions on branches leading to *dead-ends* (Glowalla & Colonius,

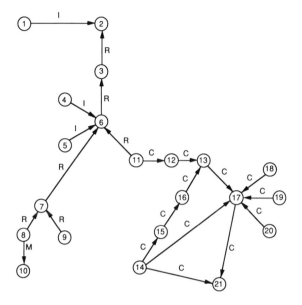

FIG. 6.1.   Network representation of **A thirsty ant went to a river and became carried away by the rush of the stream.** Proposition numbers refer to the idea units in Table 6.3. The propositions are linked by the relations of Reason (R), Initiate (I), Consequence (C), and Manner (M). *Source:* Adapted from Graesser, Robertson, & Anderson, 1981, Figure 1, p. 9. Adapted by permission.

1982; Omanson, 1982; Trabasso et al., 1984; Trabasso & Sperry, 1985). For example, in Fig. 6.1, the goal of DRINKING WATER (unit 6) is on the main causal chain of ideas 1-2-3-6-11-12-13-17, whereas the subsidiary goal of GOING TO THE RIVER (unit 7) is not.

Empirical Evidence.   Like hierarchical level and connectivity, there is evidence that causal chain membership influences both thematic judgments and recall. Trabasso et al. (1984) performed causal analyses of stories, and applied these analyses to existing recall data for these stories (Stein & Glenn, 1979). They found that causal chain ideas were recalled better than dead-end ideas. Furthermore, across different stories, the overall level of recall improved as a function of the number of events in the stories that appeared in the main causal chain. There was also a very high correlation $(r > .9)$ between the participants' importance ratings of story components and the proportion of the components' events that appeared in the causal chain (see also Omanson, 1982).

Signals.   It may be the case that causal chain membership is affected by propositional content. In this regard, Trabasso and Sperry (1985) proposed there are some systematic differences between the content of causal chains and dead-ends. In particular, only dead-ends were observed to include conversational asides, as well as information about time and places.

Processes.   It can be seen in Fig. 6.1 that the causal chain members tend to be more richly connected than dead-end events. This raises the question of whether causal chain membership and connectivity are independent structural indexes of theme. If they are not independent, then the processes that account for the recall and importance-rating advantages of richly connected propositions probably apply as well to causal chain members. However, Trabasso and van den Broek (1985) provided evidence that the two factors are to some degree independent. Processing differences between causal chain and dead-end events may be related to differences in their content.

Conclusions

Recognizing that hierarchical level, connectivity, and causal chain membership are all structural indexes of the theme, researchers have attempted to compare their relative contributions to representation, comprehension, and memory (Omanson, 1982; Trabasso & van den Broek, 1985). This problem is complicated by the fact that these three features may not be independent of one another. For example, the possible lack of independence of connectivity and causal chain membership was addressed in the last section. Similarly, it is conceivable that hierarchical level and connectivity are likewise not independent. That is because high level propositions tend to be more richly connected than low level ones. Several investigators have adopted the strategy of creating formulas of theme that combine level, connectivity, and causal chain membership. For example, Omanson (1982) created a measure of *centrality* based on hierarchical level, connectivity, and causal chain membership, plus "main character of the discourse." Goetz' (1977) ratings of the *importance* of text ideas referred to hierarchical level and connectivity. In summary, it is likely that several structural indexes must be considered to yield a satisfactory analysis of discourse theme.

At the outset of this chapter, the concepts of sentence topic and discourse theme were distinguished. Although the relationship between topic and theme has not received extensive consideration, the literature offers some suggestions about this problem. One hypothesis is that propositions that are topicalized in one or many sentences of a discourse become candidates to play the role of discourse theme. There are at least two reasons that this might be the case. First, the theme is often selected from one of the first sentences of a message (initial mention). In particular, the topic of the first sentence of a discourse might be assigned to the superordinate position in the text base (Kieras, 1978, 1981a, 1981b). Then, understanders will begin with this proposition in the retrieval of the message. Furthermore, because this proposition is available from the outset, it will constitute given information, and will likely become richly interconnected with other discourse ideas (Bock, 1980; Kieras, 1978; Kozminsky, 1977).

Second, among the concepts retained in working memory during discourse comprehension are the topics of recent sentences. The longer a proposition remains in working memory, the more likely it is to be linked to subsequent discourse ideas (Kintsch & van Dijk, 1978; Lesgold et al., 1979). As a result, propositions that function as sentence topics are likely to be high in connectivity.

THEME AND MACROSTRUCTURE

Macrostructure and Macrorules

As discussed in chapter 2, the text base of a message is a hierarchical network linking the propositions conveyed by the message. The *macrostructure* of a discourse is another organized network of propositions, one that particularly captures the theme of the message (Kintsch & van Dijk, 1978; van Dijk, 1977; van Dijk & Kintsch, 1983). Like the summary of a message, the macrostructure includes many fewer idea units than the complete propositional representation. For contrast, what we have until now called the text base of a message may be referred to as the *microstructure*. Its elements are called *micropropositions*. The text base representation of a discourse consists of the microstructure and the macrostructure.

The macrostructure is constructed during comprehension, by the application of certain mental operations to the microstructure. These operations are called macrorules, and the construction of the macrostructure is called *macroprocessing*. Several macrorules are as follows (van Dijk, 1977):

1. Selection: Some micropropositions are particularly important or relevant, and are adopted into the macrostructure.
2. Deletion: Micropropositions that are unimportant, irrelevant, or

redundant are "delete(d) from the macrostructure" (Kintsch & van Dijk, 1978, p. 372), although they remain in the microstructure.

3. Generalization: If a set of propositions suggest a generalization, then this generalization may appear in the macrostructure. For example, the propositions DONNA LIKES BASKETBALL, DONNA LIKES HOCKEY, and DONNA LIKES SWIMMING may be generalized to DONNA LIKES SPORTS.

4. Construction: A macroproposition may be constructed from several propositions that mutually imply it. For example, AL WROTE A DEPOSIT SLIP, AL APPROACHED THE TELLER, and AL GOT A RECEIPT yield the construction, AL DID SOME BANKING.

Most macrorules have the effect of reducing the number of micropropositions that appear in the macrostructure. Deletion, Generalization, and Construction all have this effect. As a result, the macrostructure consists of many fewer propositions than the microstructure.

The organization of macropropositions into the macrostructure is guided by the knowledge of the understander. Of particular importance is one's knowledge of the usual form of familiar text types, such as the story, and content areas, such as baseball. For example, understanders implicitly know that stories typically consist of a Setting, a Theme, a Plot, and a Resolution (Mandler & Johnson, 1977; Thorndyke, 1977; see chapter 8). Suppose that one or more macropropositions extracted from the initial sentences of a story include reference to people, places, and times. Then, these macropropositions can be related to the Setting component of one's *story schema* (van Dijk & Kintsch, 1983). The text schema permits the understander to distinguish between relevant and irrelevant propositions. Knowledge about a particular topic can play a similar role. For example, baseball experts are more able to distinguish relevant and irrelevant facts in the description of a baseball game than are baseball novices (Spilich et al., 1979).

Psychological Reality of the Macrostructure

Researchers have empirically distinguished the macrostructure, and its corresponding processes, from the microstructure. Both on-line and memory measures of comprehension have been used to make this distinction. One hypothesis about macroprocessing states that reading time is likely to be greater for high level than for low level *micropropositions*. The reason for this is that, being more important, high level micropropositions are better candidates for Selection into the macrostructure; and Selection is a time-consuming process. In support of this analysis,

Schmalhofer and Glavanov (1986) found that reading time was greater for high level micropropositions than for low level ones, but only when the readers performed a reading task that encouraged the construction of a macrostructure (see also Cirilo & Foss, 1980).

The *coherence graph model* of discourse comprehension (Kintsch & van Dijk, 1978) has provided another index of on-line macroprocessing (see also chapter 10). In particular, it has been estimated that people can maintain four to six macropropositions in working memory at any one time, as compared with only two or three micropropositions (Kintsch & van Dijk, 1978; Singer, 1982; Vipond, 1980). This result suggests that there are separate working memory *buffers* for macropropositions and micropropositions. The larger capacity of the macrostructure buffer is consistent with the proposed importance of the macropropositions of a discourse.

Several memory measures of comprehension have likewise supported the macrostructure–microstructure distinction. First, in free recall, people reproduce a higher proportion of macropropositions than micropropositions (Kintsch & van Dijk, 1978; Singer, 1982; Vipond, 1980). For example, Singer (1982) reported that, immediately after reading a newspaper article, people recalled 44% of the text macropropositions and 22% of the micropropositions. Other individuals, who recalled the article after 6 weeks, reproduced 10% of the macropropositions and 5% of the micropropositions. Second, the macropropositions of a text mutually prime one another more than do comparable micropropositions (Guindon & Kintsch, 1984; Ratcliff & McKoon, 1978; see also chapter 2). This is consistent with the view that macropropositions are privileged memory units and therefore are strong sources of priming. In summary, reading times, estimates of working memory capacity, and recall measures all support the psychological validity of the macrostructure.

The Dynamics of Macroprocessing

Although important, macroprocessing does not always accompany comprehension. There is evidence that discourse macroprocessing is influenced by the form of a message, by the goals of the understander, and by individual differences among readers.

Consider first the form of a message. Because the construction of the macrostructure is guided by relevant knowledge, the understander needs to be able to access that knowledge in order to engage in macroprocessing. This ought to be easiest for well-organized messages. *Well-organized* means that the message clearly represents a particular type of discourse, such as a story, newspaper article, research report, or puzzle; or a particular content area, such as science, history, or sports. In fact, there is considerable evidence that people can construct the macrostructure of well-organized messages (Hayes & Simon, 1974; Kintsch & Greeno, 1985; Kintsch & van Dijk, 1978; Thorndyke, 1977; van Dijk & Kintsch, 1983). On the other hand, macroprocessing should be curtailed if a message is disorganized or vague (Kintsch & van Dijk, 1978). To test this hypothesis, investigators have presented readers with text fragments that conceal the structure of the complete texts. In this condition, neither measures of memory performance (Kintsch & van Dijk, 1978, p. 388) nor reading time (Cirilo, 1981) distinguished between the macropropositions and micropropositions of the text. Likewise, presenting the sentences of a text in a disorganized or scrambled order prevents the extraction of the macrostructure (Lorch, Lorch, & Matthews, 1985; Vipond, 1980).

Second, understanders can approach discourses with many different goals and strategies, and these can influence the degree of macroprocessing. Suppose that you set about to read a text with the intention of summarizing it when you are done. Summarizing particularly requires that you identify the theme of the message, and so ought to encourage macroprocessing. In contrast, tasks that require that the understander pay attention to the superficial features of a message require little or no macroprocessing. For example, a person who proofreads a text for spelling and punctuation errors does not need to extract the main gist of a text. The same might be true for someone performing simultaneous translation. Experimental evidence has revealed that people who read in order to summarize a text engage in extensive macroprocessing (Brown & Day, 1983; Lorch et al., 1985; Schmalhofer & Glavanov, 1986), whereas those performing superficial understanding tasks do not (Cirilo, 1981; Mayer & Cook, 1981). It is important to note that people who approach a message with what might be thought of as typical goals, such as understanding and remembering, perform extensive macroprocessing (Cirilo, 1981; Kintsch & van Dijk, 1978; Mayer & Cook, 1981; Singer, 1982).

Finally, people differ from one another on many dimensions that affect comprehension, including verbal ability, age, and knowledge about the topic of the discourse. Individual differences on these dimensions affect the course of macroprocessing. Consider the knowledge of the understander. It should be easier for a person knowledgeable about the discourse content to distinguish the important and unimportant ideas of a message than for a less knowledgeable individual. Spilich et al.'s (1979) study of people high and low in baseball knowledge bears on this proposal. After hearing a description of a baseball half-inning, high-knowledge understanders exceeded low-knowledge understanders in their retention of the ideas relevant to baseball goals, such as scoring runs and winning. However, the two groups did not differ in their retention of less relevant information, such as a description of the weather. Likewise, characteristics such as the verbal ability and the age of understanders affect their relative emphasis on macroprocessing and microprocessing (e.g., Craik & Simon, 1980; Dixon, Hultsch, Simon, & von Eye, 1984; Lorch, Lorch, & Morgan, 1987).

SUMMARY

The theme of a message serves as a pointer to relevant world knowledge, and imposes organization on the discourse ideas. This chapter focused on the latter function. Discourse theme is signaled by factors including the title, initial mention, frequency of mention, the grammatical role of ideas, content, and explicit markers. Ideas that are identified as thematic by these factors are remembered better and are judged to be more important than other discourse ideas.

Three structural features of message representations account for the retrieval and importance-judgment advantages of thematic ideas. First, ideas mentioned in the title and at the outset of a message are likely to be assigned to high levels of the discourse representation. High level ideas have a retrieval advantage because people may begin searching the representation at or near the top. Second, frequently mentioned ideas are richly interconnected with other discourse ideas. As a result, these ideas are highly likely to be integrated into the text base, and to be activated for retrieval by other ideas. Third, some discourse ideas appear in the main causal chain underlying a message, whereas others are assigned to dead-end branches. Ideas on the causal chain are retrieved more effectively and judged to be more important than dead-end ideas. The retrieval advantage of causal chain ideas may be due to their high connectivity and to their content.

The theme of a discourse is particularly captured by an organized, hierarchical network of propositions called the macrostructure. The macrostructure is constructed by applying macrorules to the (micro)propositions of the discourse. Macrorules such as Selection, Deletion, Generalization, and Construction generate fewer macropropositions than the micropropositions underlying the discourse. The microstructure and the macrostructure together form the discourse text base.

The psychological validity of the macrostructure is supported by measures of reading time, recall, and by evidence for separate working memory buffers for micropropositions and macropropositions. The course of macroprocessing is influenced by the form of a text, the understander's task, and individual differences among understanders.

7

Inference Processes

Consider the sentence, **Carol forgot about the turkey she was roasting.** The text base representation of this sentence consists of an integrated network of the propositions P1 (FORGET, CAROL, P2), P2 (ROAST, CAROL, TURKEY). The theorists who first presented this view soon considered the possibility that the resulting network might include propositions and propositional arguments that were not mentioned in the message (e.g., Johnson, Bransford, & Solomon, 1973; Kintsch & Keenan, 1973). For the sentence about Carol, it seems sensible to consider the possibility that the consequence that THE TURKEY BURNED is also stored in memory. Likewise, one might deduce that an oven was used to roast the turkey. The term *inference processes* will refer to the mental operations whereby the language understander extracts from a message implied propositions such as THE TURKEY BURNED and implied concepts such as OVEN.

A little reflection suggests that inference processing pervades language understanding. For example, from the sentence, **The farmer entered the pen,** it is by inference that one decides that *pen* refers to an enclosure rather than a writing implement. From the sentence, **The old man the boats,** it must be inferred that **old** is a noun rather than an adjective. For the sentence, **Sam angered Bill because he broke the window,** complex inferential procedures are required to determine that the pronoun *he* probably refers to Sam and not to Bill (Caramazza et al., 1977). When one is asked **Do you have a watch?** it must be inferred that the questioner wants to know the time and not literally whether you possess a watch. Examples of this sort are inexhaustible. In fact, inference has been called the "core of the understanding process" (Schank, 1976, p. 168).

This chapter focuses on inferences that add propositions or propositional arguments to the text base of a message. This approach deemphasizes low level inference processes, such as those contributing to spoken and written word recognition. To illustrate, in one word recognition experiment, people heard the sentence, **It was found that the *eel was on the orange,** in which the speech sound [p] was replaced with a nonspeech sound. However, the participants reported hearing the word **peel** (Warren & Warren, 1970). This chapter also deemphasizes high level inferences of complex problem solving, reasoning, and the construction of situation models (Collins, Brown, & Larkin, 1980; Rickheit, Schnotz, & Strohner, 1985; see also chapter 2). Finally, reconstructive discourse memory, which is inferential in nature but strictly a retrieval phenomenon, was examined in chapter 4.

The remainder of the introduction presents the definition of inference that is adopted in this chapter. The next section examines the issue of when, during the course of comprehension, inferences are drawn. Then, the text and reader factors that guide inference processing are considered.

Defining Inference

Inferring Propositions and Arguments. The term *inference* refers both to activities on the part of the understander, and to the ideas that result from those activities. For example, upon reading the sentence, **The wine bottle tipped,** one might infer that the wine spilled. In this event, the resulting idea, THE WINE SPILLED, constitutes an inference.

The present chapter examines the inference processes of the text base representation. These are processes that result in *the addition of arguments or entire propositions* to the propositions that are explicitly conveyed by a message. For example, underlying the sentence, **The tailor swept the floor** is the proposition, (SWEEP, AGENT:TAILOR, OBJECT:FLOOR). The inference that the tailor used a broom to sweep the floor adds the argument BROOM, resulting in the proposition (SWEEP, AGENT:TAILOR, OBJECT:FLOOR, INSTRUMENT:BROOM). If one inferred that the floor was consequently clean, the proposition (CLEAN, FLOOR) would be added to the text base representation.

Whereas "inference" refers to the understander's processes, *implication* refers to an activity of the speaker or writer. In some circumstances, the intention of the speaker to make an implication is especially clear. If, after a terrible movie, your companion says, "What a great film," the intended sarcasm is likely to be apparent. "Implication" can also refer to a characteristic of the message itself. For example, the sentence, **The wine bottle tipped,** carries the implication that the wine may have spilled.

Encoding Versus Activation.   The distinction between activation and encoding is important for the present purposes. Words in a message activate related concepts. For example, the word *nail* activates the concept NAIL, which in turn activates the related concept, HAMMER. Although the activation of HAMMER may contribute to the encoding of the argument HAMMER in the text base (McKoon & Ratcliff, 1986; Walker & Yekovich, 1984), it does not guarantee it (Corbett & Dosher, 1978, p. 480; Dosher & Corbett, 1982). This proposal is supported by the finding that the words of a message activate even those associated concepts that are unrelated to the meaning of the message. For example, the word **bug** results in the transient activation of the concept INSECT even when **bug** is encountered in the context of spying (Swinney, 1979). However, no one would propose that INSECT would consequently appear in the message text base. The present treatment emphasizes inferences that are propositionally encoded and not merely activated.

Logical Versus Pragmatic Inferences.   The implications of a message are either logical or pragmatic in nature (Harris & Monaco, 1978). Logical implications are 100% certain, and are based on some identifiable set of rules. For example, **Susan had nine oranges and she gave two to Bill** logically implies that Susan was left with seven oranges. We can be sure of this because of our knowledge of the rules of arithmetic. Pragmatic implications, in contrast, are probable, but not certain. Furthermore, they are based on our knowledge and experience rather than on formal rules. For example, **The cat ran from the dog** pragmatically implies that the cat was scared. The understander may draw this inference because a cat in this circumstance is ordinarily scared. However, it is conceivable that the animals in question were playing and that the cat was not scared.

The logical–pragmatic distinction helps to categorize many types of implication. For example, **The squirrel is older than the bear, and the bear is older than the fox** logically implies that the squirrel is older than the fox. This is true because of the *transitive* nature of the age relationship. On the basis of category relations, **Ed saw five Cadillacs** logically implies that Ed saw five cars. On the other hand, **The rock struck the window** pragmatically implies the *consequence* that the window broke. Likewise, **Stan had his hair cut** pragmatically implies the participation of the agent, BARBER.

Logical and pragmatic implications may be distinguished by a *but-*

not test (Brewer, 1975; Harris & Monaco, 1978). To apply the test, a statement is linked to its implication using the phrase "but . . . not." If this results in a self-contradiction, then the implication in question is a logical one. For example, the sentence, **Betty swatted a fly BUT she did NOT swat an insect,** is self-contradictory. Therefore, **Betty swatted a fly** logically implied that she swatted an insect. If, on the other hand, the result is sensible, the implication is pragmatic. For example, **Joe dropped the glass BUT it did NOT break** makes a sensible statement. Therefore, **Joe dropped a glass** pragmatically implies that the glass broke. One restriction of the *but-not* test is that it should not be applied to unrelated ideas, as in **Denmark is in Europe BUT it did NOT rain on Tuesday.**

The psychological validity of the logical–pragmatic distinction is somewhat limited (e.g., Keenan, 1978). It receives support from the fact that people agree that the logical implications of a sentence are more likely to be true than its pragmatic implications (Harris, 1974). On the other hand, consider the tempting hypothesis that, because of their certainty, logical inferences are more likely to accompany comprehension than are pragmatic inferences. There are several reasons that this is unlikely to be accurate.

First, the limitations of cognitive resources (Kahneman, 1973; Norman & Bobrow, 1975) prevent the computation of all of the logical implications of a message. Even the simplest sentences carry many implications. For example, from the sentence, **The girl ate the chocolate bar,** one could infer, THE GIRL ATE CANDY, THE GIRL ATE FOOD, and THE YOUNG FEMALE HUMAN BEING ATE THE CHOCOLATE BAR. There is almost no end to such possibilities. Futhermore, each inference might in turn suggest others. If one were to draw every logical inference suggested by a sentence, an *inference-explosion* would result (Charniak, 1975; Rieger, 1975).

A second reason that logical inferences might not accompany comprehension is that many of them either require that the understander engage in time-consuming problem solving, or they are simply beyond the capability of the understander. For example, even though **Linda correctly computed the derivative of X^2** logically implies that she arrived at the answer $2X$, one could draw this inference only if one possessed knowledge of calculus.

Conversely, because of the simplicity of many pragmatic implications, it is likely that some of them accompany comprehension. In short, even though the logical–pragmatic distinction helps us to categorize inference types, it does not provide a clear answer to the question of which inferences accompany comprehension.

WHEN ARE INFERENCES DRAWN?

Inference During Comprehension or Retrieval?

A central problem of inference processing concerns the question of when inferences are drawn. After reading **The delicate vase fell to the floor,** most people would agree that the vase probably broke, an implied idea. That agreement, however, does not determine whether the inference reliably accompanies comprehension, or whether it occurs only later, when the understander has reason to wonder about the fate of the vase.

In one relevant experiment, people heard a list of passages that included complex sentences, such as (1).

(1)   John was pounding the nail when his father came out to watch him.

An unexpected recognition test followed. The test sentences were either identical to ones in the original list, such as sentence (1), or they introduced a pragmatic implication of one of the original sentences, as in (2):

(2)   John was using the hammer when his father came out to watch him.

The participants claimed to have heard the identical test sentences and implicational test sentences about equally often (Johnson, et al., 1973). A comparable finding is that *implicit* cues, such as **hammer,** effectively remind 5th-grade children of sentences that they have heard, such as, **My father struck his finger instead of the nail** (Paris & Lindauer, 1976).

These results indicated that the participants were engaging in inferential processing. Johnson et al. (1973) distinguished two alternate hypotheses about the exact course of processing. First, the *inference-during-comprehension* hypothesis states that the listeners inferred the use of a hammer during the comprehension of (1). According to this view, the text base representation of (1) includes the proposition, (POUND, AGENT:JOHN, OBJECT:NAIL, INSTRUMENT:HAMMER). In this event, people incorrectly recognize test sentence (2) because its propositional form resembles the representation of (1). Likewise, the implicit cue, **hammer,** would provide access to the argument HAMMER in the stored proposition, and so prompt the recall of the original sentence.

The second hypothesis about the course of inference processing is the *inference-at-retrieval* view. It states that the inference about the hammer does *not* accompany comprehension, and occurs only at test time. In this event, the propositional representation of **John was pounding the nail** is simply (POUND, AGENT:JOHN, OBJECT:NAIL). According to this position, people report recognizing sentence (2) because it is judged to be consistent with the meaning of sentence (1). Similarly, the implicit cue, **hammer,** may, at test time, remind the understander of related actions, such as hitting a nail. This, in turn, provides access to the stored proposition.

Corbett and Dosher (1978) presented evidence that helped to choose between the inference-at-comprehension and inference-at-retrieval hypotheses. Their participants read antecedent sentences that named probable or improbable instruments or no instrument at all. For example, during learning, people read either the Explicit Probable instrument sentence (3), the Implicit instrument sentence, (4), or the Explicit Improbable instrument sentence, (5):

(3)   The accountant dried his hands with the towel.
(4)   The accountant dried his hands.
(5)   The accountant dried his hands with the shirt.

In the test session, all participants received the probable instrument, **towel,** as a recall cue. This cue prompted the recall of the Explicit Probable sentences and the Implicit sentences 72% of the time each, replicating the finding of the effectiveness of implicit cues (Paris & Lindauer, 1976). However, the Explicit Improbable sentences were recalled 73% of the time! In other words, **towel** helped people recall **The accountant dried his hands with the shirt.**

How can this result be explained? When one reads, **The accountant dried his hands with the shirt,** it does not make sense to infer that the accountant used a towel. That would be a direct contradiction. For **towel** to cue the recall of (5), it must suggest the act of drying, which in turn provides access to (5). If this mechanism can work for the Explicit Improbable sentences, it can do likewise for the Implicit sentences. Therefore, the fact that **towel** reminds people of the implicit sentence **The accountant dried his hands** does not prove that the use of a towel was inferred during comprehension.

Although this finding clarified the role of implicit recall cues, it did not clearly favor either the inference-at-comprehension or inference-at-retrieval hypothesis. However, Corbett and Dosher (1978) presented some evidence that addressed these hypotheses more directly. It was reasoned that if people infer probable instruments during sentence comprehension, then they should subsequently include them in their free recall reports. It was found that people *seldom* include probable implied instruments in their recall. This outcome favored the inference-at-retrieval hypothesis.

In another study, people read brief passages that stated or implied the use of highly probably instruments. For example, sentence (6) states the use of a broom, whereas (7) implies it (Singer, 1979a).

(6) The sailor swept the floor with the broom.
(7) The sailor swept the floor.

Twenty minutes after reading, the participants were timed while they made judgments about test sentences. All of the test sentences had the explicit form, such as sentence (6). The participants performed either a recognition task, or judged the truth of the test sentences. In both tasks, implicit test sentences were accepted about as often as explicit ones, replicating the finding of Johnson et al. (1973). However, it took about one-fifth of a second more to respond affirmatively to implicit than to explicit test sentences (see Table 7.1). A similar result was obtained when each passage was *immediately* followed by its corresponding test sentence. The answer-time difference suggests that the crucial inferences, such as the one about the broom, were drawn at the time of retrieval.

Of relevance to the inference-at-retrieval hypothesis is the proposal that even the explicit ideas of sentences are weakly encoded if they convey predictable information (Garnham, 1982; Spiro & Esposito, 1981). The rationale of this view is that predictable information can be reconstructed on the basis of one's world knowledge. For example, sentence (8b) presents predictable information when it is preceded by (8a).

TABLE 7.1
Time Needed to Judge the Explicit Statements and Implications of Brief Passages (Milliseconds)

Task	Statement Type	
	Explicit	Implicit
Recognition	2545 (.79)[a]	2732 (.70)
Verification	2422 (.91)	2685 (.86)

Note: Proportion of affirmative answers in parentheses.
Source: The data of Singer (1979a). Reprinted by permission.

(8) a. The karate champion hit the block.
     b. The block broke.

If predictable explicit ideas are encoded weakly, then it should not be surprising to discover that predictable *implications* are also encoded either weakly or not at all.

In a test of the weak-encoding hypothesis, people read sequences such as (8), or the alternative, (9).

(9) a. The karate champion had a fight with his wife earlier. It was impairing his concentration.
     b. The karate champion hit the block.
     c. The block broke.

If (9a) precedes **The karate champion hit the block,** then it seems less predictable that the block will break. Therefore, the proposition, THE BLOCK BROKE, ought to be encoded more strongly in sequence (9) than (8). The results of a recognition test supported this hypothesis: People were more certain that **The block broke** had been explicitly mentioned in sequence (9) than in sequence (8) (Spiro & Esposito, 1981). This outcome is consistent with the failure to encode predictable implications during comprehension: that is, it is consistent with the inference-at-retrieval hypothesis.

Other experimental techniques have similarly supported the inference-at-retrieval hypothesis (Dosher & Corbett, 1982; Mandler & Murachver, 1985; McKoon & Ratcliff, 1986; Singer, 1979b). This outcome might strike us as puzzling. At the beginning of this chapter, the pervasiveness of inference in comprehension was considered. Likewise, chapter 4 emphasized that language understanding proceeds with reference to one's world knowledge. Therefore, one might expect that the understander's reference to world knowledge would result in inferences during comprehension.

One explanation of these findings is that the reliable encoding of even highly probable inferences would result in the inference-explosion that was discussed earlier (Charniak, 1975; Rieger, 1975). An inference-explosion would quickly overwhelm the understander's cognitive resources, especially in view of the many subtasks of language analysis required in listening and reading comprehension.

Conclusions

Research during the 1970s revealed that there are limits on the inference processing that accompanies comprehension. This suggests that there must be factors that determine which implications of a message are inferred by the understander. Researchers have tried to identify the characteristics of messages and readers that guide inference processing during comprehension (Goetz, 1979). The next two sections of this chapter will take up these issues.

MESSAGE CHARACTERISTICS THAT GUIDE INFERENCE PROCESSING

In view of the limitations on the inference processing that accompanies comprehension, it stands to reason that the form of a message constrains the inferences that are computed. In this section, four message character-istics are considered: coherence requirements, thematic structure, dis-tance among ideas, and interestingness.

Coherence Requirements

Bridging Inferences Versus Elaborative Inferences.   The distinction between bridging and elaborative inferences (also called backward and forward inferences, respectively) is an important one in the inference literature (Clark, 1977; Graesser, Haberlandt, & Koizumi, 1987; Just & Carpenter, 1978; Singer, 1980; Thorndyke, 1976). A bridging inference is a proposition or argument that is constructed to bridge two sentences, such as (10a) and (10b).

(10)   a.   The tooth was pulled painlessly.
       b.   The dentist used a new method.

Upon examining (10b), it becomes necessary to find a referent for the given element, DENTIST (Clark, 1977; Haviland & Clark, 1974). Because (10a) includes no direct referent for DENTIST, an indirect referent is identified by the process of bridging. For sequence (10a)-(10b), it is a simple matter to draw the bridging inference that the dentist was the agent who pulled the tooth. As discussed in chapter 5, constructing a bridge between the current sentence and the preceding discourse preserves the coherence of the discourse.

The importance of drawing bridging inferences is illustrated by the contrasting sequence, **The tooth was pulled painlessly. The tailor used a new method.** Because there is no obvious knowledge that bridges TAILOR and PULLING A TOOTH, this sequence strikes us as inco-herent.

In contrast to bridging inferences, elaborative inferences add sensible information to a message text base, but they are not essential to the coherence of the message. For example, if, upon reading **The tooth was pulled painlessly,** one infers that the tooth was pulled by a dentist, then a simple elaborative inference has been drawn. If you briefly reconsider the previous section, "When are Inferences Drawn?", you will see that the inferences that it examined were elaborative inferences.

It is conceivable that, upon reading (10a)-(10b), one would draw an elaborative inference about the dentist as soon as (10a) is examined. The important point is that if the reader does not draw this elaborative inference, then a bridging inference *must* accompany the comprehension of (10b) for coherence to be preserved.

Experimental Comparisons of Elaborative and Bridging Inferences. There is considerable evidence of the psychological validity of the distinction between elaborative and bridging inferences. In particular, numerous studies indicate that bridging inferences reliably accompany comprehension, whereas elaborative inferences do not.

In one study, people read either sequence (11), (12), or (13), and then verified test item (14) (Singer, 1980).

(11)   The pitcher threw the ball to first base. The runner was halfway to second. (explicit antecedent)

(12)   The pitcher threw to first base. The ball sailed into the field. (bridging inference antecedent)

(13)   The pitcher threw to first base. The runner was halfway to second. (elaborative inference antecedent)

(14)   The pitcher threw a ball. (test item)

Consider the proposition underlying (14), (THROW, PITCHER, BALL). Sequence (11) expresses this *explicitly.* Sequence (12) requires that the reader construct the bridging inference, (THROW, PITCHER, BALL), in order to link the word **ball** in the second sentence with the first sentence. Finally, sequence (13) permits an *elaborative inference* about the pitcher throwing the ball. However, the coherence of (13) does not depend on this inference.

The verification times for sentence (14) were 1884, 1897, and 2136 msec in the explicit, bridging inference, and elaborative inference conditions, respectively. The similar scores for the explicit condition and the bridging inference condition were interpreted to indicate that the bridging inferences had accompanied comprehension. In contrast, the longer verification times for elaborative inference test sentences indicate that the elaborative inferences were drawn only at retrieval time. The difference between the explicit and elaborative inference conditions replicated the findings about elaborative inferences presented in the previous section of this chapter (e.g., Corbett & Dosher, 1978; Johnson et al., 1973; Singer, 1979a, 1979b).

In another study of complex bridging inferences, people read stories that included sentences such as (15) (Thorndyke, 1976).

(15)   The hamburger chain owner was afraid that his love for french fries would ruin his marriage.

It was proposed that understanding (15) might lead to inferences such as those expressed by (16a) and (16b), sentences that did not appear in the story.

(16)   a.   The hamburger chain owner was very fat.
        b.   The hamburger chain owner's wife didn't like french fries.

Later in the story, the participants encountered sentence (17).

(17)   The hamburger chain owner decided to join weight-watchers in order to save his marriage.

Thorndyke argued that to understand (17), people would need to draw a bridging inference to link (17) to (15). He pointed out that (17) supports inference (16a), but not (16b).

The data bore out this analysis (Thorndyke, 1976, Experiment 2). After reading the story, people incorrectly reported recognizing the appropriate inference, (16a), 57% of the time. This reflects the fact that, to understand the relation between sentence (17) and sentence (15), the reader had to draw the bridging inference, (16a). In contrast, inappropriate inferences, such as (16b), were recognized only 6% of the time.

Several other investigations have supported the conclusion that bridging inferences accompany comprehension (Black & Bern, 1981; Hayes-Roth & Thorndyke, 1979; Just & Carpenter, 1978; Singer & Ferreira, 1983). Conversely, numerous studies have indicated that elaborative inferences are not reliably drawn during the encoding of a message (e.g., Belmore, Yates, Bellack, Jones, & Rosenquist, 1982; Corbett & Dosher, 1978; Dosher & Corbett, 1982; Downey, 1979; Just & Carpenter, 1978; Mandler & Murachver, 1985; Potts, Keenan, & Golding, 1988; McKoon & Ratcliff, 1986; Singer, 1979a, 1979b, 1980; Singer & Ferreira, 1983). As discussed earlier, the drawing of elaborative inferences is probably limited by the constraints of cognitive resources.

Inferring Causal Connections.   The causal relations among ideas are especially important to the gist of a message (e.g., Schank & Abelson, 1977). In the study of cause and inference, it is necessary to distinguish between inferences about the events and states that function as causes, as opposed to inferences about the causal connections between events. For example, upon reading, **The snowman melted,** one might infer the causal event that the temperature climbed above freezing. In contrast, from the sequence, **The child stuck the balloon with the pin. The balloon burst,** one might infer a connection between the two events: Namely, sticking the balloon caused it to burst. Inferring a causal event is an elaborative inference whereas inferring a causal connection is a bridging inference.

There is considerable evidence that people draw bridging inferences about causal connections during comprehension. In one study, it was proposed that readers draw bridging inferences based on causal relations more reliably than ones based on temporal (time) relations (Black & Bern, 1981). In the experiments, people read causal sequences, such as (18), and temporal sequences, such as (19).

(18) a. The cat leapt up on the kitchen table.
      b. Fred picked up the cat and put it outside.

(19) a. The cat rubbed against the kitchen table.
      b. Fred picked up the cat and put it outside.

In a subsequent recall test, the participants received sentences such as (18a) and (19a) as recall cues. Sentence (18a) cued the recall of (18b) more effectively than (19a) cued (19b). Furthermore, in free recall, individual causal sentences and pairs of causal sentences were recalled more frequently than their temporal counterparts. Black and Bern (1981) concluded that people infer the causal connections between sentences, resulting in the integration of the underlying ideas (see also Brewer & Dupree, 1983).

In a related study, norms were collected that specified four degrees of causal relation among pairs of sentences. Sentences (20a) and (20b) illustrate close causal relatedness, whereas (21a) and (21b) are only distantly related.

(20) a. Joey's big brother punched him again and again.
      b. The next day his body was covered with bruises.

(21) a. Joey went to a neighbor's house to play.
      b. The next day his body was covered with bruises.

Then, it was demonstrated that reading time for the second sentence in the pairs varied as a function of causal relatedness: namely, the closer the relationship, the faster the reading time (Keenan et al., 1984). This outcome supports the conclusion that people construct causal bridging inferences during comprehension. In particular, the less causally related two sentences are, the longer it takes to bridge them.

Trabasso and Sperry (1985) provided evidence that inferred causal connections play an important role in text representation. They analyzed the causal structure of a story, and determined the number of explicit and implicit causal connections in which each story proposition participated. Readers' judgments about these propositions revealed that rated importance varies systematically with the number of causal connections of a proposition. Because only a subset of the causal connections were explicitly stated in the story, the readers must have inferred the others. Only in this way could importance rating have been so directly related to the number of causal connections.

Theme and Inference

The *inference-theme* hypothesis states that inference processing is concentrated on thematic ideas in a discourse. One rationale of this proposal is that, in view of the limitations on inference processing, focusing on thematic ideas generates those inferences most useful to the understander.

In chapter 6, we considered three structural correlates of theme: namely, hierarchical level, connectivity, and causal chain membership. Consistent with that analysis, researchers investigating the inference-theme hypothesis have frequently defined "theme" in terms of these structural features.

To evaluate the inference-theme hypothesis, investigators have compared people's judgments about the implications of thematic and peripheral discourse ideas. In most of these studies, ideas have generally been identified as thematic or peripheral on the basis of their role in the story structure, rather than their content. For example, Walker and Meyer (1980) presented readers with a text that included sentences (22a) and (22b).

(22)   a.   The Spring Episode was the first revolution in Morinthia.
       b.   All Morinthian revolutions were failures.

Across different text versions, the ideas underlying (22a) and (22b) were either at high or low levels of the text base: that is, they were either thematic or peripheral.

Later, the participants judged the truth of implied facts, such as (23), called an inference by direct reference (Clark, 1977).

(23)   The Spring Episode was a failure.

Consistent with the inference-theme hypothesis, people were more accurate in their judgments of inferences derived from thematic than peripheral facts. People also take less time to verify the true implications of ideas thematized by frequent reference, than those of peripheral ideas (Eamon, 1978-79). Finally, as described in chapter 6, Goetz (1979) manipulated the thematic status of text ideas by coupling them with important consequences or unimportant ones. For example, as a result of missing a plane, a character could either be late for her business meeting, or avoid death in a plane crash. The readers made a greater number of accurate judgments about the implications of thematic ideas than peripheral ones.

The inference-theme hypothesis has also been examined using the measure of comprehension time (Cirilo, 1981). People were timed while they read sequences such as (24) and (25).

(24)   a.   The warrior said he would help her by turning her tears into gold.
        b.   Then the tears fell on the ground.

(25)   a.   The warrior said he would help her as her tears splattered her dress.
        b.   Then the tears fell on the ground.

The concepts TEARS is thematic in (24a) and peripheral in (25a). It was predicted that people would need less time to comprehend **Then the tears fell on the ground** when it followed (24a) than (25a). The rationale was that it should take less time to identify the referent of *tears* in the thematic case. Consistent with this analysis, comprehension time was faster for sentences presenting thematic than nonthematic ideas.

Although thematic variables thus influence a reader's judgments of implied ideas, is it correct to also conclude that these inferences accompany comprehension? There is some evidence to support such a proposal, but it is necessary to be cautious. For example, Walker and Meyer (1980, p. 273) reported that true thematic inferences, such as sentence (23) were verified as quickly as comparable explicit statements. However, this was the case only when the two statements yielding the inference were adjacent to one another in the text. Similarly, Eamon's (1978-79) participants verified thematic implications faster than some explicit statements, but it is unclear that the implicit and explicit statements were completely comparable.

A processing explanation of why inference processing focuses on thematic ideas is that high level propositions in a text base are more likely to be retained in working memory than low level ones (Kintsch & van Dijk, 1978). This is especially so because thematic ideas are relatively likely to be adopted as macropropositions, and the working memory buffer for macropropositions is large (Vipond, 1980). As a result, thematic ideas remain in working memory, available to be inferentially combined with subsequent discourse ideas.

Distance

The distance between discourse ideas should affect the likelihood of constructing bridging inferences between them. That is, it should be easier to identify the conceptual referent of a word when the referent has appeared recently (near) in the text than when it has appeared much earlier (far). This is because most propositions are deleted from working memory shortly after they are presented in a message (Kintsch & van Dijk, 1978). Therefore, the greater the distance between two propositions in the text, the less likely that the earlier one will remain in working memory to provide the referents necessary to complete bridging inferences.

To examine the impact of distance on inference processing, Hayes-Roth and Thorndyke (1979) presented two related facts either in the same text, the near condition; or in two different texts, the far condition. Sentences (22a) and (22b), previously considered, illustrate a pair of related facts.

(22) a. The Spring Episode was the first revolution in Morinthia.
      b. All Morinthian revolutions were failures.

The integration of (22a) and (22b) results in the logical inference, (23).

(23) The Spring Episode was a failure.

People were more accurate in their judgments about implication (23) in the near condition than the far condition (Hayes-Roth & Thorndyke, 1979). In a similar study, people were more likely to report *recognizing* implications such as (23) when they could be derived from near statement pairs than far statement pairs (Walker & Meyer, 1980). They also took more than 2 seconds longer to correctly judge the implications of far than near facts. Likewise, comprehension time for test sentences with near referents is less than that of test sentences with far referents (Cirilo, 1981).

The data of Ehrlich and Johnson-Laird (1982), discussed in chapter 5, bear on the role of distance in inference processing. Their participants read descriptions of the spatial positions of several objects, and then drew diagrams of the layout. The texts were either continuous, such as **The knife is in front of the pot. The pot is on the left of the glass. The glass is behind the dish;** or discontinuous, such as **The knife is in front of the pot. The glass is behind the dish. The pot is on the left of the glass.** One feature of the discontinuous sequences is that the second sentence intervenes between the third sentence and its referent, *pot*, in the first sentence. People drew more accurate diagrams of objects described by continuous than discontinuous sequences, and needed about 4 seconds less to read the third sentence of continuous sequences than discontinuous sequences. These results support the role of distance in drawing bridging inferences.

Interestingness

Consideration of the motivations of understanders suggests that the interestingness of a message may guide inference processing. This hypothesis has not received extensive experimental testing, but detailed arguments supporting it have been presented. Schank (1979) proposed that emotional topics such as power, sex, money, and death, plus events of personal relevance, are inherently interesting. Also interesting are unexpected events. In this regard, most of what happens in the course of doing laundry is not interesting. However, if the washing machine overflows and the janitor throws a temper tantrum, there is greater interest, because these events are unusual in the laundry context (Graesser et al., 1979).

Interestingness has also been defined in terms of the relation between the understander's knowledge and the events described in a discourse (Kintsch, 1980). To be most interesting, a text would have to present ideas that are somewhat but not overly familiar to the reader. For example, one might expect an adult amateur astronomer to enjoy magazine articles on astronomy. However, neither a child's book on astronomy, nor a journal article on astrophysics, is likely to hold much interest for such an individual.

Because the reader is assumed to attend more carefully to that which is interesting, interestingness should influence inference processing (Kintsch, 1980; Schank, 1979). In one study that indirectly bears on this issue, the role of a specific statement was varied across different versions of a story (Nezworski, Stein, & Trabasso, 1982). In one story, for example, Mary lies to Peter about why she cannot play with him. The critical information is that Mary is making a secret trip to buy Peter a birthday present. In different versions of the story, information about the shopping trip was presented in different parts of the story, such as the setting, the consequence, or the character's reaction. However, memory for the crucial fact did not differ across these versions. This indicates that the interestingness of the content of a text idea affects its memorability. It is reasonable to propose, in turn, that interestingness will likewise affect inference processing.

READER CHARACTERISTICS THAT GUIDE INFERENCE PROCESSING

Individuals vary along many dimensions, including verbal ability, degree of knowledge, age, available cognitive resources, and the goals that are applied to a comprehension task. Because inference processing is based on one's relevant knowledge, therefore the particular knowledge that understanders possess, and their ability to retrieve it, is likely to have a considerable impact on these processes. The present section examines several understander characteristics that have been hypothesized to affect inference.

Orienting Tasks in Reading

There are many different tasks that one can perform in the act of reading. One may read with the intention of learning, solving a problem, summarizing, or simply enjoying. Several investigators have examined the effect of the reader's task on inference processing. These studies have invoked the principles of depth of processing (Craik & Lockhart, 1972), transfer-appropriate training (Morris, Bransford, & Franks, 1977), and the more general notion of *orienting tasks*.

In a landmark paper, Craik and Lockhart (1972) advanced the notion that a stimulus may be processed at deep or shallow levels. In general, deep processing involves the extraction of meaning, whereas shallow processing refers to the examination of the superficial features of a stimulus. It was proposed that deeper processing results in stronger and longer-lasting memory traces. In reading, counting the number of nouns in a text would constitute shallow processing, whereas judging the degree of activity conveyed by a text would exemplify deep processing.

The levels of processing analysis raised the possibility that inference processing might be curtailed in shallow tasks. To test this hypothesis, people were assigned to read ambiguous passages with one of two tasks in mind (Schallert, 1976). Consider, for example, the following passage:

> In the last days of August, we were all suffering from the unbearable heat. In a few short weeks, our daily job had turned from a game into hard labor. "All we need now," said the manager in one of his discouraged moods, "is a strike." I listened to him silently but could I not help him. I hit a fly. "I suppose things could get even worse," he continued. "Our most valuable pitchers might crack in this heat. If only we had more fans, we would all feel better, I'm sure. I wish our best man would come home. That certainly would improve everyone's morale, especially mine. Oh well, I know a walk would cheer me up a little." (Schallert, 1976, pp. 621–622)

This passage could be interpreted as referring to the worries of a baseball manager or the manager of a glass factory. Each reader was informed of one of these themes or the other, or was not given a theme. Furthermore, the participants were instructed either to judge the degree of ambiguity of the passage (deep task), or to count the number of pronouns (shallow task). In a subsequent multiple choice test, the participants incorrectly recognized implicational sentences related to their theme more often than those related to the other theme. However, this result was obtained only when the readers performed the deep task.

In another study, people read sentences such as, **The youngster watched the program** (Till & Walsh, 1980). One group rated the pleasantness of the sentences, a deep processing task. A second group counted the words in the sentences, a shallow task. In a subsequent cued recall task, the participants received cues that were either explicit (e.g., **program**) or implicit (e.g., **television**) with reference to the sentences. The deep processors recalled as well with implicit cues as explicit ones, whereas the shallow processors showed a deficit with the implicit cues. This outcome indicates either that the deep processors generated the implied concept during comprehension, or that the shallow processors generally encoded the meaning of the sentences less effectively than the deep processors.

A different analysis of processing depth states that shallow processing does not yield inherently weaker memory traces than deep processing, but rather that the memory results of shallow processing are pertinent to different types of transfer tasks (Morris et al., 1977). Pursuing this notion of transfer-appropriate training, Mayer and Cook (1981) asked some participants ("shadowers") to repeat the words of a passage about radar as they listened to it, and asked others to simply listen normally. Afterwards, the participants were tested on their memory for the wording, syntax, and meaning of the passages, and on their ability to apply the information of the passage in a new context. Those individuals who listened normally scored better than the shadowers only on the *application* of the information. Applying the information required the participant to generalize the information from the passage, which can be viewed as an inferential activity. Conversely, the shadowers were marginally better than the normal listeners in their memory for the precise wording of the passage. This outcome supported the principle of transfer-appropriate training, and it also elaborated the role of the reader's task on inference processing.

One shortcoming of the depth of processing notion is that it seems inevitable that if one prevents a reader from attending to text meaning, inference processing will be curtailed. Some of those who have studied the impact of reading tasks have, therefore, not invoked the depth of processing principle. Instead, they have attempted to identify specific sets of goals that are associated with different reading *orienting tasks* (e.g., Cirilo, 1981; Walker & Meyer, 1980). They have predicted that these goals will guide the construction of quite different representations of text meaning, and result in different patterns of inference processing.

To study the impact of the orienting task on inference, Walker and Meyer (1980) (who also examined the factors of theme and distance) instructed one group of individuals simply to read passages at a normal pace. A second group was instructed to reread the text if necessary, so that they might learn the details of the passage. The "learners" were more accurate than "readers" in verifying implications such as **The Spring Episode was a failure,** examined earlier. The learners also produced these implications in a free recall task more often than did the readers.

It may be that the understander's task affects inference processing by regulating the amount of macroprocessing. As discussed in chapter 6, tasks such as summarizing promote macroprocessing, whereas reading with the intention to learn enhances microprocessing (Brown & Day, 1983; Cirilo, 1981; Schmalhofer & Glavanov, 1986). Tasks requiring macroprocessing might enhance inferences such as those due to generalization and construction. For example, a person who reads in order to summarize might construct the macroproposition, THE YOUNGSTER WATCHED TELEVISION from the sentence, **The youngster watched the program.** In contrast, tasks requiring extensive microprocessing are likely to ensure the drawing of bridging inferences, which are needed to maintain a coherent micropropositional text base.

Knowledge

Inferences result when understanders use their knowledge to extrapolate beyond the ideas directly stated in a message. Accordingly, the particular knowledge of the understander is likely to affect inference processing. Evidence to this effect was considered in chapter 4. For example, Anderson, Reynolds, et al. (1976) reported that people's interpretations of ambiguous passages were influenced by their background. In one case, weight-lifters understood an ambiguous passage as referring to a wrestling match, whereas music students saw a prison interpretation. In this respect, the readers' knowledge influenced their inferential decisions about word sense.

Likewise, after listening to a lengthy baseball passage, people high in their knowledge of baseball exceeded low knowledge listeners in their recall of game-relevant statements. However, there were no differences in memory for game-irrelevant statements, such as advertisements (Spilich et al., 1979). These findings were extended to the study of inference processing (Post, Greene, & Bruder, 1982). Post et al. asked people high or low in baseball knowledge to read the description of an entire baseball game! Test sentences were constructed to probe numerous types of inference in relation to baseball. These sentences referred to nongame information, such as the weather; various types of information pertinent to the game, such as a batter striking out; and the integration of game information, such as how many hits a player had.

Measures of verification accuracy and verification time revealed similar patterns of results. High knowledge readers had large advantages over low knowledge readers in their judgments of implications about game information. The two groups did not differ for nongame information. Perhaps surprisingly, there was also no difference for test sentences probing the integration of game information. What the last result means is that even high knowledge participants do not keep a running count of the number of hits of each player, or the number of pop-flies during the game. Because the readers were not tested on explicit text statements as well, it is impossible to determine which game-information inferences of the high knowledge readers accompanied comprehension. Nevertheless, the results indicate that the pertinent knowledge of the reader plays a large role in the computation of inferences either during or after reading.

It is likely that the understander's knowledge guides inference processing by its influence on macroprocessing. Schemata relevant to the genre and content of a discourse guide the construction of the macrostructure. For example, knowledge about baseball permits the understander to distinguish between the relevant and irrelevant statements in the description of a game. The judgment of relevance determines whether a particular proposition will be selected for the macrostructure, or deleted. In turn, the appearance of relevant propositions in the macrostructure is likely to affect the course of inference processes.

Age

Changes in cognitive functioning across the adult lifespan have been the focus of considerable attention (e.g., Craik & Byrd, 1981; Craik & Simon, 1980). Investigators have raised the issue of whether the comprehension deficits of the elderly may be linked to impoverished inference processing. The ability of young and elderly people to make simple and complex deductions was examined by Cohen (1979). In the experiment, young (age range 20–29 years) and old (age range 65–95 years) individuals listened to brief passages. For example, one passage stated that Mrs. Brown goes to the park on nice days, and also that it had rained for the past 3 days. An inference question asked, **Did Mrs. Brown go the park yesterday?** (no). Young readers made more errors on inference questions than explicit questions, but this difference was considerably larger in elderly listeners.

In a second experiment, people were instructed to detect anomalies in passages (Cohen, 1979). For example, one passage described a house-wife as having run out of bread, but later stated that she made sand-wiches. Young adults were better at detecting these errors than elderly adults, which suggests that the young more effectively discern the con-nection between related ideas in messages (see Hayes-Roth & Thorn-dyke, 1979; Walker & Meyer, 1980).

Till and Walsh (1980) asked young (age range 18–22 years) and old (age range 65–81 years) adults to listen to a list of 16 sentences, including items such as **The student carefully positioned the thumbtack on the chair.** Afterwards, each participant received either a free recall or cued recall test. The recall cues were concepts that represented implicational generalizations from the sentences, such as the word **prank** (cf. McKoon & Ratcliff, 1986; Paris & Lindauer, 1976). The young listeners recalled more sentences in cued recall than free recall, but the reverse was true for the old listeners. This outcome indicated a deficit on the part of the elderly participants to detect implicit relationships between the cues and the corresponding sentences.

Although Cohen (1979) found that elderly people experience more difficulty with implicational test items than do the young, this is not the case in all tasks. Belmore (1981) presented messages to young and old participants, followed by a timed sentence verification task. People needed more time to judge implicit than explicit test items, and the difference was similar in magnitude for the two age groups. The similar-ity between the performance of the two age groups may have been due to the fact that sentence verification is closely related to recognition, a memory task in which the elderly display little or no deficit (e.g., Craik

& Byrd, 1981). These findings underline the need to link deficits of inference processing in the elderly to general proposals concerning cognition and aging. For example, Craik and Byrd (1981) proposed that the elderly have a smaller reservoir of cognitive resources to divide among all cognitive tasks. Because only controlled processes (Schneider & Shiffrin, 1977; see also chapter 1) draw upon these resources, Craik and Byrd's proposal implies that the elderly should exhibit deficits in controlled but not automatic inference processing. Inference researchers will need to address hypotheses such as this.

Conclusions

The last two sections examined several text and reader variables that influence inference processing. Several conclusions seem warranted. First, the approach of identifying and studying the factors that guide inference processes is a fruitful one. Second, we have examined only a subset of the variables influencing inference. For example, other message factors, such as the number of times an idea is implied (Walker & Yekovich, 1984), and other reader characteristics, such as verbal ability (Hunt, 1978) and the amount of available cognitive resources (Britton, Holdredge, Curry, & Westbrook, 1979), are likely to exert important effects.

Third, inference factors of the sort that were examined here interact with one another in complex ways. For example, we saw that people recognize theme-relevant implicational test sentences more than theme-irrelevant ones, but only when they have performed a reading task requiring deep processing (Schallert, 1976). This amounts to what is called an *interaction* between the reader characteristic of orienting task and the message characteristic of theme. Likewise, knowledge and theme interact: For example, high knowledge readers outperform low knowledge readers in their judgments about theme-related (baseball) inference statements, but not for nontheme inferences (Post et al., 1982). Other interaction patterns of this sort were detected by Walker and Meyer (1980) and Cirilo (1981).

Finally, to achieve a true understanding of inference processing, it will be necessary to explain, within the framework of general models of language comprehension, how all of these factors exert their effects. Although the achievement of this goal lies in the future, the experience of the past two decades has provided some useful strategies for approaching it.

SUMMARY

For language comprehension to proceed, one must draw inferences about the content of a discourse, on the basis of one's world knowledge. The present chapter focused on the inference of propositions and arguments that contribute to the text base representation of a message. For example, if told, **Carol forgot about the turkey she was roasting,** the listener might infer the proposition, THE TURKEY BURNED, and also infer the use of an OVEN.

During the course of comprehension, the words of a discourse activate related concepts. This activation contributes to but does not guarantee the text base encoding of an inference about the concept.

Logical inferences are certain, and are based on an identifiable set of rules. Pragmatic inferences, in contrast, are probable but not certain. They are based on one's knowledge and experience. The understander does not draw all possible logical inferences during comprehension, because to do so would overwhelm the available cognitive resources. Furthermore, some logical inferences are beyond the capability of many understanders.

The experimental study of pragmatic inferences has indicated that even highly probable inferences do not reliably accompany comprehension. This outcome prompted investigators to identify the factors that guide inference processing. Four discourse factors were considered. First, many inferences that bridge the ideas expressed by a message accompany comprehension, probably because they are essential to coherence. In contrast, inferences that sensibly elaborate a message but that do not contribute to coherence are not reliably computed. Second, there is evidence that inference processing focuses on thematic rather than nonthematic discourse ideas. Third, ideas nearby to one another in a discourse are more likely to be inferentially bridged than are distant ideas. Fourth, it is hypothesized that interestingness influences inference processes.

The computation of discourse inferences is also guided by several understander characteristics. One's task and knowledge affect the extent of inferential macroprocessing that one performs. The age of the understander regulates the amount of cognitive resources that may be applied to controlled inference generation. The discourse and understander factors that guide inference processing are likely to interact with one another in complex ways.

8

Understanding Stories

A central goal of the study of discourse processes is to provide an account of the comprehension of complex messages. No text genre has received more attention in the psychological literature than the story. In many cultures, stories are used to entertain and to convey lessons or morals. In our culture, in particular, stories typically describe the trials and tribulations of one or more main characters. The main character is faced with a problem to solve, a goal to attain, or an obstacle to overcome. Table 8.1 presents a simple story, called "The King and his Daughters," in outline form (Mandler & Johnson, 1977). This story presents the goal of the heroes of rescuing the daughters, and recounts their attempts to achieve the goal. Statements 1 to 20 each convey a small number of propositions.

Two types of knowledge schema play a central role in the analysis of story understanding. First, the story schema captures people's knowledge about the typical form of stories. This knowledge guides the organization of the ideas encountered in a story, and particularly contributes to the representation of the story macrostructure (Kintsch & van Dijk, 1978; see chapter 6). Second, scripts represent people's knowledge about stereotypical situations, such as eating in a restaurant. Whenever a story refers to such a situation, the appropriate script may be called into play.

The first section of this chapter examines the role of the story schema in comprehension. The second section considers the role of specialized schemata of cause, goals, and plans in story understanding. The third section inspects genres other than the story. The fourth section presents an analysis of the comprehension of stories that invoke scripts. The final section addresses the coordination of the different schemata underlying a text.

THE STORY SCHEMA

The Story Grammar Model

The *story schema* is a mental structure that represents one's knowledge of the form of a typical story (Bower, 1976; Kintsch, 1977; Mandler & Johnson, 1977; Rumelhart, 1977; Thorndyke, 1977). One sort of formal model that describes the contents of the story schema is the *story grammar* (Mandler and Johnson, 1977; Thorndyke, 1977). Story grammars consist of a set of rewrite rules, similar in form to the rewrite rules of phrase structure grammar (see chapter 3). Table 8.2 presents the story grammar of Thorndyke (1977). Rule 1, for example, states that the symbol, Story, is rewritten as the string, Setting + Theme + Plot + Resolution. This is analogous to the phrase structure rule S → NP VP, that rewrites a sentence as a noun phrase plus a verb phrase. Rule 1 addresses

TABLE 8.1
The Story, "The King and his Daughters"

1	There once was a king
2	who had three lovely daughters
3	One day the three daughters went walking in the woods.
4	They were enjoying themselves so much
5	that they forgot the time
6	and stayed too long.
7	A crimson dragon came
8	and kidnapped the three daughters.
9	As they were being dragged off they cried for help.
10	Three heroes heard the cries.
11	and set off to rescue the daughters.
12	The heroes played their flutes to lure the dragon from its lair.
13	but the dragon paid no attention.
14	Then the heroes came
15	and fought the dragon,
16	and they killed the dragon
17	and rescued the maidens.
18	The heroes then returned the daughters safely to the palace.
19	When the king heard of the rescue
20	he rewarded the heroes.

Source: Adapted from Mandler & Johnson, 1977, Table 2, p. 121. Adapted by permission.

TABLE 8.2
Story Grammar Rules for Simple Stories

(1)	STORY →	SETTING + THEME + PLOT + RESOLUTION
(2)	SETTING →	CHARACTER + LOCATION + TIME
(3)	THEME →	(EVENT)* + GOAL
(4)	PLOT →	EPISODE*
(5)	EPISODE[a] →	(SUBGOAL) + (DESIRED STATE) + ATTEMPT* + OUTCOME
(6)	ATTEMPT →	{ EVENT* { EPISODE
(7)	OUTCOME →	{ EVENT* { STATE
(8)	RESOLUTION →	{ EVENT { STATE
(9)	SUBGOAL GOAL } →	DESIRED STATE
(10)	CHARACTERS LOCATION TIME } →	STATE

Source: Adapted from Thorndyke, 1977, Table 1, p. 79. Adapted by permission.
[a]Analysis of EPISODE presented by Glenn (1978).

people's knowledge that a story typically consists of a setting, theme, plot, and resolution.

Figure 8.1 applies the story grammar of Table 8.2 to "The King and his Daughters." The grammar imposes a hierarchical organization upon the statements of the story. For example, the Story constituent, at the top of the hierarchy, generates the symbol, Theme, at the second level. Theme, in turn, generates a Goal at the third level, which generates a Desired State at the fourth level. Furthermore, the idea units under certain nodes, such as ideas 3 to 10, are linked to one another by temporal or causal relations.

Story grammar rules have several special characteristics. First, strings of symbols are entered into the analysis in a distinct sequence. This sequential feature is denoted by the plus sign, +. Components appearing in parentheses are optional, and components marked by an asterisk, *, may be repeated two or more times. Consider Rule 3, Theme → (Event)* + Goal. Because Event is optional (enclosed in parentheses), the Theme can consist simply of a goal. For example, "The King and his Daughters" might have begun with a goal, such as, **Once, three heroes set off to rescue the daughters of the King**. Alternatively, the Theme can consist of a single event plus a goal, as in **Once, a crimson dragon kidnapped**

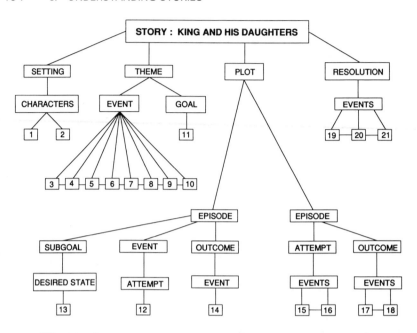

FIG. 8.1. Story grammar analysis applied to "The King and his Daughters."

the three daughters of a king. Three heroes set off to rescue them. As presented in Table 8.1, the Theme consists of events 3–10, plus goal 11.

Tests of the Story Grammar Model

The grammar approach to the story schema suggested numerous hypotheses concerning the comprehension and memory retrieval of stories. The resulting findings may be treated under the headings of sequential effects, hierarchical effects, and story category effects.

Sequential Effects.   Many story grammar rules, such as Rule (1) in Table 8.2, rewrite one story category as a sequence of categories. This suggests that story comprehension will be facilitated when story ideas are presented in their usual order. In a test of this hypothesis, Schwarz and Flammer (1981) examined people's memory for different versions of a story. In the normal version, the story sentences were ordered according to the rule, Story → Setting + Theme + Plot + Resolution. In a slightly disorganized version, the theme of the story was moved to the end. In a third version, the story sentences were completely randomized. Consistent with the story grammar analysis, people recalled the greatest number of story propositions in the regular version, and the fewest in the random version.

Of course, it would be unusual to encounter a story in completely random order. On the other hand, in many stories, the order of ideas does not exactly follow the one specified by the story grammar. Instead, authors frequently use narrative devices, such as flashbacks, which cause the serial order of ideas to deviate from the most typical one. However, the availability of the story schema should make it easier to understand a random story, as long as the story obeys some of the usual conventions of the genre.

To evaluate this analysis, Kintsch (1977) asked people to read stories that were either tightly or loosely structured with reference to the story schema of Western culture. In the tight story, the poisoning death of Pasquino directly leads to the trial of his lover, Simona. In the loose story, Rinaldo is robbed and is subsequently sheltered by a lady. However, the two episodes of the Rinaldo story are not closely connected.

In the experiment, both the tight and the loose stories were presented in either normal or randomized order. After reading, the subjects wrote abstracts of the stories. The experimenter could not tell whether the abstracts of tight stories had been derived from the normal or randomized order. This means that people were able to organize the ideas of tight stories regardless of whether they were normal or random. The readers' story schemata must have contributed to their analyses. In contrast, abstracts of loose stories in normal order could be distinguished from those in random order. Because the loose stories did not conform well with the story schema, people could not organize the story ideas presented in a random order.

Hierarchical Effects.   The hierarchical organization that story grammars impose on story ideas (see Fig. 8.1) suggests that high level story ideas will be remembered better than low level ideas. Such an observation would parallel the microstructure levels effects described in chapter 2 (e.g., Kintsch et al., 1975). Consistent with this proposal, story recall reveals a distinct levels effect (Thorndyke, 1977, Fig. 4; see also Graesser et al., 1981; Graesser, Robertson, et al., 1980).

The story levels effect could be an encoding or a retrieval phenomenon. During story comprehension, high level story ideas might be encoded more effectively than low level ideas. During retrieval, on the other hand, the understander might proceed from the top of the hierarchy, and occasionally fail to retrieve ideas low in the hierarchy.

The encoding and retrieval explanations of the story levels effect can be distinguished by substituting recognition for recall. If low level ideas are weakly encoded, then a levels effect should appear in a recognition test. If low level ideas are encoded but not effectively retrieved, then a recognition test ought to eradicate the levels effect. Consistent with the retrieval alternative, story recognition tests reveal no levels effect (Kintsch & Young, 1984; Yekovich & Thorndyke, 1981). This finding is consistent with the observation that the microstructure levels effect is likewise a retrieval phenomenon (Alba et al., 1981; Anderson & Pichert, 1978; Britton et al., 1980).

Story Category Effects.   The status of story grammar categories, such as theme and goal, differ on dimensions other than hierarchical level. For example, settings, attempts, and outcomes are recalled better than mental states and internal reactions (Glenn, 1978; Mandler & Johnson, 1977). This is in spite of the fact that some of the better and worse recalled categories occupy the same level of the story hierarchy. For example, attempts and states are both introduced at Level 3, by Rule 5 (Table 8.2). Similarly, people are more sensitive to story grammar violations that result from the deletion of actions than the deletion of states (Kemper, 1982; see also Graesser et al., 1981).

To illustrate, consider statements 3–6 of "The King and his Daughters": (3) **One day the three daughters went walking in the woods** (4) **They were enjoying themselves so much** (5) **that they forgot the time** (6) **and stayed too long.** It would not seem surprising if **They were enjoying themselves so much**, which conveys the mental state of the daughters, were omitted from one's recall of this sequence. This deletion does not significantly change the meaning of the story.

It is important to ask whether effects of story category are independent of hierarchical level. That is, it can be seen in Fig. 8.1 that memorable categories, such as attempts, generally appear at higher hierarchical levels than less memorable ones, such as states. At the end of the following section, a comparison is made among the factors influencing story comprehension.

Conclusion.   There is considerable evidence that the story schema, which represents people's knowledge about the usual form of a story, guides story comprehension. The story grammar is a formal technique for describing the contents of the story schema. However, it has been proposed that the story schema cannot completely account for the phenomenon of story understanding. The next section examines other factors that contribute to story comprehension. Then, the following section proposes that much of the content of stories is understood with reference to schemata of cause, plans, and goals.

Other Factors Influencing Story Representation

There are several features of story representation and retrieval that are not captured by the story grammar analysis. Two of these, connectivity and causal-chain membership, were shown to play a central role in the definition of discourse theme (chapter 6). In addition, the content of story ideas has a qualitative impact on story representation.

Connectivity.   In story grammar analysis, story ideas are primarily connected by links between the different hierarchical levels (see Fig. 8.1). Furthermore, ideas within levels are sometimes connected by temporal and causal links (Mandler & Johnson, 1977; Thorndyke, 1977). A different approach to story analysis places a greater emphasis on the causal links among story ideas (Graesser et al., 1981; Trabasso et al., 1984; Trabasso & Sperry, 1985). This analysis generates story representations that take the form of networks rather than strict hierarchies. The representations include all of the causal relations among ideas that are explicitly stated in a story. Furthermore, story comprehenders may infer additional causal relations. One example, the causal analysis of the "Ant" fragment, was shown in Fig. 6.1.

The connectivity of a story idea is an index of the number of links that connect it to other ideas. Story ideas with high connectivity are recalled more frequently (e.g., Graesser, Robertson, et al., 1980; Graesser et al., 1981; Omanson, 1982). One explanation of this effect is that ideas with numerous connections are likely to receive activation from other ideas during recall (e.g., Graesser, Robertson, et al., 1980). Ideas with high connectivity are also judged to be more important than those with low connectivity (Omanson, 1982; Trabasso & Sperry, 1985).

Causal Chain Membership.   The causal analysis of stories permits a distinction between ideas that appear on the main causal chain of events, as compared to dead-ends (Glowalla & Colonius, 1982; Graesser et al., 1981; Omanson, 1982; Trabasso et al., 1984; Trabasso & Sperry, 1985). Setting information, such as **In a kingdom far away . . .** , and descriptive ideas, such as **The dragon was crimson** may appear off the main causal chain. Likewise, failed attempts, such as **The heroes played their flutes to lure the dragon from its lair but the dragon paid no attention**, are typically dead-ends.

Causal chain membership has been shown to influence story representation and memory. Children recall a much higher proportion of causal chain ideas than dead-end statements (Trabasso et al., 1984). Likewise, Fig. 8.2 illustrates that the proportion of ideas in a story that fall on the main causal chain is an excellent predictor of children's

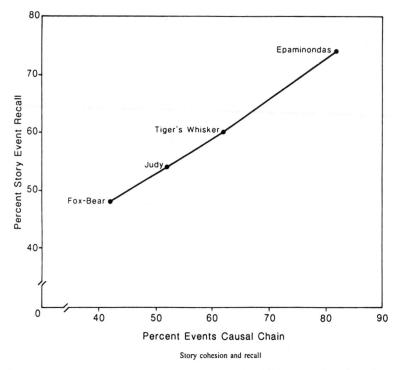

FIG. 8.2.   Percent of story events recalled by children as a function of the percent of the events that appeared on the main causal chain of four stories. *Source:* Trabasso, Secco, & van den Broek, 1984, Figure 3.9, p. 99. Reprinted by permission.

recall of story events (Trabasso et al., 1984). Finally, adult judges have been shown to rate causal chain propositions as more important that dead-end statements (Trabasso & Sperry, 1985).

Story Content.   There are indications that story understanding and memory are influenced by story content. For example, one feature of story content that might affect comprehension is interestingness (Kintsch, 1980; Schank, 1979; Waters, 1983). Interestingness refers to the emotional impact, unexpectedness, personal relevance, and familiarity of an idea (see chapter 7). For example, in "The King and his Daughters," the statement, **A dragon came and kidnapped the three daughters**, is unexpected, and it has the emotional impact of relating to danger.

One problem with the proposal that content influences story representation is that content varies systematically across story grammar categories, such as Setting, Theme, Plot, and Resolution. Therefore, it

is difficult to determine whether observed story comprehension effects
are due to differences among the categories, or their content. To address
this issue, researchers have controlled story content across categories
(Nezworski et al., 1982; Omanson, 1982; Thorndyke, 1977). Consider a
story called "The Tiger's Whisker." In one version of the story, the
sequence, **One day her husband became very sick and a doctor told
her to make medicine with a tiger's whisker for him,** functioned as
an initiating event (Nezworski et al., 1982). In another version, the
comparable sequence, **She knew that her husband was very sick and
that he needed a medicine made with a tiger's whisker** appeared as an
internal reaction of the woman. School children heard the stories and
then recalled them. For those ideas whose story category was varied
across versions, there were no differences in recall as a function of story
category. This indicates that it was the content that determined the
probability of recall. For other ideas, whose category was not controlled,
the familiar category effect was detected: Namely, settings and outcomes
were recalled better than internal reactions and states.

This result might suggest that effects of story category are due solely
to systematic differences in their content. However, Nezworski et al.
(1982) also observed that people who retell stories frequently transform
ideas they encounter in one story category, such as the internal reaction,
into another category, such as the initiating event. This indicates that
people associate certain types of content with particular story categories. It was concluded that, although content exerts a measurable impact
on story representation, the story schema likewise affects the interpretation of story ideas, causing them to conform with the typical form of a
story (see also Mandler, 1987).

Comparing the Factors of Story Representation.   The story representen-
tation factors that influence comprehension and retrieval are not independent of one another. As was just mentioned, story content varies
with story category. Likewise, content is correlated with causal chain
membership: For example, descriptions, and time and location information, tend to appear in dead-ends rather than on the causal chain (Trabasso & Sperry, 1985). Dead-end ideas generally have lower connectivity
than causal chain ideas (Trabasso et al., 1984). Finally, story categories
also systematically vary in connectivity: For example, initiating events
are likely to be more richly connected than internal reactions.

In view of these interrelations, it is necessary to determine whether
these factors exert independent effects. Trabasso and van den Broek
(1985) used regression analysis (see chapter 5) to address this issue (see
also Black & Bower, 1980; Omanson, 1982; Trabasso et al., 1984). The
analysis assessed the impact of causal chain membership, story cate-

gory, and connectivity on the measures of immediate and delayed story recall, importance rating, and summarization (Omanson, 1982; Stein & Glenn, 1979). First, it was found that causal chain membership, story category, and connectivity make independent contributions to most of the measures of retrieval and comprehension. Second, the relative contributions of the three factors to each measure are quite consistent: Causal chain membership typically makes the largest contribution, story category is next, and connectivity is last. On the basis of these findings, Trabasso and van den Broek (1985) presented a model of story representation that accommodates the contributions of all three factors.

SCHEMATA OF CAUSE, PLANS, AND GOALS

To overcome a goal or obstacle, the main character of many stories must formulate a plan, and carry out the actions specified by the plan. The resulting actions are causally interrelated in complex ways.

Previous chapters have addressed the central role of causal relations in discourse meaning. It has been proposed that plans and goals likewise have a privileged status in the representation of stories and other messages (Schank & Abelson, 1977). According to this position, a plan explains the causal interrelations between events and goals.

These observations raised the possibility that many story comprehension effects arise from the organizational impact of schemata for causes, plans, and goals, rather than the story schema (e.g., Brewer & Lichtenstein, 1981). To evaluate this hypothesis, it is useful to consider evidence concerning the existence of schemata for causes, plans, and goals.

People's sensitivity to *causal relationships* was addressed in chapter 7. During reading, comprehension time varies with the difficulty of causal bridging inferences needed to link text ideas (Keenen et al., 1984). This indicates that readers strive to establish the causal links among ideas. During retrieval, causally related ideas mutually prompt the recall of one another more effectively than do temporally related ideas (Black & Bern, 1981). People can distinguish legitimate causal sequences from flawed ones. These findings suggest the existence of a schema of causal interrelations.

The psychological validity of the *plan schema* was examined by Brewer & Dupree (1983; see also Lichtenstein & Brewer, 1980). They proposed that a plan schema imposes organization on a character's goal-oriented actions, with special reference to a relationship called *in-order-to*. In terms of "The King and his Daughters" story, the heroes fight the dragon in-order-to kill the dragon, and, in turn, kill the dragon in-order-to rescue the daughters. In contrast, had the heroes tied their horses to a tree, this action would not have been organized by the plan schema, because it does not bear the in-order-to relation to rescuing the daughters.

Brewer and Dupree (1983) used an elegant design to test these hypotheses. They constructed episodes consisting of a subordinate action and a goal action. Each subordinate action bore the in-order-to relation to the goal. For example, one episode involved a woman plugging two electric cords together in-order-to achieve the goal of sharpening a pencil with an electric pencil sharpener. Videotapes were made of the episodes, but the main goals of half of the episodes were edited out. Accordingly, some experimental participants saw an actress plug the two cords together and then sit down at a desk. Of course, plugging two electric cords together does not bear the in-order-to relation to sitting at a desk.

It was predicted that subordinate actions would be remembered better if they constituted part of a plan: That is, if they led to a goal action. Recall data bore this out. Recall was 70% for subordinate actions embedded in a plan and 30% for nonplan subordinates. Furthermore, nonplan subordinates were recalled 58% of the time when subjects inferred their own plan, compared with 21% when no plan was inferred.

It is interesting that recognition performance (Brewer & Dupree, 1983, Experiment 1), in contrast to recall, was equivalent for plan and nonplan subordinate actions. This indicates that the failure to recall nonplan subordinate actions is a retrieval rather than an encoding phenomenon. This is consistent with findings for other schematic effects, such as the story levels effect.

Additional though less direct support for the plan schema is provided by research concerning the psychological validity of the *episode*. The episode is a story grammar category (Mandler & Johnson, 1977; Thorndyke, 1977) that consists of a plan plus the actions used to execute the plan (Glenn, 1978). Children's recall performance reveals that they are very sensitive to the episode structure of stories (Glenn, 1978): In particular, children's episode recall does not vary either with story length or as a function of whether episodes are separate or intertwined. Also supporting the psychological validity of the episode is the observation that adults spend more time reading story statements at the beginning and ends of episodes than those in the middle (Haberlandt et al., 1980).

There are different ways to think of *schemata for goals*. On one hand, goals appear as a component of the plan schema: For example, according to Brewer and Dupree (1983), a plan consists of a subordinate action executed to accomplish a goal. Second, theorists have proposed the existence of schemata that represent a rank order of the goals that guide behavior (Rule & Bisanz, 1987; Schank & Abelson, 1977).

Does the psychological validity of schemata of cause, plans, and goals indicate that story comprehension effects are not due to the role of the story schema? There is evidence that discourages this conclusion. In particular, investigators have shown that, even when one takes into account the effect of content (Nezworski et al., 1982), centrality (Omanson, 1982), and causal chain membership and connectivity (Trabasso & van den Broek, 1985), story schema categories still exert a measurable impact. Furthermore, even those researchers who have presented evidence for autonomous cause and plan schemata assert that knowledge about narrative structure is likely to exert independent effects. If this analysis is accurate, then it is necessary to ask how the roles of different types of schemata are coordinated. This problem is taken up toward the end of this chapter.

NONNARRATIVE DISCOURSE

Schemata of Expository Texts and Newspaper Articles

In the examination of schemata for familiar texts, it has been convenient for researchers to focus on stories because of their relatively consistent structure. However, people understand many types of discourse, including expositions, newspaper articles, descriptions, recipes, conversations, and lists. Therefore, it is useful to extend schema analyses to these discourse types.

Expository text appears in many contexts, including text books, technical manuals, and scientific essays. It is designed literally to "expose" a topic. Theorists have expressed agreement that there is no general, well-defined schema that captures the form of expository prose (Kinstch & Young, 1984; Miller, 1985; Thorndyke, 1977). For example, in an analysis of one expository passage, Miller (1985) identified numerous components, in the following order: the statement of a problem, a description, a further specification of the problem, a result of the problem, two examples, another result, and a cause of the problem. Miller proposed that if an exposition schema exists, then, at the very least, it must be very flexible in nature.

Newspaper and magazine articles appear intermediate to stories and expositions in their structural consistency. Many articles begin with the most important and interesting information, and progress to less important details (Thorndyke, 1977). However, this structure destroys the temporal and causal arrangement of the presented facts (Thorndyke, 1979). As a result, the organization of newspaper articles is less predictable than that of stories.

Certain other texts, however, may be argued to have a well-defined schema. For example, recipes consist of an ingredient list and a set of instructions. In baking recipes, the ingredient list is further divided into sets of "wet" and "dry" ingredients. Scientific reports likewise have a definite structure. For example, the major constituents of psychology research reports are the introduction, method, results, and discussion (see Kintsch & van Dijk, 1978).

Understanding Nonnarrative Discourse

One hypothesis derived from the schematic analysis of nonnarrative discourse is that the superior organization of the story schema ought to be reflected by a recall advantage for narratives. To test this proposal, Thorndyke compared the recall of stories with that for expository text (Thorndyke, 1977) and for news articles (Thorndyke, 1979). In both studies, superior recall was detected for the stories, even though content was held constant across text types.

This analysis was extended by Kintsch and Young (1984). They constructed narrative passages and two types of expository passages, using the same content. Embedded in the passages were *target sentences* that concerned the financial well-being of a seafood restaurant. In the narrative passage, the main characters were described as having a meal at the restaurant, and the target sentences were, accordingly, unimportant to the main thrust of the story. The expository passages concerned either the finances of the restaurant in particular, or the stock market in general. As a result, the target sentences were relevant in the expository passages.

It was predicted that overall recall would be better for the narrative passage, in view of the well-formed story schema. This is because the story schema ought to select some story ideas for the text macrostructure. However, the readers were expected to recall the target sentences better in the expository than in the narrative condition. The reasoning was that the target sentences were irrelevant to the story schema but relevant to the content of the expository passages. The data supported both of these predictions.

If comprehension and retrieval are affected by the degree of organization of a discourse schema, then nonnarrative discourses with well-formed schemata should exhibit the same behavior as stories. One feature of the data of Kintsch and van Dijk (1978) bears on this prediction. They measured psychology students' recall of a psychology research report, which has a well-defined schema. The recall data revealed a distinct levels effect: That is, ideas pertinent to high level schema categories were recalled better than low ones. This outcome parallels the story levels effect discussed earlier (Graesser, Robertson, et al., 1980; Graesser et al., 1981; Thorndyke, 1977).

Finally, because the main role of the discourse schema is to guide macroprocessing, schema organization should not influence the construction of the microstructure. Support for this hypothesis was derived from the comparison of narrative history texts and expository science texts (Kintsch et al., 1975). First, there was a distinct microstructure levels effect for both text types. Second, people recalled a smaller percentage of propositions when both types of passage included many rather than few different arguments. Third, for both text types, reading time per proposition was faster in the few- than in the many-arguments condition (see chapter 2).

Conclusion

Both theoretical analysis and experimental evidence indicate that there is less schematic support for the comprehension of nonnarrative than narrative texts. This raises the issue of how nonnarrative texts are understood. One possibility is that, to understand such texts, people rely more heavily on schemata for causes, goals, and plans, which apply across many contexts (Miller, 1985). Second, understanding expository and other nonnarrative texts particularly requires the application of the content-specific knowledge of the understander. As a result, a reasonably well-informed reader might be able to assimilate useful information from such texts, whereas novices might find them almost incomprehensible.

UNDERSTANDING SCRIPT-BASED STORIES

Scripts are schemata that represent people's knowledge of familiar, stereotypical situations. Many stories are set in familiar contexts of this sort. In this event, the relevant script contributes to story comprehension. In chapter 4, it was proposed that, during encoding, scripts serve to integrate the ideas of a message. This section examines specific hypotheses of how this occurs during story comprehension. First, we must consider the organization of scripts. Then, a model of understanding script-based stories is described and evaluated with reference to existing evidence.

The Organization of Scripts

Scripts consist of a title, a list of props, roles, entry conditions, results, and a sequential chain of the events that make up the script activity (Schank & Abelson, 1977; see also Table 1.2). The sequential chain is the crucial feature of the script. A person who performs the sequence of actions engages in the activity in question. That is, by virtue of sorting the clothes, loading the washer, washing and then drying the clothes, and finally folding them and putting them away, one has DONE THE LAUNDRY.

There is evidence that scripts possess hierarchical as well as sequential organization (Abbott et al., 1985; Barsalou & Sewell, 1985; Galambos & Rips, 1982). Abbott et al. (1985) presented a model that captures both the sequential and hierarchical features of scripts. Consider the restaurant script. At the top of the hierarchy is the script title, EATING AT A RESTAURANT. At the next level are essential components called *scene headers*. For the restaurant script, these include ENTERING, ORDERING, EATING, and EXITING (Bower et al., 1979; Schank & Abelson, 1977). Each scene header is further analyzed to sets of *scene actions*, which form the lower levels of the hierarchy.

In this model, the sequential properties of the script are captured by temporal links that appear only *within* the hierarchical levels. The result is a modified hierarchy, illustrated in Fig. 8.3 (Abbott et al., 1985). The present subsection examines evidence about script organization that bears on this model.

Sequential Organization of Scripts. The sequential structure of scripts is supported by measures of recall, production of script actions, and judgments about script actions. Consider first the *recall* evidence. Many scripts seem to be associated with a specific sequence of actions,

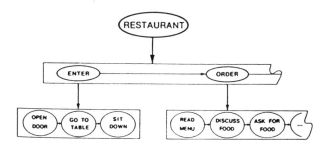

FIG. 8.3. Modified-hierarchical organization of the Restaurant script. *Source:* Abbott, Black, & Smith, 1985, Figure 1, p. 183. Reprinted by permission.

but some, such as grocery shopping, are not (Anderson et al., 1978; Bower et al., 1979). To examine the representation of sequential information in scripts, Bower et al. (1979, Experiment 5) measured people's ability to recall script actions in their exact position of occurrence in a story. In unordered-script stories (e.g., grocery shopping, house cleaning), people scored 30% on this measure. Stories based on ordered scripts (e.g., eating at a restaurant, going to a movie) yielded different results. Actions that appeared in their typical positions in the stories were recalled in the correct position 50% of the time. However, ordered-script actions that occurred out of sequence in the story were recalled in the correct position only 18% of the time. These results indicate that ordered scripts influence people to recall story actions in their typical positions. This results in very high accuracy for actions that appear in their typical position in ordered-script stories, and very low accuracy for misplaced actions.

Barsalou and Sewell (1985) used a *production* technique to examine script organization. People were asked to list the actions associated with different scripts. They were instructed to use one of four production strategies: namely, to generate the actions (a) in the order they came to mind, the unconstrained strategy; (b) from most to least central, the centrality strategy; (c) from first to last, the forward strategy; or (d) from last to first, the backward strategy. It was reasoned that, using the unconstrained strategy, people should be guided by the predominant type of script organization. Furthermore, the forward strategy is congruent with the sequential organization of scripts, whereas the centrality strategy is congruent with the hierarchical organization of scripts. Therefore, if sequential information predominates, more actions should be produced in the unconstrained and forward conditions than in the centrality and backward strategies. On the other hand, if script actions are organized primarily with respect to centrality, then it is the unconstrained and centrality strategies that should yield the most actions.

To examine these alternatives, Barsalou and Sewell (1985) measured the number of script actions that people could list in a 20-second period. The results indicated that sequential organization predominates in scripts: An average of 7.9 actions was produced in the unconstrained and forward conditions, as compared with only 6.3 in the centrality and backward conditions.

If scripts represent a sequence of actions, then it should be easier to make *judgments* about script-action sequences in their forward than in their backward order. To test this hypothesis, Haberlandt and Bingham (1984) asked people to judge whether two simple sentences were related or not. The related pairs were drawn from the same scripts, such as the CAMPFIRE script. The sentence pairs were presented either in the forward order, such as, **He got some logs. He lit the wood,** or the backward order, such as **He blew on the flame. He lit the wood.**

The crucial measure was the time needed to read and to judge the relatedness of the second sentence of each pair. Across two experiments, people needed 1691 msec for the forward pairs, and 1888 msec for the backward pairs, a substantial difference of about ²⁄₁₀ of a second. This indicates that sequential information represented in scripts affects people's access to script actions and their judgments about them.

Hierarchical Organization of Scripts.   The actions of scripts vary in their status. When instructed to rate script actions, people agree on their centrality (Bower et al., 1979; Galambos & Rips, 1982), typicality (Barsalou & Sewell, 1985; Graesser et al., 1979), and necessity (Galambos & Rips, 1982; Graesser et al., 1979). These status differences suggest that script actions may be hierarchically organized.

What is meant by the centrality of script actions? Galambos and Rips (1982) identified two underlying components of centrality, namely *necessity* and *distinctiveness* (see also Graesser et al., 1979). For example, EATING FOOD is a necessary action in the restaurant script. In contrast, READING THE MENU is not, because a customer may decide beforehand what she wants. Distinctiveness refers to the extent to which an action is associated with one particular script. READING THE MENU is very distinctive of the restaurant script. In contrast, EATING FOOD is not distinctive of the restaurant script, because it can occur in virtually any setting.

To assess the contributions of necessity and distinctiveness to script-action centrality, Galambos and Rips (1982) asked different people to rate script actions on the dimensions of centrality, necessity, and distinctiveness. This revealed that necessity ratings are correlated with centrality ratings, but distinctiveness ratings are not. Therefore, necessity is the more important determinant of script-action centrality.

Differences in script-action centrality that emerge from rating studies are corroborated by judgment-time measures. For example, in one experiment (Galambos & Rips, 1982, Experiment 2), people judged whether actions belonged to particular scripts. On each trial, a script title, such as SHOPPING FOR GROCERIES, was displayed above an action, such as UNLOAD THE CART. Correct judgment time was faster for actions with high than with low centrality ratings. In a second experiment, people judged whether or not pairs of actions were related to the same script. This took less time for central pairs than for peripheral pairs. It was concluded from the latter result that script titles activate central actions more than peripheral ones (Galambos & Rips, 1982).

Scripts as Modified Hierarchies.   Evidence to evaluate the hierarchical and sequential features of the model of Fig. 8.3 was presented by Abbott et al. (1985). In one experiment, people read script-based stories. In different versions of each story, the presence and absence of a scene header and one of its scene actions were varied. For example, the restaurant-meal story included either scene action (1a), scene header (1b), both, or neither.

(1)   a.   They discussed what they wanted to eat. (scene action)
      b.   They ordered their meal. (scene header)

It was reasoned that if scripts have a hierarchical structure, then the mention of a scene action should activate its scene header. After all, it would be unusual for people in a restaurant to discuss what they want to eat and not subsequently order. However, the opposite is not true: Ordering the meal does not require prior discussion. Thus, according to the modified-hierarchy model, mentioning a scene header should not activate its subordinate scene actions. According to an alternate model that states that scripts include sequential but not hierarchical information, there would be only one path through the script. Then, scene headers and scene actions would mutually activate one another.

In a test of these hypotheses, an unexpected rated-recognition test followed the reading of the stories. Of greatest interest is the recognition of (1a) and (1b) in two conditions: when *Neither* (1a) nor (1b) has appeared in the story, and when only the *Other* of the two had appeared. Scene headers received higher recognition ratings when the Other (its scene action) had appeared in the story than when Neither had occurred. This suggests that the scene action activated its header. In contrast, the recognition of scene actions was about equal when its scene header had appeared (Other) and when Neither had occurred. These results supported the prediction derived from the modified-hierarchy model, and are consistent with the proposal that scripts represent both sequential and hierarchical information.

The reading time data of Smith (1981) are also relevant to the evaluation of the modified-hierarchy model. Smith (1981) proposed that, if scripts represent sequential information, then comprehension time of a target sentence should vary with its sequential distance from its antecedent in the story. According to this view, it should take longer to comprehend **The customer ate the meal** in sequence (2a)–(2b) than in (3a)–(3b). Such an outcome is called the *gap-size* effect.

(2)   a.   The customer entered the restaurant.
      b.   The customer ate the meal.

(3) a. The customer placed his order.
     b. The customer ate the meal.

All of Smith's (1981) sentence sequences were derived from a single hierarchical level: either the level of scene headers or scene actions. The reading time of target sentences revealed a distinct gap-size effect for scene headers. For scene actions, comprehension time initially increased with gap size but then leveled off. The difference between these patterns supports the distinction between scene headers and scene actions. When sentence pairs are formed *between* hierarchical levels, in contrast, no gap-size effect is detected (Bower et al., 1979, Experiment 6).

A Text Base Plus Script Model of Script-Based Stories

Evidence that script knowledge influences language comprehension and that scripts take the form of modified hierarchies permits the formulation of models of the representation of script-based stories. Bower et al. (1979) proposed that the representation of script-based stories consists of a two-part memory trace. The first part includes the specific propositions of the story: This is the text base microstructure. The second part is a distinct pattern of activation that the story sets up in the relevant script. The present subsection describes a model, called the *text base plus script* model (TBS), which combines features of the analyses of Abbott et al. (1985), Bower et al. (1979), and Walker and Yekovich (1984). In the following subsection, the TBS model is evaluated, and compared with some alternative models.
    Consider the following episode:

> Don decided to have lunch at a restaurant. He took his seat, and ordered his favorite, the tuna sandwich. He straightened his collar while he waited. When the food arrived, Don ate hungrily. When the waiter brought the cheque, he accidentally spilled coffee on Don. Don was very upset and left without paying.

This passage obviously invokes the restaurant script. Equally obviously, it describes events that do not typically occur when one eats in a restaurant. The representation of the passage is shown in Fig. 8.4. Figure 8.4a shows the text base microstructure of the passage. Figure 8.4b outlines the restaurant script. Understanding the "coffee spill" passage creates a pattern of activation among the statements of the script. (The term *script statement* will be used to refer to script information at

(A)

```
P1     (HAVE, DON, LUNCH)
P2     (DECIDE, DON, P1)
P3     (LOCATION:AT, P1, RESTAURANT)
P4     (TAKE, DON, SEAT)
P5       (AND, P4, P6)
P6     (ORDER, DON, TUNA-SANDWICH)
P7       (FAVORITE, TUNA-SANDWICH)
P8     (STRAIGHTEN, DON, COLLAR)
P9       (TIME:WHILE, P8, P10)
P10    (WAIT, DON)
P11      (ARRIVE, TUNA-SANDWICH)
P12        (TIME:WHEN, P11, P13)
P13    (EAT, DON)
P14      (HUNGRILY, P13)
P15    (LOCATION:ON, P16, DON)
P16      (SPILL, WAITER, COFFEE)
P17        (TIME:WHEN, P16, P18)
P18      (BRING, WAITER, COFFEE)
P19    (UPSET, DON)
P20      (VERY, P19)
P21        (AND, P19, P22)
P22    (LEAVE, DON)
P23      (MANNER, P22, P24)
P24    (PAY, DON)
P25      (NOT, P24)
```

(B)

Restaurant Script

Title	Scene Headers	Scene Actions
9* Restaurant meal	7* Entering	7* Enter restaurant
		1* Look for table
		1* Decide where to sit
		1* Go to table
		9* Sit down
	9* Ordering	1* Read menu
		1* Make selection
		9* Order food
		9* Wait for food
		1* Cook prepares food
	9* Eating	3* Waiter brings food
		9* Eat food
	9* Exiting	9* Waiter brings bill
		1* Customer leaves tip
		1* Go to cashier
		9* Pay cashier
		9* Exit restaurant

FIG. 8.4.   Text base plus script representation of the "coffee spill" passage. Part (A) shows that the propositional network (text base) includes four hierarchical levels. Part (B) shows that statements in the related script are activated from 1* (unmentioned scene actions) to 9* (mentioned scene headers and scene actions).

any hierarchical level.) The pattern of activation is determined by the following principles:

Principle 1. The activation of script statements ranges from a low of 0* to a high of 9*. The number of levels of activation is somewhat arbitrary, but 10 levels is a convenient choice.

Principle 2. When a script is invoked, the script title is fully activated to 9*. Scene headers receive almost full activation, namely 7*. All other script statements are slightly activated, to 1* (Abbott et al., 1985; Sharkey & Mitchell, 1985; Walker & Yekovich, 1984).

Principle 3. When a story statement corresponds to a script statement at any script level, that script statement is fully activated to 9*.

Principle 4. Each time a script action is implied but not explicitly stated, its activation is raised by one unit, up to a limit of 6* (Walker & Yekovich, 1984).

Following these principles, understanding the "coffee spill" episode creates the pattern of script activation that is shown in Fig. 8.4b: The script title is activated to 9*. The scene header, Entering, is activated by 7*, as specified by Principle 2. The remaining scene headers, Ordering, Eating, and Exiting, are activated to 9*, by virtue of being directly mentioned in the story. For example, the clause, **He ordered his favorite**, mentions the Ordering scene header. Likewise, the scene actions Sit Down, Order Food, Wait for Food, Eat Food, Pay Cashier, and Leave Restaurant are activated to 9* because they are directly expressed in the story.

All of the remaining script actions are activated to 1* when the script is activated. However, following Principle 4, WAITER BRINGS FOOD has an activation level of 3*. It is activated two units above 1* because two statements, **while he waited** (for the waiter to bring the food) and **when the food arrived**, imply the idea of the waiter bringing the food.

One might argue that the PAY CASHIER scene action should not be activated to 9*, because Don did not pay. However, according to Principle 3, the direct mention of a script statement fully activates it. Therefore, the phrase, *without paying*, activates PAY CASHIER. The fact that Don did not pay is recorded only in the text base.

In what follows, evidence bearing on the TBS model is examined. Then, two models that compete with the TBS model are considered.

Evaluation of the Text Base Plus Script Model

Numerous studies of the retrieval of script-based stories bear on the TBS model. To show how the TBS model accounts for phenomena of story memory, it is necessary to consider the roles of *forgetting* and of the *strategies of retrieving* story information. Bower et al. (1979) described the processes of forgetting in a two-trace (e.g., text base plus script) story representation. First, propositions in the microstructure decay over time, with high level propositions being more resistant to decay. Second, script statements lose their activation as time elapses. Therefore, story memory is eventually based only on an impoverished text base and a relatively unactivated script.

To retrieve story information, people can use either the strategy of *directly retrieving* a fact from the text base, or of *judging the plausibility* of a fact on the basis of the relevant script (Reder, 1982, 1987; Reder & Ross, 1983; Reder & Wible, 1984). The strategies can be combined: For example, after failing to retrieve a fact from the text base, one may proceed next to examine the relevant script (e.g., Lehnert, 1977).

One variable that influences the choice between these retrieval strategies is test delay (Reder, 1982, 1987). At short delays of 1 hour or less, people attempt direct retrieval from the message text base. According to the TBS model, this ought to reveal a relatively detailed microstructure. If retrieval fails, the inspection of the activated script might follow. At long intervals of a day or more, the plausibility strategy is preferred. In this event, retrieval is based on a script in which activation has diminished.

Memory for Script-Based Stories: Short Test Intervals. In the study of memory for script-based stories, researchers have frequently distinguished between story ideas that are central and peripheral (also called *typical* and *atypical*) in the pertinent script. For example, sentence (4) is central with regard to the restaurant script whereas sentence (5) is peripheral.

(4)   Don entered the restaurant.
(5)   He straightened his collar.

Graesser et al. (1979) examined the representation of script-based story statements. People read script-based stories and performed a recognition test 1 hour later. The test sentences were either central, such as (4), or peripheral, such (5). Furthermore, the test sentences either had or had not been presented in the story.

According to the TBS model, central and peripheral ideas that are Presented in the story are both represented in the text base. However, only central ideas activate a script statement: That is, there is no script statement for **He straightened his collar** to activate. Furthermore, because of the short testing delay, people should consult the text base before the script.

In the Presented condition, central and peripheral test sentences should be recognized equally, because both are represented in the text base. In the Unpresented condition, in contrast, neither central nor peripheral ideas appear in the text base, and any attempt to retrieve them fails. After this failure, the pertinent script may be examined. Unpresented peripheral sentences are readily rejected, because they do not appear in the script. For Unpresented central sentences, however, there are corresponding statements in the script. For example, when the test sentence, **Don entered the restaurant,** is encountered as a test sentence in the Unpresented condition, a search of the script reveals the scene header, Entering, activated to 7*. As a result, Unpresented central statements are predicted to sometimes be incorrectly recognized.

The combined recognition data of two experiments (Graesser et al., 1979), shown in Table 8.3, support this analysis. As predicted, the recognition ratings of Presented central and Presented peripheral sentences were similar, but Unpresented central sentences had higher recognition ratings than Unpresented peripheral ones. It is also important that Presented central sentences had higher ratings than Unpresented central ones. This indicates that, at short test intervals, the text base of a story is a more reliable source of information about which ideas appeared in the story (see also Bower et al., 1979, Experiment 4; Light & Anderson, 1983; Nakamura, Graesser, Zimmerman, & Rhia, 1985).

The free recall of script-based stories yields parallel findings. In one study, people read a lengthy multi-script story and performed a free recall task 30 minutes later (Smith & Graesser, 1981). The data are shown in the *Short Interval* columns of Table 8.4. As predicted, the central and peripheral Presented statements were reproduced about equally often, 29% each. In contrast, Unpresented central statements were reconstructed more often than Unpresented peripheral ones. Furthermore, the subjects produced many more Presented central statements than Unpresented ones. Likewise, in a study that examined only central

TABLE 8.3
Recognition of Central and Peripheral Story Statements
On a 6-Point Scale

	Central	*Peripheral*
Presented	4.97	4.76
Unpresented	3.83	2.11

Source: Based on data of Graesser, Gordon, & Sawyer, 1979. Reprinted by permission.

TABLE 8.4
Percent of Central and Peripheral Story Statements Recalled
as a Function of Test Interval

	Interval			
Sentence	Short		Long	
Presentation	Central	Peripheral	Central	Peripheral
Presented	29	29	22	5
Unpresented	12	0	16	0

Source: Adapted from Smith & Graesser, 1981, Table 1, p. 553. Adapted by permission.

script statements, Bower et al. (1979, Experiment 3) found that people recalled an average of 3.0 Presented statements as compared with only .8 Unpresented statements.

Peripheral story statements may be either relevant or irrelevant to the main point of the story (Bower et al., 1979). In this regard, **He accidently spilled coffee on Don** is very relevant in the "coffee spill" story, whereas **He straightened his collar** is irrelevant. Bower et al. (1979, Experiment 7) predicted a high recall rate for relevant but peripheral story ideas. Consistent with this prediction, people recalled 53% of relevant peripheral statements in a short-delay test. In contrast, only 38% of central statements and 32% of irrelevant peripheral statements were recalled. The similar recall of central statements and irrelevant peripheral statements parallels Smith and Graesser's (1981) finding of 29% recall for both central Presented and peripheral Presented statements (Table 8.4), because Smith and Graesser's peripheral statements were irrelevant to the main point of the story.

The recall advantage of relevant peripheral statements (Bower et al., 1979) is probably due to the fact that these statements are selected into the story macrostructure by story categories. For example, **He accidently spilled coffee on Don** might be identified with a story schema category called "Cause" (Mandler & Johnson, 1977).

Memory for Script-Based Stories: Long Test Intervals. At lengthy test delays, the representation of a script-based story consists of a text base in which some propositions have decayed, and a script in which activation has diminished. Suppose that, after some interval, the activation level of the script statements were reduced by about half, with a minimum activation reduction of 1*. The script activation pattern for the "coffee spill" passage might be portrayed by Fig. 8.5.

As discussed earlier, with the passage of time, people increasingly

Restaurant Script

Title	Scene Headers	Scene Actions
4* Restaurant meal	3* Entering	3* Enter restaurant
		1* Look for table
		1* Decide where to sit
		1* Go to table
		4* Sit down
	4* Ordering	1* Read menu
		1* Make selection
		4* Order food
		4* Wait for food
		1* Cook prepares food
	4* Eating	1* Waiter brings food
		4* Eat food
	4* Exiting	4* Waiter brings bill
		1* Customer leaves tip
		1* Go to cashier
		4* Pay cashier
		4* Exit restaurant

FIG. 8.5. Script representation of the "coffee spill" passage at a long retention interval.

favor the strategy of consulting the relevant script rather than the text base. Suppose one examined the restaurant script of Fig. 8.5 in an attempt to recall the "coffee spill" episode. In this script, it is difficult to discriminate Presented and Unpresented statements from the story because of their similar levels of activation. Therefore, the TBS model predicts that Presented and Unpresented central statements will be recalled about equally often. Consistent with this analysis, at long intervals (2 days to 3 weeks), central Presented statements were recalled 22% of the time and central Unpresented statements were recalled 16% of the time (Smith & Graesser, 1981; see Table 8.4, long-interval columns). This outcome represents a convergence from the short interval scores of 29% for central Presented versus 12% for central Unpresented.

This analysis also predicts that peripheral Presented statements will seldom be recalled, because they do not appear in the script. Table 8.4 confirms that, at long intervals, Peripheral presented statements were recalled only 5% of the time.

Recognition of Implied Script Statements.   Principle 4 of the TBS model was suggested by Walker and Yekovich (1984). They proposed that each time a script concept is implied by a verb in a story, the activation of that script concept is raised. For example, the phrase, **He ate hungrily**, implies the central concept, FOOD. The increase in activation should have a greater impact on peripheral than on central script concepts. In terms of the TBS model, five implications of an unpresented peripheral script concept would raise its activation from 1* to 6*. In contrast, because central concepts are activated to 7* whenever the script is accessed, additional implications can raise their activation level only from 7* to 9*.

To examine these hypotheses, Walker and Yekovich (1984) presented people with a series of script-based stories. Across two experiments, the stories made 0, 1, 3, or 5 implications about central and peripheral script concepts. It was predicted that the recognition of peripheral script concepts would vary with the number of times that they were implied.

Table 8.5, which combines the data of the two experiments (Walker & Yekovich, 1984, Tables 1 and 2), supports this analysis. As predicted, the number of implications has a greater impact on the recognition of peripheral than central concepts. It is interesting that recognition was slightly higher for frequently than for infrequently implied central concepts (64% and 55%, respectively). This suggests that the activation level of central concepts can be slightly raised by frequent implication.

Across the same two experiments, explicitly mentioned concepts were recognized 90% of the time, much higher than any of the implied concepts (Walker & Yekovich, 1984). This indicates that, consistent with the TBS model, explicitly mentioned concepts are more strongly activated than implied ones.

Alternative Models.   Two other models of the representation of script-based stories merit consideration. The *script-only* model states that the representation of a script-based story consists of a copy, in memory, of the pertinent script (e.g., Anderson et al., 1978; Carbonnell, 1978; Charniak, 1975). Statements from the story raise the activation of the corresponding script statements. Furthermore, specific story information results in the filling of *script slots*. For example, in the "coffee spill" story, the FOOD slot would be filled with the concept, TUNA

TABLE 8.5
Percent Recognition of Implied Concepts as a Function
of the Number of Implications and Centrality

	Number of Implications			
Centrality	0	1	3	5
Central	55	52	66	64
Peripheral	14	26	49	53

Source: Adapted from Walker & Yekovich, 1984, Tables 1 and 2, p. 361 and p. 363. Adapted by permission.

SANDWICH. The script-only model does not specify the creation of a story text base.

Two sources of evidence work against the script-only model. First, according to this model, peripheral statements, such as **He straightened his collar**, are not incorporated into the script copy, because they do not correspond to any script statement. Therefore, the script-only model cannot account for high recognition and recall rates of peripheral story statements at short test intervals (e.g., Bower et al., 1979; Graesser et al., 1979; Light & Anderson, 1983; Smith & Graesser, 1981; see also Tables 8.3 and 8.4). Second, according to the script-only model, a separate script copy is created for every script-based story that one understands. Therefore, encountering several stories based on the same script should not pose any difficulty in memory tasks. However, Bower et al. (1979, Experiments 3 and 4) reported that people who had read several stories based on the same script experienced interference. They made more reconstructions in a recall task, and committed more false alarms in recognition, than people who read only one story per script.

The TBS model can account for interference between sets of stories based on the same script. As discussed earlier, understanding stories results in the construction of text bases and in script activation. For stories that refer to a common script, activation accumulates in the scene headers of that script and in the script statements that are mentioned and implied in the stories. During story retrieval, people who have understood several stories based on the same script tend to consult the pertinent script rather than the text bases, even at short test intervals (Reder, 1987). This reveals many activated script statements, with little indication of which story was the source of activation. As a result, the understander makes numerous reconstructions in recall and false alarms in recognition (Bower et al., 1979).

The other alternative model is the *script pointer plus tag* model (Graesser et al., 1979; Nakamura et al., 1985; Smith & Graesser, 1981). This models states that the representation of a script-based story includes a script copy whose slots have been filled with corresponding story information, such as the filling of the FOOD slot with TUNA SANDWICH. The representation also includes a set of tags to story propositions that are peripheral to the script.

Unlike the script-only model, the script pointer plus tag model can account for the recall of peripheral story statements: in particular, these are recovered via the tags. However, the script pointer plus tag model cannot explain the fact, discussed earlier, that relevant peripheral script statements are recalled better than either central script statements or irrelevant peripheral ones (Bower et al., 1979, Experiment 7). This latter result may be attributable to the appearance of relevant peripheral statements either in the macrostructure or at high levels of the microstructure of the text base. The script pointer plus tag model not does not refer to a text base representation. A second shortcoming of the script pointer plus tag model is that it hypothesizes a separate script image for each story. Therefore, it cannot account for interference between stories based on the same script (Bower et al., 1979).

COORDINATING DIFFERENT SCHEMATA

Evidence supporting the psychological reality of scripts, story schemata, and schemata of cause, plans, and goals raises the issue of how these knowledge structures are coordinated during comprehension. This problem may be illustrated with reference to the following story synopsis (Lehnert, Dyer, Johnson, Yang, & Harley, 1983):

> Richard, a lawyer, met his old college roommate, Paul, at a restaurant for lunch one day. Richard felt bad about having long ago failed to repay some borrowed money to Paul, so he agreed to give Paul some free legal advise about his impending divorce. When they went over to Paul's to talk it over, they found Paul's wife in bed with another man. They were shocked, but Richard realized that this would help Paul's divorce case.

This story's simple meaning veils its underlying complexity. At one level of analysis, it constitutes a story. It invokes a variety of familiar scripts, such as the restaurant script. Embedded in the story are simple plans, such as giving free legal advice in-order-to repay a debt. In addition, the story makes reference to complex concepts such as borrowing money, repaying favors, and the emotional reaction of being shocked.

Rumelhart and Ortony (1977) identified two principles of coordinating the schemata underlying a message. First, schemata are embedded in one another. For example, the episode schema is embedded in the story schema, and the fast-food restaurant script is embedded in the restaurant script. One advantage of schema-embedding is that a schematic situation or concept can be comprehended without examining the structure of its subschemata. This is consistent with the finding, discussed earlier, that mentioning scene headers does not activate their subordinate script actions (Abbott et al., 1985).

The second principle of schema coordination states that there are schemata at many levels of analysis (Rumelhart & Ortony, 1977). In this regard, it has been proposed that high level schemata, called *memory organizational packets* (MOPs), identify the interrelations among goals, intentions, and script-like action sequences (Schank, 1979, 1982). For example, Lehnert et al. (1983) proposed that the concept of DIVORCE is better represented as a MOP than as a script. At even higher levels of abstraction are schemata for concepts such as LEGAL DISPUTE and PROFESSIONAL SERVICE.

These proposals are consistent with the phenomenon of interference between stories based on similar scripts (Bower et al., 1979). For example, people's confusion of statements from separate passages about visiting a doctor and visiting a dentist could result from the fact that both the doctor and dentist scripts make reference to a higher-order MOP about visiting a health professional.

These analyses reflect a growing consensus that language comprehension requires the coordination of a complex array of schemata at various levels of abstraction. Theoretical treatments of this problem are at an early stage of development, and systematic experimental examinations of this problem have yet to be carried out.

SUMMARY

Research concerning the comprehension of complex discourses has particularly focused on story understanding. Story understanding is guided by the story schema, which captures one's knowledge of the typical form of stories.

The story grammar is one formal technique for describing the contents of the story schema. A story grammar consists of a set of rules that describe the rewriting of story-idea categories in terms of sequences of other categories. The story grammar technique receives support from findings of sequential, hierarchical, and story category effects in story comprehension. However, story comprehension is also influenced by the causal chain status, the connectivity, and the content of story ideas. These results indicate that story grammars do not address all features of story comprehension.

There is evidence that people possess schemata of abstract concepts such as cause, plans, and goals. The cause schema guides people's integration of related text ideas. The plan schema likewise integrates actions and goals, with reference to the relation in-order-to. The goal schema may be a subschema of the plan schema. These schemata are likely to contribute to the understanding of stories and other types of discourse.

Schemata contribute to the understanding of texts such as newspaper articles, expositions, and recipes as well as stories. However, nonnarrative schemata are likely to be less well organized than the story schema. Consistent with this analysis, people exhibit better retrieval for narrative than nonnarrative messages, but this advantage is restricted to text statements that are relevant to the schema. Furthermore, nonnarrative texts that do have well-defined schemata, such as scientific research reports, do not exhibit a retrieval disadvantage.

Scripts play a role in the understanding of stories that are set in one or more stereotypical situations. Scripts have a hierarchical organization in which the script title forms the superordinate node, scene headers appear at the next level, and scene actions form the lower levels. Within each level of the hierarchy, the script statements are sequentially organized. This analysis is supported by people's ratings of script statements and by their timed judgments about the components of scripts.

According to the text base plus script model, script-based stories are represented in terms of a text base plus a pattern of activation in the pertinent script. In the script, the title and all mentioned statements are activated to the highest level, 9*. Unmentioned scene headers are activated to 7* and unmentioned scene actions receive activation only to 1*. Each implication about an unmentioned script statement raises its level of activation by one unit. This model receives support from numerous studies of the retrieval of script-based stories. These studies have varied both the centrality of the story statements in relation to their scripts, and the relevance of the story statements. Retrieval has been examined using both recall and recognition tests administered at short and long test intervals.

Understanding ordinary stories requires the coordination of schemata of text type, familiar situations, and content. Two principles address the coordination of schemata. First, one schema may be embedded in another. Second, there are schemata for concepts at many levels of analysis. Understanding may require frequent shifts from one of these levels to the other.

9

Question Answering and
Sentence Verification

Consider the following passage, previously examined in chapter 4.

> Last night, Fred was washing some shirts in his apartment building laun-
> dromat. While reading his magazine, he realized that he had no coins left
> for the dryer. It took Fred twenty minutes to get some change from a
> building acquaintance. When he got back, Fred found that his washer had
> overflowed. The place was a mess and the janitor was furious.

After reading this passage, there are many questions that would pose
little difficulty for the average adult understander. Questions (1) and (2)
seem trivial—their answers are directly stated in the passage.

(1) What did Fred wash?
(2) Where was Fred washing his shirts?

Indeed, if the understander could not state that Fred was washing shirts
in his apartment building laundromat, one would doubt whether the
passage had been understood at all (Lehnert, 1977). Question (3), however is more demanding.

(3) Why did Fred leave the laundromat?

Correctly answering (3) requires the recognition that Fred did leave, a
fact that is not explicitly stated. It also depends on understanding that
Fred's leaving was caused by his lack of change. Question (4) is even

221

more complicated and yet most people would judge that the shirts did not end up satisfactorily clean.

(4)   Were Fred's shirts clean at the end of the episode?

Consider next question (5):

(5)   Why did the washer overflow?

The passage clearly gives no indication of the cause of the overflow. Although one could make general or specific speculations, such as **The machine was faulty** or **A drain was blocked**, many people would simply respond, **I don't know.** How the reader comes to that decision, however, is by no means obvious.

The principal role of language is to convey meaning from one individual to another. For this function to be properly fulfilled, the understander must be able to retrieve the meaning of a message at a later time. The ability to answer questions about a message has been characterized as the overriding criterion of understanding, more important than the ability to summarize or to paraphrase (Lehnert, 1977).

Accordingly, the goal of this chapter is to examine the processes that permit people to successfully answer questions and verify sentences. Particular emphasis is placed on the answering of questions about discourse. However, researchers have also examined people's ability to answer questions with reference to their general and autobiographical knowledge (e.g., Bahrick, Bahrick, & Wittlinger, 1975; Gentner & Collins, 1981; Reiser, Black, & Abelson, 1985; Rips, Shoben, & Smith, 1973). Indeed, there are many similarities between the processes of answering questions with reference to discourse and to general knowledge (e.g., Galambos & Black, 1985; Graesser & Murachver, 1985). Items (6) through (8) exemplify general knowledge questions.

(6)   Is a bat a bird?
(7)   What is the capital of Pakistan?
(8)   Is rice grown in Brazil?

Question (9) is an autobiographical question.

(9)   Where were you at noon on February 19, 1985?

The remainder of this chapter is organized as follows: First, the processing stages of question answering are inspected. The second section presents a class of models that addresses the coordination of the stages of question answering. Finally, question answering processes are compared with those of a related activity, fact retrieval (Anderson, 1976).

STAGES OF QUESTION ANSWERING

Theoretical analysis suggests that question answering consists of a number of stages or components (e.g., Clark & Clark, 1977; Graesser & Murachver, 1985; Lehnert, 1977; Singer, 1985). These stages include question encoding, question categorization, selection of an answering strategy, search of the discourse representation and of general knowledge, comparison of the retrieved information, and response. This arrangement is outlined in Fig. 9.1. Processing at each stage is influenced by the answerer's knowledge. For example, question encoding is influenced by one's implicit knowledge of syntax. Likewise, response formulation is guided by knowledge about the content of the question, and by pragmatic knowledge of the intentions of the questioner.

The stage analysis oversimplifies question answering in several ways (Graesser & Murachver, 1985; Lehnert, 1977). First, it is unlikely that the stages are executed in a strictly serial manner. For example, although Fig. 9.1 shows encoding as preceding categorization, the understander is likely to categorize **Who did some washing?** as a question about an agent before a full propositional encoding has been accomplished. Second, there is interaction among the stages that is not captured in Fig. 9.1. For example, failure of the memory search might result in a recategorization of the question or a change of answering strategy. In spite of the oversimplification, the stage analysis helps to identify the component problems of question answering.

Question Encoding

Question encoding involves the identification of a question's propositional content. As usual, propositional encoding requires the parsing of the question, the construction of the corresponding propositions, and

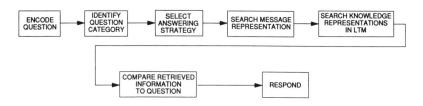

FIG. 9.1. Stage analysis of question answering.

the distinction between given and new information. The given–new distinction is an especially important aspect of question meaning, because the new component is the idea that the questioner wants to know about. For example, in question (1), **What did Fred wash?**, it is given that Fred washed something. The new component is the unknown thing that was washed.

What did Fred wash? may be represented as (WASH, AGENT:FRED, OBJECT:X?) (Anderson, 1976; Kintsch, 1974; Singer, 1984). The argument X? signifies that the questioner wants to know what concept corresponds to the variable X. This approach may be extended to yes–no questions. For example, **Did Fred wash some shirts?** may be represented as (WASH, AGENT:FRED, OBJECT:SHIRTS?). Once again, the question mark modifies the interrogated concept. In general, it will be assumed that the general principles of propositional analysis extend to the representation of questions.

As in other sentences, given and new questions components are distinguished by factors such as syntactic construction, intonational stress, and the use of pronouns. However, this analysis is not complete. For example, questions (10) and (11) have similar grammatical structures, but they do not appear to focus on equivalent elements (Lehnert, 1977, p. 56).

(10)   Why did John fly to Siberia?
(11)   Why did John crawl across the street?

Most people judge *Siberia* to be the focus of (10), and the act of crawling to be the focus of (11). Lehnert proposed that, in each question, the unusual element (**Why to Siberia? Why crawl?**) is judged to be the focus. The judgment of what is unusual, of course, requires reference to one's world knowledge.

Similarly, consider question (12):

(12)   Why did Sam eat dinner at the Copper Beach Restaurant?

It may focus either on why Sam ate dinner, why Sam ate at a restaurant, or why Sam ate at that particular restaurant (Galambos & Black, 1985). Therefore, the analysis of given and new question information requires an understanding of the relation between questions and pertinent world knowledge.

Question Categories and Question Categorization

Most questions are sentences that request that the understander either supply one or more ideas, or indicate whether certain ideas are accurate. Questions are typically signaled by interrogative pronouns, such as *who* or *what*, or interrogative adverbs, such as *how, where,* and *when.* Categorizing questions by their interrogative terms is called *lexical categorization* (Lehnert, 1977). However, the relationship between interrogative words and the type of question they signal is not one-to-one. For example, the questions **How many shirts did Fred wash?, How was Fred able to get some change?,** and **How did Fred wash his shirts?** all begin with the word *how,* but they ask about the concepts of quantity, enablement, and instrument, respectively (Lehnert, 1977). Furthermore, the utterance, **You went to the store',** spoken with rising intonation on the word *store,* functions as a question, in spite of the fact that it does not begin with an interrogative word at all. Although lexical categorization of questions has descriptive value, it does not provide a useful basis for understanding the processes of question answering. Categorizing questions in terms of the conceptual category they ask about is more suitable for the present purposes.

Using this conceptual approach, several investigators have presented taxonomies of question categories. For example, Lehnert (1978) listed 13 conceptual question categories, which are illustrated by questions (13a)–(13m) (see also Graesser & Murachver, 1985; Trabasso et al., 1984).

(13) a. Why did Fred's clothes get dirty? (causal antecedent)
     b. Why did Fred get some change? (goal orientation)
     c. How was Fred able to get some change? (enablement)
     d. What happened when Fred left the laundromat? (causal consequent)
     e. Did Fred have change for the dryer? (verification)
     f. Was Fred or Carol at the laundromat? (disjunctive)
     g. How did Fred wash his shirts? (instrumental procedure)
     h. What did Fred wash? (concept completion)
     i. Why didn't the episode end satisfactorily? (expectation)
     j. What should Fred do to make it up to the janitor? (judgmental)
     k. How many shirts did Fred wash? (quantification)
     l. What color were the shirts? (feature specification)
     m. Can you hand Fred his shirts? (request)

Consider a few of these categories. Causal antecedent questions, such as (13a), ask about the conditions that have resulted in a particular state of affairs. Verification questions, such as (13e), ask about the truth or accuracy of particular ideas or concepts. Concept completion questions, such as (13h), request that the listener supply the information filling a semantic case. Quantification questions, such as (13k), ask for a number or amount.

These question categories can be further analyzed to an interrogative idea, plus a discourse category (Graesser & Murachver, 1985; Graesser et al., 1981). Interrogative ideas are concepts with labels such as HOW, WHY, SIG(nificance), and CON(sequence) (Graesser & Murachver, 1985). Some of these ideas, such as HOW and WHY, directly correspond to interrogative words. Others, such as CONS, meaning **What is the consequence of?** do not. Discourse categories, such as actions, events, and states, are comparable to the story categories discussed in chapter 8. For example, the question proposition of **How did Fred wash his shirts?** is (WASH, FRED, SHIRTS). This proposition has the discourse category of an action in the "flooded laundry" episode.

According to this analysis, question (13a), **Why did Fred's clothes get dirty?** is categorized as a WHY⟨event⟩ question (Graesser & Murachver, 1985). Therefore, WHY⟨event⟩ questions correspond to the category of causal antecedent questions. In contrast, WHY⟨action⟩ questions, such as (13b), **Why did Fred get some change?**, ask about one's motivation for performing an action. They correspond to Lehnert's (1978) goal orientation questions.

Although verification questions are identified as a separate category (e.g., 13e, **Did Fred have change for the dryer?**,) it is possible to formulate verification questions about any conceptual category. For example, (14a), (14b), and (14c) are verification, or yes–no, questions about causal antecedents, goal orientation, and enablement, respectively.

(14) a. Did Fred's clothes get dirty because he was working in the garden?
      b. Did Fred get some change because he wanted to buy a chocolate bar?
      c. Did Fred get some change from the change machine?

Strategies of Question Answering

Direct Retrieval Versus Plausibility Judgments.   Before proceeding to search for requested information, it is necessary to select an answering strategy. As discussed in chapter 8, one alternative is to *directly retrieve* the requested information from memory (Reder, 1982, 1987). Alternatively, one may *judge the plausibility* of a questioned fact on the basis of stored knowledge (Camp, Lachman, & Lachman, 1980; Gentner & Collins, 1981; Kolodner, 1983; Lehnert, 1977; Reder, 1982, 1987).

Reder (1982, 1987) presented a model of answering strategies. This model questions the assumptions of other investigators that direct retrieval is always more efficient than plausibility judgment and that direct retrieval always precedes plausibility judgment. Some of the central principles of the model are as follows:

Principle 1. There is a distinct stage of strategy selection in question answering.

Principle 2. People do not always adopt the explicit strategy of an answering task. For example, people who have been assigned to perform a recognition task, which ostensibly requires direct retrieval, may use either direct retrieval or plausibility judgment.

Principle 3. Strategy selection is influenced by variables *intrinsic* to the question, such as the familiarity of the question and the activation of the question concepts.

Principle 4. Strategy selection is influenced by variables *extrinsic* to the question, such as instructions to adopt a particular strategy, and the delay between learning and questioning.

Reder (1982) conducted a series of experiments to test these proposals. People read brief passages and then made timed judgments about statements that had either been presented or not presented in the passages. The test delay was either 0 or 20 minutes, or 2 days. Individuals were instructed either to recognize the test sentences (direct retrieval), or to perform plausibility judgments. Finally, the test sentences were of either high or medium plausibility. For example, in the context of the "flooded laundry" episode, **Did Fred add detergent to the wash?** has high plausibility, and **Did Fred add bleach to the wash?** has medium plausibility.

Consider the impact of test delay, an extrinsic question factor. Reder (1982) proposed that direct retrieval is more efficient than plausibility judgment only at short delays, when verbatim traces and/or details of the text microstructure are still available. Reder reasoned that attempting to directly retrieve the test fact after the message details have decayed ought to result in a prolonged search. Judgment times supported this analysis. Table 9.1a shows that recognition was faster than plausibility judgment only in immediate testing. At delays of 20 minutes and 2 days, recognition was not more efficient than plausibility judgment.

Reder (1982) proposed that, regardless of task instructions, people tend to employ direct retrieval at short test intervals and the plausibility

TABLE 9.1
Sentence Judgment Times (seconds) as a Function
of Assigned Task, Test Delay, and Sentence Presentation

(A) Assigned Task	Delay		
	0 Minutes	20 Minutes	2 Days
Recognition	2.51	2.65	2.85
Plausibility	3.21	2.68	2.61

(B) Assigned Task	Presented	Not Presented	Presented	Not Presented	Presented	Not Presented
Recognition	2.33	2.69	2.57	2.72	2.66	3.09
Plausibility	2.74	3.67	2.55	2.81	2.51	2.71

Source: Adapted from Reder, 1982, Table 1, p. 259. Adapted by permission.

strategy at long intervals. Two features of her data bear on this proposal. First, it should take longer to judge unpresented than presented test statements only if one uses the direct retrieval strategy. This is because plausibility judgments about presented and unpresented statements ought to take the same amount of time. However, Table 9.1b, which presents data for the 0-minute delay, reveals that plausibility judgments took an average of 3.67 seconds for unpresented statements as compared with only 2.74 seconds for presented statements. This indicates that, in immediate testing, people in the plausibility condition sometimes adopted the recognition strategy (Reder, 1982, p. 260).

Conversely, at long intervals, people assigned to a recognition task tend to shift from direct retrieval to plausibility judgments. This is supported by the effect of statement plausibility in Reder's (1982) study. It should take less time to make plausibility judgments about statements of high than of medium plausibility. Plausibility should have no effect on the time needed to directly retrieve statements from memory. However, at the 20-minute and 2-day delays, people in the direct retrieval condition took longer to judge test items of medium plausibility than of high plausibility (Reder, 1982, Table 1; not shown in Table 9.1). Reder concluded that the "recognizers" sometimes shifted to the plausibility strategy at lengthy delays.

To summarize, people tend to employ direct retrieval at short test intervals and plausibility judgments at long test intervals. Furthermore, the impact of the test interval partially overwhelms other variables influencing strategy selection, such as strategy instructions. In any given condition, people are able to mix the direct retrieval and plausibility judgment strategies.

Questions Strategies and Reconstruction Effects.   Direct retrieval and plausibility judgment are predominantly recognition strategies. They correspond respectively to reproduction and reconstruction in recall (see chapter 4). Some of the reconstruction effects examined in chapter 4 may be interpreted with reference to Reder's (1982, 1987) strategy principles. First, Sulin and Dooling (1974) asked people to read a passage alternately titled "Helen Keller" or "Carol Harris." Only those who received the "Helen Keller" title incorrectly reported recognizing the new sentence, **She was deaf, dumb, and blind.** In Reder's terms, this was a plausibility judgment. This outcome indicates that one can perform plausibility judgments only if one possesses knowledge pertinent to the test item.

Second, with increased test interval, there is a convergence of reproduction and reconstruction in discourse recall (Kintsch & van Dijk, 1978; see also Fig. 4.1). This trend indicates that, with increased test delay, people abandon the attempt to directly retrieve the ideas stated in a text, and, instead, reconstruct the message from world knowledge. The only difference between this observation and those of Reder's (1982, 1987) is that, in a delayed recall condition, people are not presented with test sentences to evaluate. Instead, they retrieve their own recall statements from world knowledge.

Third, if, at lengthy test delays, a perspective change (e.g., *burglar* to *homebuyer*; see chapter 4) prevents people from reconstructing a message, they reproduce more of the message than would otherwise be the case (Anderson & Pichert, 1978; Hasher & Griffin, 1978). This finding reflects Reder's proposal that people are flexible in their selection of strategies and combinations of strategies. Even though the preferred strategy at lengthy test intervals is plausibility judgment, people can apparently revert to direct retrieval if they are deprived of the knowledge on which to base their plausibility judgments.

Memory Search Procedures in Question Answering

After selecting a search strategy, the understander can proceed to retrieve the requested information. In part, this requires the application of the given–new strategy (Clark & Haviland, 1977). For example, to answer **What did Fred wash?**, a referent for the given component, FRED WASHED SOMETHING, is sought in the message representation. Once a referent has been accessed, search for the new information can be initiated.

The materials in (15)–(17) help to illustrate that there are different memory search procedures for different question categories.

(15) The burglar climbed the drainpipe. He pried the window and the lock broke. Then, he opened the window, entered the house, and stole the jewelry.

(16) WHY did the burglar enter the house?

(17) HOW did the burglar enter the house?

Questions (16) and (17) both have the same given component, THE BURGLAR ENTERED THE HOUSE. However, it is obvious that (16) and (17) demand different answers. This means that, after matching the given component with the message representation, the answerer must search the representation of (15) differently for (16) and (17). For question (16), a goal orientation question, the answerer must search memory for the events that chronologically *followed* the given idea. This search yields answers such as **To steal the jewelry** (Graesser, Robertson, et al., 1980). In contrast, question (17), an enablement question, initiates a search for events that chronologically *preceded* the given idea. As a result, one might answer, **By climbing the drainpipe.** In order to provide the questioner with the appropriate information, the correct search procedure must be executed.

Matching the Given Question Information.   To find a referent for the given information, one may examine either the discourse text base or a knowledge structure related to the discourse. This choice is influenced by the answering strategy. For example, direct retrieval usually requires the examination of the discourse text base. The failure to match the given information to a text base proposition can sometimes be overcome by reinstating a matching idea from long-term memory (Kintsch & van Dijk, 1978; Lesgold et al., 1979), or by constructing a bridging inference between the given idea and the discourse representation (Haviland & Clark, 1974).

People do not appear to carefully scrutinize the accuracy of the given component of the question before seeking a referent for it. For example, in one study, people viewed a film of a car accident in which no broken headlight was shown. They subsequently were asked either **Did you see THE broken headlight?,** which falsely presupposes the existence of a broken headlight, or **Did you see A broken headlight?,** which does not (capitals added). More people incorrectly answered *yes* to the former question than to the latter (Loftus & Zanni, 1975). Similarly, the given component of **How many animals of each kind did Moses take on the Ark?** is MOSES TOOK SOME ANIMALS ON THE ARK. This is inaccurate, because it was Noah who sailed the ark. Nevertheless, this question usually evokes the response, *two* (Erickson & Mattson, 1981).

People are less prone to overlook inaccuracies in the new component of the question than in the given. Upon viewing, for an instant, a picture of a girl holding a dog, people incorrectly responded *yes* to **Is it a girl that is holding the cat?** This question included the inaccurate given idea, SOMEONE IS HOLDING THE CAT. In contrast, with the same picture, people did not answer "yes" to **Is it a boy that is holding the dog?** which includes the inaccurate new idea, IT WAS A BOY (Hornby, 1974; see also Harris, 1973; Loftus, 1975; Loftus & Palmer, 1974).

Question Search Procedures.   After retrieving a referent for the given question component, the answerer proceeds to search for the requested information. Graesser and his colleagues (e.g., Graesser & Clark, 1985; Graesser & Murachver, 1985; Graesser et al., 1981) have developed a four-part procedure for identifying the search procedures associated with different question categories. First, people are intensively questioned about the ideas of a text. Second, their answers are used to construct a representation of the text. At the third and crucial step, an inventory of the search procedures that yielded the original answers is compiled. Fourth, the analysis is evaluated. It is useful to consider this procedure in some detail.

At the first stage, normative answering data are collected from people who read narratives (Graesser & Murachver, 1985; Graesser et al., 1981). Each person is assigned an interrogative idea, such as WHY, and answers a question based on that idea about *every statement* in the story. For example, with reference to the narrative fragment (15), people in the WHY group would answer questions such as **Why did the burglar climb the drainpipe?** and **Why did the burglar pry the window?**

(15)   The burglar climbed the drainpipe. He pried the window and the lock broke. Then, he opened the window, entered the house, and stole the jewelry.

People are encouraged to provide several reasonable answers to each question. A list is then made of every answer provided by two or more readers.

At stage two of the research, expert judges construct a causal text representation from the answer protocols. Figure 9.2 illustrates that the representation of sequence (15) includes the discourse categories Action and Event, and the links Reason (R), Consequence (C), and Enable (E). This representation is not strictly hierarchical in nature.

Third, a list is made of the types of links or link-sequences connecting each node to its answer. Suppose that the WHY⟨event⟩, or causal antecedent, question, **Why did the lock break?** receives the answer, **Because the burglar pried the window.** Figure 9.2 shows that the shortest path from THE LOCK BROKE to BURGLAR PRIED THE WINDOW is labeled by a backward consequence link. Using this *shortest path* criterion, Graesser and Murachver (1985) computed the frequency of link-types for numerous question categories. For example, the frequencies for WHY⟨event⟩ questions were 84% for backward consequence links and 16% for all other links. Similarly, WHY⟨action⟩ questions are predominantly answered by tracing forward reason links. Therefore, the WHY

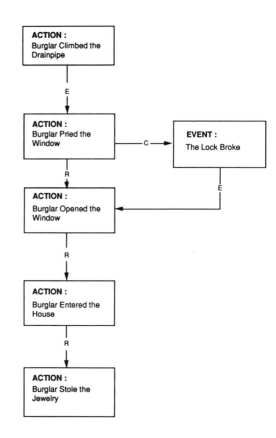

FIG. 9.2. Network representation of the "burglar" narrative fragment. The propositions are linked by the relations of Reason (R), Consequence, (C), and Enable (E).

⟨action⟩ question **Why did the burglar pry the window?** receives answers such as, **To open the window** (Graesser & Murachver, 1985, p. 47).

Using methods similar to Graesser's, Trabasso et al. (1984) proposed search procedures for four categories of *why* questions. Each procedure involved the tracing of backward consequence links, plus the identification of the node categories of candidate answers. The predictions derived from this analysis fit the question answering data that Stein and Glenn (1979) had collected from both adults and children (see also Galambos & Black, 1985).

According to these analyses, both single legal paths and combinations of legal paths yield satisfactory answers. For example, **Why did the burglar pry the window?** is satisfactorily answered following a path of two forward reason links, yielding **To enter the house**. However, there are limits to the distance between the question node and its satisfactory answers (Goldman, 1985; Graesser & Murachver, 1985). Furthermore, answers may be *tuned* to the level of detail of a question. In this regard, it seems more satisfactory to answer **Why did the burglar open the window?** with *To enter the house* than with **To steal the jewelry** (Galambos & Black, 1985).

The fourth and last stage of Graesser's analysis involves the evaluation of the question search procedures. Graesser has used three measures to accomplish this. First, Graesser and Murachver (1985) found that 95% of the answers appearing in the original answer norms (stage 1) were consistent with the derived search procedures. Second, Graesser's theory distinguishes between admissible and inadmissible answers to a question. People judge answers, which, according to the theory are admissible, to be more "acceptable" than the inadmissible ones (Graesser et al., 1981). However, on the third measure, the theory does not fare quite as well: Only 20% of the answers admissible to the theory were actually given by any person (Graesser & Murachver, 1985; but see Graesser, Koizumi, Vamos, & Elofson, 1985).

Similar procedures have been used to study the answering of questions with reference to one's world knowledge. For example, Galambos and Black (1985) studied the mechanisms of answering questions about script actions. Their analysis was based on a pool of thousands of sample answers obtained in a norming study. They distinguished among six different script-action categories, and identified the categories of reasons that people provide in answer to WHY⟨action⟩ questions. Whether particular question categories initiate the same search procedures when they refer to scripts and to discourse representations is a problem in need of further examination.

Choosing an Answer. It is tempting to think that formulating a response is a trivial matter once the requested information has been retrieved. However, the choice of response is influenced by several pragmatic factors. First, the speech act of the question must be considered. For example, **Can you hand Fred his shirts?** has the indirect speech act of a request, and does not demand the answer *yes* or *no*.

Second, response selection is guided by politeness (e.g., Clark & Schunk, 1980). Consider question (18).

(18)   Does Montana have a significant cattle industry?

Although the answer to this question is *no*, it would be impolite to answer so curtly in ordinary conversation. Instead, in keeping with Grice's (1975) maxims of quantity and manner, (19) is a more appropriate reply (Lehnert, 1977, p. 52).

(19)   No, there are a number of sheep ranches, but most of the land is too barren to support cattle.

When one determines that the answer to a yes–no question is negative, one generates a *secondary question*, and includes the reply to the secondary question in one's answer (Lehnert, 1977). Thus, for (18), one generates the secondary question, **Why doesn't Montana have a significant cattle industry?** However, the mechanism of generating secondary questions is not obvious. For example, when the answer to **Did John eat a hotdog?** is negative, is the secondary question **What did John eat?**, **Who ate a hotdog?** or **Why didn't John eat a hotdog?** Like identifying the focus of a question, generating secondary questions probably requires considering the discourse context.

A third pragmatic factor that guides response selection is the shared knowledge of speaker and listener (Clark & Marshall, 1981; Sperber & Wilson, 1986). For example, people give different answers to **Where is the Empire State Building?** depending on whether the question is posed in Europe, in Brooklyn, or on a Manhattan subway (Norman, 1973). In this case, answer selection depends on the answerer's assumptions about the knowledge of the questioner.

PROCESS MODELS OF SENTENCE VERIFICATION
AND QUESTION ANSWERING

This section presents an analysis of sentence verification and yes–no questions, and considers process models derived from this analysis. These models address the coordination of the processing stages examined in the last section. In addition, they examine the processing stage of *comparing* retrieved information with the question statement (see Fig. 9.1). This stage is essential in the answering of yes–no questions.

When asked the concept completion question, (13h), **What did Fred wash?** one must search memory for the requested information. A successful search permits the registration of the answer, **some shirts**. The situation is different for the closely related yes–no question, **Did Fred wash some shirts?** To answer this question, one must again search memory to determine what Fred washed. However, the retrieved information must next be compared with the new element of the question, namely, SHIRTS. If the retrieved information matches the new question element, one may answer *yes*. However, if a mismatch is detected, then the correct answer is *no*. As discussed earlier, it is possible to ask yes–no questions about every conceptual category.

The processes of answering yes–no questions were first examined in tasks of *sentence verification*. Sentence verification requires a truth judgment about a statement. For example, the truth of **Fred washed some socks** may be evaluated with reference to the "flooded laundry" passage. It is apparent that sentence verification and answering yes–no questions are closely related.

Gough (1965, 1966) examined the verification of simple sentences with reference to corresponding pictures. Each picture showed either a boy hitting a girl, or vice versa. Particular combinations of sentences and pictures yielded different conditions. Consider sentences (20a)–(20d) in relation to a picture of a girl hitting a boy.

(20) a. The girl is hitting the boy. (true affirmative)
      b. The boy is hitting the girl. (false affirmative)
      c. The boy is not hitting the girl. (true negative)
      d. The girl is not hitting the boy. (false negative)

Sentence (20a) is an affirmative sentence, and is true of the picture: Therefore, it is a true affirmative sentence. Similarly, (20b) is a false affirmative, (20c) is a true negative, and (20d) is a false negative.

The time that people needed to correctly verify these sentences with reference to the picture revealed an interesting pattern of results: For affirmative items, verification time was longer for false items than true items. For negative sentences, the pattern was just the opposite: Answer time was greater in the true negative condition than the false negative condition (see also McMahon, 1963; Slobin, 1966; Wason, 1961, 1965).

You can get a sense of this result by mentally verifying sentences (21a) and (21b):

(21) a. A giraffe is not short.
      b. A lion is not fierce.

Sentence (21a) is a true negative sentence, and (21b) is a false negative sentence. In agreement with Gough's (1965, 1966) findings, most people find it easier to verify (21b) correctly than (21a).

Additive-Stage Models of Sentence Verification

Several investigators independently suggested an explanation for these sentence verification effects (Clark & Chase, 1972; Trabasso, Rollins, & Shaughnessy, 1971). Clark and Chase (1972) presented a process model of sentence verification that is outlined in Fig. 9.3

This model was developed to address the comparison of sentences and pictures, but it can be explored with reference to sequence (15), examined earlier.

(15)   The burglar climbed the drainpipe. He pried the window and the lock broke. Then, he opened the window, entered the house, and stole the jewelry.

(23)   a.   The burglar pried the window. (true affirmative)
        b.   The burglar pried the door. (false affirmative)
        c.   The burglar did not pry the door. (true negative)
        d.   The burglar did not pry the window. (false negative)

Consider the verification of (23c), which is a true negative in the context of sequence (15). Before the onset of the processes of Fig. 9.3, an internal *response index* is initialized with the value, TRUE (Clark & Chase, 1972). Processing begins with the encoding of sentence (23c) as

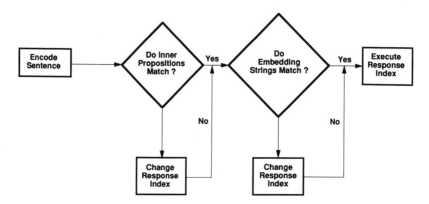

FIG. 9.3.   Process model of sentence verification. *Source*: Adapted from Clark & Chase, 1972, Table 1, p. 480. Adapted by permission.

P1 (NEG, P2) P2 (PRY, BURGLAR, DOOR). This can be expressed more simply as (NEG(PRY, BURGLAR, DOOR)). (PRY, BURGLAR, DOOR) is called the *inner proposition*, and the negative predicate, NEG, is called the *embedding string*.

Next, the reader compares the test sentence to the corresponding discourse proposition, AFFirmative(PRY, BURGLAR, WINDOW). Each time a mismatch is detected, the response index is changed from TRUE to FALSE or back. First, it is determined that the inner proposition of (23c), (PRY, BURGLAR, DOOR), mismatches the discourse proposition, (PRY, BURGLAR, WINDOW). As a result, the truth index is changed from TRUE to FALSE. The embedding string of (23c), NEG, likewise mismatches that of the discourse, AFF. Therefore, the response index is switched back to TRUE. To answer, the reader reports the response index. In an experiment, this might be accomplished by pressing buttons labeled "true" and "false."

Table 9.2 shows the mismatches that are detected in verifying sentences in the different conditions. Inner proposition mismatches occur in the false affirmative and true negative conditions. Embedding string mismatches occur in the true negative and false negative conditions. Each mismatch requires a time-consuming change of the response index. Therefore, this analysis predicts that verification times will be longest in the true negative condition. The observations presented in Table 9.2 support this prediction for sentence-picture verification (Clark & Chase, 1972; see also Gough 1965, 1966). Similar observations are detected in many other verification tasks (Carpenter & Just, 1975).

Individual Differences in Sentence Verification

People use different strategies to perform sentence-picture comparisons. In one such task, people examine a sentence such as (24) for as long as

TABLE 9.2
Verification of sentences with reference to pictures:
Predicted inner proposition and embedding string mismatches,
and observed judgment times (milliseconds)

	Do the Inner Propositions Mismatch?	Do the Embedding Strings Mismatch?	Observation
True affirmative	No	No	1744
False affirmative	Yes	No	1959
True negative	Yes	Yes	2624
False negative	No	Yes	2476

Source: Adapted from Clark & Chase, 1972, Table 2, p. 482. Adapted by permission.

they wish. Upon pressing a button, they are then shown a corresponding picture, as follows (Clark & Chase, 1972):

(24)   The plus is not above the star.   *

                                                  +

The sentence judgment is registered by pressing either a "true" or a "false" button. This procedure permits the separation of sentence encoding time and verification time (MacLeod, Hunt, & Mathews, 1978; Mathews, Hunt, & MacLeod, 1980).

Using this method, Mathews et al. (1980) found that the data of 43 of their 70 participants were well-fit by analyses of sentence verification such as the one that was presented in Fig. 9.3 (Carpenter & Just, 1975; Clark & Chase, 1972). ("Well-fit" means that their data matched the predictions.) This is reflected by the high true-negative verification times shown in Fig. 9.4 for the well-fit group. However, the data of 16

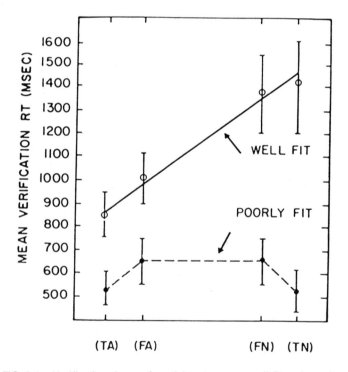

FIG. 9.4. Verification times of participant groups well-fit and poorly-fit by the analysis that assumes the propositional encoding of the sentence. *Source:* Mathews, Hunt, & MacLeod, 1980, Figure 1, p. 538. Reprinted by permission.

other individuals were poorly-fit by the model. Figure 9.4 reveals that the data of both groups were quite orderly, although in different ways. Mathews et al. proposed that, whereas the well-fit participants encoded the sentences propositionally, the poorly-fit individuals encoded the sentences by forming a pictorial representation, or image. Negation, of course, cannot be encoded in an image. Therefore, the image strategy should simply result in longer verification times for false trials than for true trials. That is what Fig. 9.4 shows for the poorly-fit group.

The well-fit group and poorly-fit groups did not differ in verbal ability, but the poorly-fit group had significantly higher spatial ability than the well-fit group. Mathews et al. (1980) concluded that spatial ability influences the strategy that one uses to perform sentence-picture comparisons.

Sentence Verification and Question Answering

I extended the principles of sentence verification (Carpenter & Just, 1975; Clark & Chase, 1972; Trabasso et al., 1971) to tasks of sentence verification and question answering about ordinary sentences and messages (Singer, 1981, 1984, 1986). Consider sentences (25a)–(25c), and corresponding question (26).

(25) a. The hunter shot the deer.
      b. The hunter shot the bear.
      c. The hunter shot with the gun.

(26) Did the hunter shoot a deer?

Question (26) has the answer *yes* after (25a) and *no* after (25b). After (25c), question (26) has the answer *don't know*, following the rationale there is no way of knowing what the hunter shot. Thus, this task gives people the option of using the realistic response option, *don't know*.

One of the central predictions of Singer's (1981, 1984) analysis of this task was that people would need *less* time to correctly answer *don't know* than *no*. For the *no* sequence, (25b)–(26), the new question element, *deer*, is compared with the corresponding concept, *bear*. The resulting mismatch requires that the response index be changed from YES to NO. For the *don't know* sequence, (25c)–(26), in contrast, the representation of sentence (25c) includes no concept with which to compare *deer*. The comparison operation is bypassed and the response index is immediately changed to DON'T KNOW. The absence of the comparison operation suggests that *don't know* questions ought to be answered more quickly than *no* items.

Table 9.3 presents data supporting this prediction for several verification and answering tasks (Singer, 1981, 1984, 1986). The similarity of the judgment time patterns across tasks indicates that the organization of question answering stages is similar for different question categories. These results demonstrate that principles of sentence verification can be fruitfully applied to realistic questioning tasks.

Feeling-of-Knowing.   In general, people rapidly answer *don't know* when they are confident that they have no information relevant to a question (Glucksberg & McCloskey, 1981; Nelson & Narens, 1980; Norman, 1973; Reder, 1987). When a question statement seems familiar, on the other hand, *don't know* answer times are long. Consider the following three questions:

(27)   What is your phone number?
(28)   What is your best friend's phone number?
(29)   What is Charles Dickens' phone number?

A superficial analysis suggests that the processes of answering questions (27)-(29) ought to be similar: One should search memory for the requested number, and ultimately report either the number, or the fact that it is unknown. However, it is unlikely that one actually searches memory for Charles Dickens' phone number (Norman, 1973). Instead, one understands that this is a fact that was never known. As a result, answer time for (29) is predicted to be very fast.

People's *feeling-of-knowing* a fact has been shown to predict their performance in a variety of memory tasks (Hart, 1967; Nelson, Gerler, & Narens, 1984; Nelson, Leonesio, Shimamura, Landwehr, & Narens, 1982; Nelson & Narens, 1980; Schacter, 1983). In particular, the feeling of knowing the fact expressed by a question influences the answering

TABLE 9.3
Answer Times (milliseconds) for Yes-No-Don't Know Task

Study	Task	Response		
		Yes	No	Don't Know
Singer (1981)	Verification	2087	2392	2101
Singer (1984)	Yes-no questions	2296	2561	2443
Singer (1986)	Yes-no questions			
	about causes	2362	2963	2689

processes. *Don't know* answer times are systematically greater for apparently familiar questions, such as **Who is the Prime Minister of Canada?** than unfamiliar ones, such as **Who is the Prime Minister of Zaire?** (Nelson & Narens, 1980). Reder (1987) reported that people take less time to accurately indicate that they know the answer to a question than they do to report the answer itself. This suggests that it will be important to pinpoint the role of feeling-of-knowing in question answering.

Conclusions

Several conclusions concerning the study of sentence verification and question answering are worth emphasizing.

1. Sentence verification models, such as the one presented in Fig. 9.3, help to identify the processing stages of question answering. Each stage is complex, and demands careful examination.
2. Studying the time that people need to verify sentences and answer questions exposes the *coordination* of the component mental operations in sets of related questioning tasks. This approach alerts the researcher to the importance of examining variables that may influence the individual stages (Sternberg, 1969).
3. Researchers have addressed a considerable range of answering tasks. For example, in the study of sentence-picture comparisons, researchers have examined sentence-first and picture-first tasks, have varied the picture-encoding strategy, and have instructed participants to recode negatives to affirmatives. What is particularly important is that proposed verification models have successfully addressed a range of tasks and strategies without sacrificing their basic processing assumptions. Across tasks, only minor variations concerning the stages and their organization have been proposed.
4. The processing principles of sentence verification may be fruitfully extended to the study of question answering.

FACT RETRIEVAL AND QUESTION ANSWERING

The Fan Effect

In a well-known series of studies, Anderson (1974b, 1975, 1976; King & Anderson, 1976) examined the processes of deciding whether a test fact, such as, **A lawyer is in the bank**, has appeared in a previously learned set of facts. Anderson called this activity *fact retrieval*. Because fact retrieval bears a close similarity to answering the yes–no question **Is a lawyer in the bank?**, it is important to examine the relation between fact retrieval and question answering.

In a typical experiment, people learned a set of facts, illustrated by items (30) to (32) (Anderson, 1974b, 1975, 1976).

    (30)   A lawyer is in the bank.
    (31)   A lawyer is in the park.
    (32)   A fireman is in the church.

At test time, people had to judge whether test facts, such as **A lawyer is in the bank** (true) and **A fireman is in the park** (false), were part of the learned set. Fact retrieval time consistently increased with the total number of facts in which the concepts of a test fact had participated. For example, because LAWYER appeared in two facts in set (30)–(32) and BANK appeared in one, therefore the total tally for the test fact, **A lawyer is in the bank**, is 3. Figure 9.5 shows the typical form of this effect.

The explanation of this outcome is that, upon the presentation of a test fact, every concept in the fact is activated. Then, activation spreads, or *fans out*, from those concepts (Anderson, 1974b, 1975, 1976). Accord-

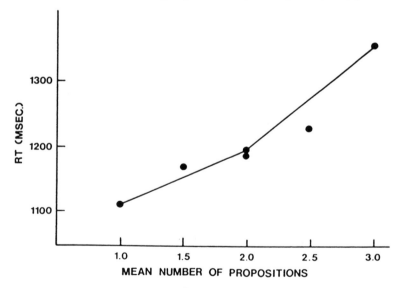

FIG. 9.5.   Mean reaction time (RT) to retrieve facts as a function of fan. Fan is the mean number of propositions to which the concepts in a fact have been connected during study. *Source:* Adapted from Anderson, 1976, Figure 8.7a, p. 278. Adapted by permission.

ingly, this result is called the *fan effect*. Consider the true test fact, **A lawyer is in the bank** and the simple representation of learned facts (30) and (31) shown in Fig. 9.6. Retrieval occurs when there is an intersection of the activation emanating from all of the concepts in the test fact: namely, LAWYER and BANK. However, the activation from each concept is divided among all of the pathways linking it to others in the learned set. Because LAWYER participated in two facts, LAWYER activates proposition nodes 1 and 2 less strongly than if LAWYER had participated in only a single fact during learning (Anderson, 1983). Dividing the activation from LAWYER increases the time needed to achieve an intersection of the activation emanating from LAWYER and BANK.

The role of spreading activation in question answering has been addressed in several ways. We turn next to these refinements.

Focused Memory Search

A strict interpretation of the fan effect states that activation automatically spreads from every concept in a test question to every other concept to which it was linked during learning. However, intuition suggests that one ought to be able to focus memory search on particular categories of concepts. Suppose one has learned the fact, **The lawyer read the magazine at the bank**. If one is then asked **What did the lawyer read?**, one should retrieve the objects of the verb **read**, such as MAGAZINE, rather than locations, such as BANK.

In one study of this *focused search hypothesis*, people learned facts such as those in set (33) (McCloskey & Bigler, 1980).

(33)   a.   The dentist likes Tokyo.
       b.   The dentist likes Vancouver.
       c.   The dentist likes Amsterdam.
       d.   The dentist likes Boston.

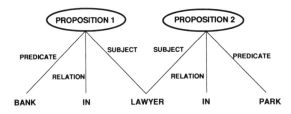

FIG. 9.6. Propositional network representation of *A lawyer is in the bank* and *A lawyer is in the park*, using the technique of Anderson, 1976, chapter 5.

e. The dentist likes London.
f. The dentist likes tigers.

Consider the true test fact, **The dentist likes tigers**, in the context of set (33). DENTIST has a fan of 6 because it was linked to six other concepts. According to the focused search hypothesis, however, people can disregard the facts about the dentist liking cities when they verify **The dentist likes tigers** (McCloskey & Bigler, 1980). As a result, they act as though they know only 1 fact about the dentist: the effective fan of DENTIST is 1. In several experiments, response time indeed varied mainly as a function of the number of concepts in the relevant category, rather than the total number of concepts linked to the character name. This outcome supported the focused search hypothesis.

A similar result was obtained by Reder and Anderson (1980). Their subjects learned facts that linked character names (e.g., *Bill*) to activities that were grouped according to either one or two themes, such as skiing and going to the circus. The time needed to judge test sentences, such as **Bill thought the clowns were very funny**, was mainly influenced by the number of facts about Bill in the relevant theme. Answer time was not influenced by whether people had learned one versus three facts about Bill in the *irrelevant theme*.

On the basis of this outcome, Reder and Anderson (1980) proposed that people group related sets of facts under thematic *subnodes*. To evaluate a test fact, one may focus on the relevant subnode and disregard irrelevant subnodes. Therefore, answer time is mainly influenced by the number of facts in the relevant category. Together, the findings of McCloskey and Bigler (1980) and Reder and Anderson (1980) clarified the role of spreading activation in question answering.

Fact Retrieval and Question Strategies

The answering strategies of direct retrieval and plausibility judgment can both be applied in fact retrieval tasks. In particular, Reder proposed that, although the intended strategy of the fact retrieval paradigm is direct retrieval, plausibility judgments are often made (Reder & Anderson, 1980; Reder & Ross, 1983; Reder & Wible, 1984). In fact, the substitution of plausibility judgments for the direct retrieval strategy should eliminate the fan effect. This is because the fan effect reflects one's attempt to directly retrieve all relevant facts.

Like answering strategies, fact retrieval strategies are influenced by factors both extrinsic and intrinsic to the test item. One extrinsic factor is the type of distractor item presented during testing. Consider the set of learned facts, (34a)–(34c) (Reder & Anderson, 1980).

(34)   a.   Alan bought a ticket for the 10:00 train.
       b.   Alan heard the conductor call, "All aboard."
       c.   Alan arrived on time at Grand Central Station.

In one experiment, some participants received distractor test items that were related to set (34), such as **Alan checked the railway schedule**. Others received only unrelated distractors, such as **Alan paid the car dealer in cash**. Of course, all of the participants viewed some test items from the learned set. Reder and Anderson (1980) proposed that, with unrelated distractors, one can correctly accept a learned fact simply on the basis of its consistency with the other facts in the learned set. This is a plausibility judgment. Only when some of the distractors are related to the learned set must one retrieve the precise learned facts. It was predicted that the familiar fan effect would appear only when the distractors were related to the learned set. The results clearly bore out this prediction.

It was likewise predicted that people would substitute plausibility judgments for direct retrieval when instructed to do so (Reder & Ross, 1983), and with longer delays between learning and testing (Reder & Wible, 1984). As predicted, answer time did not increase as a function of fan in these two conditions.

These results permit the conclusion that the basic mechanisms of spreading activation contribute to sentence verification and question answering. Whether the fan effect is detected in a particular study, however, depends on factors that require and permit people to adopt a strategy of direct retrieval. When plausibility judgments are substituted for direct retrieval, the fan effect is reduced or eliminated (cf. Myers, O'Brien, Balota, & Toyofuku, 1984).

Differences Between Fact Retrieval and Question Answering

The fact retrieval paradigm consists of a highly specific arrangement of learning and testing sessions. The generality of fact retrieval findings may be limited by systematic differences between that paradigm and natural question answering. Several differences appear to exist. First, the rote learning of sets of facts, such as (30)–(32), does not closely resemble the comprehension of ordinary discourse. Second, most questions clearly distinguish given and new components, and the task of the answerer is to retrieve and/or compare the new component. In studies of fact retrieval, in contrast, people are expected to examine the accuracy of all of the concepts in a test fact (Anderson, 1974b, 1975, 1976). Third, when people learn facts such as **A lawyer is in the bank** and **A lawyer is in the park**, it is not clear whether they create representations of one lawyer or two. In contrast, when one encodes an ordinary message, such distinctions would virtually always be clear. These differences certainly do not invalidate Anderson's experimental findings. However, advances in the understanding of question answering will depend on the examination of relatively natural questioning tasks.

SUMMARY

The ability to answer questions is a central feature of comprehension. Question answering requires the encoding and categorization of the question, the selection of an answering strategy, the search for and comparison of the requested information, and the formulation of a response. Although this stage analysis of question answering is an over-simplification, it has facilitated the study of answering processes.

Question encoding includes the parsing of the question and the construction of its underlying propositions. Distinguishing the given and new question propositions is important, because the question typically focuses on its new component. Question categorization is based on the conceptual category that is being asked about rather than the interrogative word of a question. Both wh- and yes–no questions may be constructed for each conceptual category.

Before memory is searched for the requested information, an answering strategy must be selected. The answerer may directly retrieve requested information or judge the plausibility of the interrogated fact. Strategy selection is influenced by factors intrinsic to the question, such as its familiarity, and the degree of activation of the question concepts. Extrinsic question factors, including the test delay and the nature of the task instructions, likewise guide the choice of strategy.

To retrieve the requested information, one must first find a referent for the given question component. Frequently, people do not check the accuracy of the given idea. Then, memory is searched for the new question element. Each conceptual category is associated with unique search procedures. For example, to answer a WHY⟨event⟩ question, one follows backward consequence links from the given question proposition to related propositions.

Formulating the response to a question is influenced by a variety of pragmatic factors. For example, some questions, such as **Can you open the window?** have the speech act of a request, and do not demand an answer at all. Because of the constraints of politeness, one would not answer **Did John eat a hot dog?** with a simple "yes" or "no." Rather, one adds additional relevant information, such as **No, he had a hamburger**.

Sentence verification models address the coordination of answering

processes, and particularly emphasize the process of comparing retrieved information with the question. A relatively small set of verification principles have been applied to the analysis of a range of verification and answering tasks. There are individual differences among the
strategies people use to verify sentences.

Fact retrieval time varies with the number of links between a test fact
and other concepts. This outcome is called the fan effect. However,
people can focus memory search on an interrogated category, in which
case answer time varies with the fan of the relevant category only. When
plausibility judgments are substituted for the direct retrieval of facts,
the fan effect disappears. Although there are systematic differences
between fact retrieval and natural question answering, the fact retrieval
paradigm has helped to identify the role of spreading activation in
question answering.

10

Natural Language Understanding by Computers—and People

Can a machine understand human language? A generation ago, this would have been regarded as an absurd question. Today, it would likely evoke a variety of answers from different people. At one end of the scale, one might object that even the most sophisticated computer could never be capable of such a complex mental feat (see Turing, 1963 for a landmark discussion). At the other extreme, a person might, naively perhaps, take it for granted that computers already understand language. After all, we are regularly bombarded with fictional human–computer dialogues, in contexts ranging from science fiction novels to an award-winning TV commercial in which a person discusses with a computer the supposedly insoluble question of whether "chunky soup" should be eaten with a spoon or a fork. Where exactly does the truth lie?

A different approach to the issue is to ask why would one want to program a computer to understand English or another natural language. In what follows, the practical and theoretical answers to this question are briefly considered.

Practical and Theoretical Advantages of Machine Understanding

Programming a computer typically requires knowledge of technical *computer languages*. Sequences (1) and (2) provide example of sequences of computer statements in the languages PAL and PASCAL, respectively.

249

(1) CLA CLL; TAD 1124; CMA; IAC; TAD 318; DCA 218
(2) BIRTHYEAR:=1973; THISYEAR:=1993; AGE:=THISYEAR −
     BIRTHYEAR

Each of these sequences instructs the computer to subtract one number from another in order to compute and store someone's age. It is apparent that PASCAL bears more similarity to English than does PAL. In spite of this, programming even in PASCAL requires knowledge of the conventions of an artificial language. If computers understood natural language, then it would be possible to instruct the computer with the sequence, **What is the difference between this year and Roger's year of birth?** Better still, one could simply ask the computer, **How old is Roger?** Similarly, when frustrated by a computerized bank teller, one might type the question **Why can't I charge my water bill to my savings account?** and receive a sensible answer.

Computer understanding would also permit computers to translate one human language into another. For human experts, translation is painstaking and expensive. Computer scientists in the 1950s expected that machine translation could be accomplished simply by equipping computers with the dictionaries of the languages in question. As discussed in chapter 1, this endeavor resulted in nonsensical and amusing outcomes, such as the translation of the English, **hydrolic ram,** to the Vietnamese, **water buffalo.** Researchers eventually realized that computer translation was impossible without understanding on the part of the computer.

One of the main themes of this book is that language understanding requires many levels of analysis, including the lexical, syntactic, referential, and semantic. By performing these analyses, the understander extracts the surface, text base, and situation representations underlying the message. This explains the enormity of the task of developing a computer capable of understanding natural language: That is, the computer system would need to be capable of all of those levels of analysis and representation performed by the human understander.

Computer understanding is of *theoretical significance* to psychologists and other scientists because the very creation of an understanding system requires a theory of language comprehension. In the computer understanding system, the theory is expressed as a running computer program, and so "performs the task it explains" (Newell & Simon, 1972, p. 10). In the study of language processes within the framework of cognitive science, there is an intimate relationship between psychology and computer science. That relationship is emphasized throughout this chapter.

Early Approaches to Computer Understanding

The failure of early machine translation projects influenced computer scientists to adopt new approaches to the creation of understanding systems. One strategy was to create programs that focused on one particular level of language analysis. Alternatively, programs were designed to function in a limited domain, such as the understanding of algebra word problems (Bobrow, 1968), or the discussion of children's building blocks (Winograd, 1972). This approach resulted in programs that ranged in ability from virtually no understanding to an impressive degree of understanding.

Consider the dialogue in Table 10.1 between the ELIZA simulation of a psychotherapist (capital letters), and a human user (lowercase letters) (Weizenbaum, 1968):

Although the computer bluffs its way through the conversation in convincing fashion, the program consists of little more than canned sentence frames that permit the computer to reflect the comments of the patient. Thus, the computer may insert the word unhappy into a frame such as **Do you think coming here will help you not be** _____. Likewise, it may repeat the phrase, **Your boyfriend made you come here.** However, these operations require no understanding of terms such as unhappy and boyfriend. Indeed, if the patient told the computer, **He says I'm gnurf much of the time,** the computer would likely respond, **I AM SORRY TO HEAR YOU ARE GNURF.**

Greater understanding was exhibited by programs constructed to function in a specific domain, using a very limited subset of English (e.g., Bobrow, 1968; Raphael, 1968). The program, STUDENT (Bobrow, 1968), communicated in the domain of algebra word problems. From

TABLE 10.1
Conversation with ELIZA (Computer statements in capitals)

Men are all alike.
IN WHAT WAY
They're always bugging us about something or other.
CAN YOU THINK OF A SPECIFIC EXAMPLE
Well, my boyfriend made me come here.
YOUR BOYFRIEND MADE YOU COME HERE
He says I'm depressed much of the time.
I AM SORRY TO HEAR YOU ARE DEPRESSED
It's true. I am unhappy.
DO YOU THINK COMING HERE WILL HELP YOU NOT BE UNHAPPY
I need some help, that much seems certain.
WHAT WOULD IT MEAN TO YOU IF YOU GOT SOME HELP

Source: Weizenbaum, 1968, pp. 172–173.

the few grammatical constructions that it was equipped to recognize, it extracted information pertinent to algebra problems, such as distances, rates, and times. However, it ignored all else. Upon solving the problem, it reported the solution in English. Although extremely limited as an understander, STUDENT did construct and manipulate a model of the "algebra situation" underlying a message.

The SHRDLU system of Winograd (1972) represented a quantum advance in this field. SHRDLU exhibited impressive capabilities of comprehension and production, in a world of children's building blocks. Table 10.2 illustrates some of the features of the system.

Consider a few of the features of the SHRDLU system. Sequence 1 of Table 10.2 indicates that SHRDLU includes a representation of the meaning of TABLE and BLOCK. Sequence 7 provides an example of pronoun resolution. Sequence 10 reveals that SHRDLU maintains a representation of its goals and the paths used to achieve them. Underlying these functions was a system of many programs that performed analyses of word meaning, syntax, semantics, answer production, and deduction. In spite of being restricted to the blocks world, SHRDLU demonstrated that computer understanding would have to be

TABLE 10.2
Conversation with SHRDLU (Computer statements in capitals)

---

1. Can the table pick up blocks?
    NO
2. Can a pyramid support a pyramid?
    I DON'T KNOW
3. Will you please stack up both of the red blocks and either a green cube or a
    pyramid?
    OK
4. Which cube is sitting on the table?
    THE LARGE GREEN ONE WHICH SUPPORTS THE RED PYRAMID
5. Is there a large block behind a pyramid?
    YES, THREE OF THEM: A LARGE RED ONE, A LARGE GREEN CUBE AND THE
    BLUE ONE
6. Put a small one onto the green cube which supports a pyramid.
    OK
7. Put the littlest pyramid on top of it.
    OK
8. Had you touched any pyramid before you put the green one on the little cube?
    YES, THE GREEN ONE
9. When did you pick it up?
    WHILE I WAS STACKING UP THE RED CUBE, A LARGE RED BLOCK AND A
    LARGE GREEN CUBE
10. Why?
    TO GET RID OF IT

Source: Winograd, 1972. Reprinted by permission.

approached by means of detailed analyses of each facet of language and meaning.

The SHRDLU system may be alternately viewed as the culmination of the first generation of computer understanding systems, or as an accomplishment that identified essential strategies for current investigators. The next section of this chapter addresses the relationship between computer models and psychological theories of understanding. Then, several recent computer understanding systems are discussed.

THE ROLE OF COMPUTER MODELS OF LANGUAGE PROCESSES

Computer Simulation of Cognitive Processes

Although machine understanding has numerous practical advantages, it is another matter to pinpoint its relevance for psychological theory. Computer simulation is pertinent to theories about all mental processing, including language processes. In general, we may think of a theory as a set of mutually consistent rules or laws that explain a set of phenomena. Ideally, the theory is parsimonious: That is, it explains many observations with few rules. We are used to seeing scientific laws being expressed in a formal way. For example, mathematical formulas are used to express physical laws, such as $force = mass \times acceleration$.

Computer languages provide scientists, regardless of discipline, with a new and powerful formal device for describing scientific rules. Beginning in the 1950s, psychologists have written computer programs that capture the essence of models of human problem solving (e.g., Newell, Shaw & Simon, 1958), learning (e.g., Feigenbaum, 1963), and language processes. When this approach is used, the resulting program *is* the theory (Quillian, 1967; Newell & Simon, 1972). Analogously, a set of mathematic rules, such as the ones that Kepler described to predict the motion of the planets of our solar system, can constitute a theory of a phenomenon.

As mentioned earlier, when a psychological theory is expressed as a computer program, the program performs the very task that it explains (Newell & Simon, 1972). This has important implications for the evaluation of computer simulations of cognitive processes. In particular, it is possible to directly compare the output of the program with the performance of human subjects. For example, a simulation program that solves chess or logic problems ought to approach a solution by a route similar to human problem solvers (Newell & Simon, 1972). The program should also be similar to people in the errors that it exhibits, such as the generation of a losing chess move. The same is true of the simulation of language processing. In a positive vein, the language comprehension program should resemble people in such tasks as recall and summarization. However, the program, like humans, should also experience problems in understanding ambiguous sentences, and should reflect the difficulty of processing a particularly complex passage.

It is possible to equip a simulation model with rules that capture a particular information processing principle. For example, evidence that people often immediately interpret the text they are reading (see chapter 3) prompted the incorporation of rules of immediate interpretation in the READER simulation of human reading (Just & Carpenter, 1987, pp. 269-270; Thibadeau et al., 1982). Likewise, the detection of systematic deviations between the performance of a simulation model and human behavior suggests the adjustment of the theory underlying the simulation (Simon & Newell, 1971, p. 146).

Advantages of Computer Simulation

Theorists have identified many benefits of the computer simulation approach to constructing psychological theories. First, and perhaps most important, it requires writing a computer program that will run. Even the most minute programming error, such as a misplaced comma, can cause a program to "crash." Therefore, the programmer must take into account every feature of the task to be simulated, be it solving chess problems, or understanding language. The result is a model that addresses rather than ignores supposedly minor considerations.

For example, a computer simulation of pronoun resolution would have to express the effects of the factors that guide this process, such as recency, number, gender, and the relevant situation. The program would also have to capture the interactions among these factors. The resulting program would be expected to identify the correct referent of all or most of the pronouns in a message. In contrast, a more traditional, qualitative explanation might mainly consist of a list of the factors believed to guide pronoun resolution (see Johnson-Laird, 1983, p. 6 for a discussion).

A second advantage of simulation modeling is that it may alert the theorist to the weaknesses of a traditional approach. At the time that Winograd (1972) created the SHRDLU system, most linguists endorsed the generative and transformational grammar proposed by Chomsky (1957, 1965). Winograd reported that transformational grammars posed distinct difficulties for the computer analysis of sentences that, like all written and spoken messages, consisted of a string of words presented in a definite order. Therefore, Winograd based SHRDLU's syntactic analysis on *systemic grammar* (Halliday, 1967, 1970), which was more suitable for the parsing of sequential strings of words.

Third, to create simulations of cognitive processes, the researcher must become aware of concepts and principles of computer science, many of which provide useful ways of analyzing human information processing. For example, artificial intelligence approaches to problem solving identified an inventory of problem solving mechanisms, some of which had relevance for a theory of human problem solving (Newell & Simon, 1972)

Finally, one might imagine that thinking through, or "hand simulating," a set of formal rules would provide the same information as programming the rules on a computer. However, because a computer can execute millions of operations per second, computer simulation can reveal ramifications of the theory that cannot otherwise be detected (e.g., Simon, 1975). In particular, only by computer simulation can it be shown whether a set of rules will result in the correct interpretation of an ambiguous sentence, the accurate resolution of a pronoun, or the determination of the intended speech act of an utterance.

Computer Simulation and Artificial Intelligence

Many computer programs solve problems, learn, or understand natural language without functioning as cognitive simulations. To serve as a cognitive simulation, a program must embody processes and representations that resemble human ones (Newell & Simon, 1972; Simon & Newell, 1971). For example, a simulation of language processes might include a small-capacity working memory buffer (e.g., Miller & Kintsch, 1980), or simulate the processing strategy of immediate interpretation (Thibadeau et al., 1982). In contrast, intelligent programs that rely primarily on the extraordinary speed and infallible memory of the computer are examples of *artificial intelligence* but not of cognitive simulation.

COMPUTER SIMULATIONS OF LANGUAGE PROCESSES

This section describes three computer simulations of language processes. Although each presents an influential theory, the three were selected primarily because they help to familiarize the reader with some of the details of simulation modeling, and to indicate the range of problems that have been addressed using this technique. The present treatment is not a technical one. The technical methods of artificial intelligence and computer simulation receive detailed treatment elsewhere (e.g., Winston, 1984).

The models surveyed here share several features. First, each generally focuses on one or a few levels of language analysis. Second, for those levels that are not the main thrust of a model, the investigators wisely borrow from existing theory, perhaps making some modifications. For example, the READER model (Thibadeau et al., 1982) uses the conceptual dependency analysis (Schank, 1972) to represent within-sentence relations. Third, in some cases, a particular level of analysis does not appear at all in a model. For example, the coherence graph model (Kintsch & van Dijk, 1978; Miller & Kintsch, 1980) includes no parser. This was bypassed by presenting the model with a list of propositions underlying a text, rather than the text itself.

Two of the three models share another characteristic—they do not converse with the user. This may strike us as puzzling. In what sense can we say that a machine understands language if it cannot converse? The answer is that the capacity of the program to construct a representation of the text base and situation model underlying a message is more important than the ability to "speak." After all, the ELIZA simulation of a psychotherapist could converse, but it was not an interesting example of machine understanding. The inability of a simulation model to converse reflects the choice of the theorist not to invest the time and effort to equip the system with a language production component. The following simulations are shown to represent text meaning, and to extract testable predictions from their processes and resulting representations. These predictions concern people's reading speed and their ability to recall different parts of a message.

Simulating the Processes of Reading

Reading time provides an on-line index of the processes of text understanding. As discussed in chapter 5, reading time can be measured for different text units, such as individual words, phrases, or complete sentences. Then, regression analysis is used to assess the impact of language variables on reading time (e.g., Haberlandt & Graesser, 1985; Just & Carpenter, 1980; Kieras, 1981a; Thibadeau et al., 1982). Studies of this sort have shown that reading time is influenced by variables at many levels of language analysis, including the word, sentence, and text; as well as by the layout of the text. These effects reflect the fact that comprehension requires the construction of several levels of representation.

A computer simulation of reading processes was presented by Thibadeau et al. (1982) (see also Kieras, 1981a). The model, called READER, was designed to understand brief expository passages. Part of one such text, the *Flywheel* passage (Thibadeau et al., 1982), is shown here:

> Flywheels are one of the oldest mechanical devices known to man. Every internal-combustion engine contains a small flywheel that converts the jerky motion of the pistons into the smooth flow of energy that powers the drive shaft. The greater the mass of a flywheel and the faster it spins, the more energy can be stored in it.

To function as a comprehensive model of reading comprehension, READER was designed to include word-, sentence-, and text-level processes. From the analyses at these levels, READER constructs linguistic, semantic, and situation representations. The READER model takes the form known in computer science as a *production system* (Newell & Simon, 1972). A production system consists of rules that relate conditions and corresponding actions. When the conditions expressed by the left-hand side of the rule are met, then the action or actions on the right-hand side are executed.

For example, productions T1 and T2 comprise a production system that describes the operation of a thermostat set to keep the temperature of a room between 68 and 70 degrees (Newell & Simon, 1972; Young, 1973):

T1:   Temperature < 68 & Furnace $=$ off $==>$ Turn-on Furnace
T2:   Temperature > 70 & Furnace $=$ on $==>$ Turn-off Furnace

The thermostat in question consists of a simple physical mechanism, and is not under the control of a computer program. However, the production system provides a convenient way of expressing the function of the thermostat. Likewise, other production systems may be used to describe language processes.

READER includes sets of production rules for word encoding and lexical access, and for syntactic, semantic, and text-schema analysis. The following production provides an example of one of READER's syntactic rules (Just & Carpenter, 1987, p. 153).

If you see a determiner   Start a new noun phrase
    (a, the) $==>$ Expect the phrase to
                                end with a noun
                                Expect that the noun
                                may be preceded by
                                modifiers

According to this rule, the appearance of a determiner conveys information about the syntax of the current phrase. In particular, it usually signals the onset of a new noun phrase, and causes the understander to anticipate encountering modifiers and a noun.

READER analyzes a text by proceeding from one word to the next. The processing of each word occurs in *cycles*. On each cycle, the actions of all of the productions whose conditions are met are executed. The condition of a rule is met if the propositions in that condition have a high level of activation. As usual, level of activation is an index of whether a proposition occupies working memory. The effect of each action that is executed is to add or delete a proposition from memory, or to raise or lower the activation of an existing proposition.

To illustrate these functions, consider READER's hypothetical analysis of **The old man the boats**. All of READER's information, including syntactic, is expressed as propositions. Therefore, if READER is temporarily fooled by this ambiguous sentence, it will believe that the word "man" is a noun. This belief can be expressed by the proposition, (IS, "MAN", NOUN). In this event, (IS, "MAN", NOUN) would initially have a high level of activation. In contrast, (IS, "MAN", VERB) might have low activation, or not appear at all. When the interpretation that "man" is a noun eventually results in an unsuccessful parse, production rules would ideally reverse the relative activation of those two propositions, resulting in a correct reading.

Each of READER's levels of analysis represents a theory. Like SHRDLU, READER includes representations of *word meaning*. These representations take the form of semantic networks, consisting of concept nodes linked to one another by labeled relations (e.g., Quillian, 1968; see also chapter 2). READER's *parser* has some of the features of an augmented transition network (ATN) (see chapter 3). In contrast with the ATN, however, READER's parser is interactive: The syntactic analysis interacts with semantic case-role assignment. The output of the parser consists of detailed propositional networks showing the relations among the concepts of the discourse. These networks are called *conceptual dependency structures* (Schank, 1972).

From its lexical, syntactic, and semantic analyses, READER extracts a referential representation, one that captures the interrelations among the entities discussed by the text. This representation has some of the features of the text base and some of the features of the situation model. Finally, READER integrates the content of the text into a schema, called MECHANISM. MECHANISM represents the functioning of either technological or biological devices, such as a flywheel. Like all schemata, MECHANISM includes slots, such as NAME, GOAL, and EXEMPLARS. On the basis of the *Flywheel* passage presented earlier, the following assignments would be made: NAME = FLYWHEEL; GOAL = THE FLYWHEEL'S GOAL IS TO STORE ENERGY; EXEMPLAR = ONE EX-EMPLAR OF A FLYWHEEL IS THE CAR-ENGINE FLYWHEEL (Just & Carpenter, 1987, p. 255). The instantiated MECHANISM schema forms part of the situation model extracted by READER.

READER embodies the principle of immediacy, which states that each level of language analysis is pursued as far as possible upon the appearance of each word (Just & Carpenter, 1980; see chapter 3). There-fore, the number of processing cycles that READER needs to process a word is a function of the processing demands of each level of analysis. For example, at the level of lexical access, the meanings of less frequent words have lower initial activation levels (Morton, 1969). Therefore, more cycles are needed to raise an infrequent meaning to its level of acceptance. Likewise, it should require more cycles to parse a syntacti-cally ambiguous sentence, such as **They are fighting dragons**, than an unambiguous one.

READER's number of processing cycles per word provides the basis for predicting people's reading time for that word. The correlation be-tween these two measures is about .85 (Just & Carpenter, 1987; Thiba-deau et al., 1982). Although this is a high value, it can largely be ac-counted for by word-length and word-frequency effects (Carrithers & Bever, 1984; Just & Carpenter, 1987). This raises some questions about the value of the numerous other details of the model.

One might also be tempted to criticize the inability of READER to converse. However, this simply reflects the decision of Thibadeau et al. (1982) not to include question answering and language production components in the model. Rather, a model such as READER might be evaluated with reference to (a) the generality of its processing principles, such as immediacy; (b) its ability to extract the different levels of repre-sentation of a text; and (c) the predictions that it generates about people's reading time, summarization, paraphrasing, and question answering (see Just & Carpenter, 1987). It will take several years to use these criteria to make a thorough comparison between READER and competing mod-els. In spite of this, READER provides an instructive example of the simulation of language processes.

The Coherence Graph Model

Elsewhere in this book, we have examined the proposal that understand-ers extract two ordered, hierarchical networks of propositions from the messages that they encounter, namely, the microstructure and the macrostructure (Kintsch, 1974; Kintsch et al., 1975; Kintsch & van Dijk, 1978). The coherence graph model (Kintsch & van Dijk, 1978; Kintsch

& Vipond, 1979) refined the assumptions about the processes that contribute to the construction of these networks, and about the resulting representations. Miller and Kintsch (1980) subsequently simulated the microprocesses of the model. The simulation had the merits of automating certain features of the model, of making the theory more precise, and of facilitating the evaluation of the model.

The Microprocesses of the Coherence Graph Model.   According to the coherence graph model, a reader analyzes a text in cycles, examining a single chunk of text on each cycle. Chunk boundaries typically coincide with major clause boundaries or with the end of a sentence. Parsing each chunk provides a list of micropropositions, whose order coincides with their appearance in the text. A coherent text base is constructed from these propositions. In the framework of the coherence graph model, coherence is defined strictly on the basis of argument overlap between the current proposition and propositions already in the network. In particular, a proposition is connected at the highest possible level of the existing network, to a proposition with which it shares an argument. This definition of coherence ignores the impact of situation models on discourse coherence (see chapter 5).

In view of the limited capacity of working memory, propositions from the current cycle are retained in a working memory buffer on the basis of importance (level in the hierarchy) and recency. The remaining propositions are stored in long-term memory, and have a certain probability of being retrievable at a later time. In the processing of a chunk of text, connections are initially detected only between the new propositions and those propositions in the working memory. If the propositions of a chunk of text do not overlap with those in working memory, then text propositions must be reinstated from long-term memory. If reinstatement also fails to reveal argument overlap, then the reader is assumed to draw a bridging inference to link the current propositions with the preceding material.

The Simulation.   The simulation (Miller & Kintsch, 1980) consists of one program that divides the text into chunks, and a second that performs the micropropositional analysis. (The simulation did not address macroprocessing.) Sentence boundaries always complete a chunk. In the absence of a sentence boundary, such as in a very long sentence, two principles come into play: First, it is assumed that a minimum number of words are read before a chunk is completed. Second, the choice of chunk boundaries is guided by a set of heuristic rules, such as "A chunk must have at least two propositions" (Miller & Kintsch, 1980, p. 338). Following these principles, the chunking program divides the following sample text into four chunks: The chunk boundaries, designated by slashes, appear at the two sentence boundaries, and after the word, *life*.

> In the request to canonize the "Frontier Priest," John Newmann, bishop of Philadelphia in the 19th century, two miracles were attributed to him in this century./ In 1923, Eva Benassi, dying from peritonitis, dramatically recovered after her nurse prayed to the bishop./ In 1949 Kent Lenahan, hospitalized with two skull fractures, smashed bones, and a pierced lung after a traffic accident, rose from his deathbed and resumed a normal life/ after his mother prayed ardently to John Newmann. (Miller & Kintsch, 1980, p. 337)

The second program, which performs the micropropositional analysis, extracts the text base of the message. On each processing cycle, the next chunk of propositions, as identified by the chunking program, is examined. These functions are outlined for two processing cycles in Fig. 10.1

At the beginning of processing (Cycle 1), the working memory, or short-term memory (STM), buffer is empty, and propositions P1-P9 are received as input. The working memory buffer was treated as having a capacity of two propositions. On the first cycle, a theme proposition must be selected to occupy level 1 of the network. In the absence of a detailed theory of theme, Miller and Kintsch (1980) designated proposition 1, (REQUEST, P2, P8), as the level 1 proposition. Then, a network is built by linking each successive proposition to the highest proposition with which it either shares an argument or in which it is embedded (see Fig. 10.1). For example, because P2 is embedded in P1, P2 appears at level 2 in the network. Sometimes, propositions have to be temporarily put "on hold" until they can be connected. For example, P3 could not be linked to P1 or P2, but was later linked to P8.

At the end of Cycle 1, important and recent propositions are selected for retention in working memory by "start(ing) with the top proposition . . . and pick(ing) up all the propositions along the graph's lower edge" (Kintsch & van Dijk, 1978, p. 379). Because the working memory capacity is two propositions, applying this rule results in the selection of propositions P1 and P2. However, due to the embedding of P8 in P1, and P7 in P8, propositions P8 and P7 are also retained in working memory. Four propositions may be retained because of the *flexible size* of the working memory buffer (Miller & Kintsch, 1980).

Cycle 2 of processing for the *Frontier-Priest* text is interesting. There is no argument overlap between the second chunk of propositions, P10-P15, and the contents of working memory. An ensuing search of long-

```
Input for Cycle 1:

        (P1 (REQUEST P2 P8))
        (P2 (CANONIZE P3))
        (P3 (ISA JOHN-NEWMANN FRONTIER-PRIEST))
        (P4 (ISA JOHN-NEWMANN BISHOP))
        (P5 (LOC:IN P4 PHILADELPHIA))
        (P6 (TIME:IN P4 19TH-CENTURY))
        (P7 (TWO MIRACLES))
        (P8 (ATTRIBUTED P7 JOHN-NEWMANN))
        (P9 (TIME:IN P8 THIS-CENTURY))

Build a graph with Proposition P1 at Level 1.
Put P2 at Level 2, pointed to by P1.
Put P8 at Level 2, pointed to by P1.
Put P9 at Level 2, pointed to by P1.
Put P3 at Level 3, pointed to by P8.
Put P4 at Level 3, pointed to by P8.
Put P7 at Level 3, pointed to by P8.
Put P5 at Level 4, pointed to by P4.
Put P6 at Level 4, pointed to by P4.

Apply the leading edge strategy.

This is Cycle 1: STM is expanded to 3 slots for
    this cycle only.

Retain Proposition P1 at Level 1.
    Proposition P2 is embedded in P1: retain
        Proposition P2 at Level 2.
    Proposition P3 is embedded in P2: retain
        Proposition P3 at Level 3.
    Proposition P8 is embedded in P1: retain
        Proposition P8 at Level 2.
    Proposition P7 is embedded in P8: retain
        Proposition P7 at Level 3.

The buffer is currently overloaded by more than
one proposition.  The embedded Proposition P3
must be deleted to remove the overload.  At the
end of Cycle 1, STM contains:

                              (continued)
```

FIG. 10.1. Cycles 1 and 2 of the analysis of the "John Newmann" passage performed by the micropropositional component of the simulation of the coherence graph model. According to the "leading edge strategy," important and recent propositions are retained in short-term memory (STM) for the next processing cycle. *Source:* Adapted from Miller & Kintsch, 1980, Appendix, pp. 353-354. Adapted by permission.

term memory leads to the reinstatement of P4, and hence to the construction of the working memory graph for Cycle 2. At the end of Cycle 2, propositions P13, P14, and P15 are held over in working memory for Cycle 3 (see Miller & Kintsch, 1980, Appendix for further details).

The most notable achievement of the coherence graph model is that it predicts the probability of recall of the individual propositions in the message, predictions that have a good level of accuracy (e.g., Kintsch &

```
Level 1:
    P1 points to (P2 P8)
    Level 2:
        P2 points to nothing.
        P8 points to P7
        Level 3:
            P7 points to nothing.

Input for Cycle 2:
    (P10 (TIME:IN P11 1923))
    (P11 (DYING EVA-BENASSI PERITONITIS))
    (P12 (DRAMATICALLY P13))
    (P13 (RECOVERED EVA-BENASSI))
    (P14 (AFTER P15 P13))
    (P15 (PRAYED NURSE BISHOP))

Add the Cycle 2 propositions to memory.

Propositions (P10 P11 P12 P13 P14 P15) cannot
    be added to STM: Search LTM for a new
    starting proposition.
The LTM search succeeded:  P4 can be reinstated
    via P15.
Bump P4's cycle counter.
Nothing from INPUTSET was placed, but the
    LTM search succeeded: P4 was found.
This counts as a reinstatement search.

Build a graph with Proposition P13 at Level 1.
Put P11 at Level 2, pointed to by P13.
Put P12 at Level 2, pointed to by P13.
Put P14 at Level 2, pointed to by P13.
Put P15 at Level 3, pointed to by P14.
Put P10 at Level 3, pointed to by P11.
Put P4 at Level 4, pointed to by P15.

    Apply the leading edge strategy.

    Retain Proposition P13 at Level 1.
    Retain Proposition P14 at Level 2.
        Proposition P15 is embedded in P14: retain
        Proposition P15 at Level 3.

    The buffer is stretched to one more than its set
    size = 3.  At the end of Cycle 2, STM contains:

Level 1:
    P13 points to P14
    Level 2:
        P14 points to P15
        Level 3:
            P15 points to nothing.
```

van Dijk, 1978; Miller & Kintsch, 1980; Singer, 1982; Vipond, 1980). This is accomplished as follows: First, the simulation specifies, in a well-defined way, the number of processing cycles during which each proposition remains in working memory. Second, the retrievability of a text proposition is assumed to be a function of its number of cycles in working memory. The success of the coherence graph model may be partly due to the rich interconnections of high level propositions, a characteristic that is a good predictor of recall (e.g., Graesser, Robertson, et al., 1980).

The simulation also determines the number of long-term memory reinstatement searches and of bridging inferences that are needed to construct the microstructure. Because both reinstatement (Lesgold et al., 1979; McKoon & Ratcliff, 1980b; O'Brien, Duffy, & Myers, 1986) and bridging (e.g., Haviland & Clark, 1974; Yekovich, Walker & Blackman, 1979) are time-consuming mental operations, the number of these operations contribute to the model's predictions of reading time and text difficulty (Kintsch & Vipond, 1979; Miller & Kintsch, 1980).

Like READER, the coherence graph model simulation does not converse with the user. Yet it is not difficult to see the implications of the model for language production. For example, the model could report "what it remembered" from a text by selecting those propositions with high retrieval probabilities, and omitting the others. Applying the same technique to the text *macropropositions* (not part of Miller and Kintsch's simulation) would result in a summary of the text (Kintsch & van Dijk, 1978).

The coherence graph model bypassed numerous levels of language processing. First, it included no parser. Second, like Kieras' (1981a) simulation, word meaning was not represented. In this regard, although the model could determine that two propositions shared an argument, such as BISHOP, it had no idea of what a bishop was. Third, the model included no higher-order schematic knowledge, which is part of the reason that Miller and Kintsch (1980) had to select the level 1 proposition on the basis of intuition. Some of these shortcomings have been addressed in more recent treatments (Kintsch, 1988; van Dijk & Kintsch, 1983, chapter 5). It is noteworthy that, despite these omissions, the simulation of the coherence graph model could test substantive hypotheses about the processes of constructing a coherent text base.

BORIS: Simulating the Role of High Level Knowledge Structures in Comprehension

Like SHRDLU (Winograd, 1972), the BORIS simulation (Lehnert et al., 1983) was designed as a comprehensive language understanding system. Its goal was to understand a small number of stories in detail. BORIS includes a parser, which, like READER, generates conceptual dependency structures (Schank, 1972; Thibadeau et al., 1982). From these structures, BORIS extracts macrostructures and/or situation models. It is also able to understand complex questions, and express the answers to the questions in English. The main emphasis of this section is on the knowledge structures that contribute to the construction of the macrostructure.

Table 10.3 illustrates the achievements of BORIS with reference to an excerpt from a story BORIS has understood, plus a subsequent question–answer dialogue.

The passage and dialogue in Table 10.3 indicate that BORIS possesses impressive skills of comprehension. The text uses complicated grammatical constructions, such as **but now he had no idea where to find his old friend**. Such constructions demand a sophisticated parser. The passage also requires extensive inferential processing. For example, it is only by inference that one knows that it was Paul who sent the letter, that the bad news appeared in the letter, and that Richard was a lawyer. More complex still is the inference that identifies the significance of Paul's small salary: Namely, he could not afford a lawyer's fees.

TABLE 10.3
Sample Passage and Conversation with BORIS
(Computer statements in capitals)

Richard hadn't heard from his college roommate Paul for years. Richard had borrowed money from Paul which was never paid back, but now he had no idea where to find his old friend. When a letter arrived from San Francisco, Richard was anxious to find out how Paul was.

Unfortunately, the news was not good. Paul's wife Sarah wanted a divorce. She also wanted the car, the house, the children, and alimony. Paul wanted the divorce, but he didn't want to see Sarah walk off with everything he had. His salary from the state school system was very small. Not knowing who to turn to, he was hoping for a favor from the only lawyer he knew. Paul gave his home phone number in case Richard felt he could help.

What happened to Richard at home?
RICHARD GOT A LETTER FROM PAUL.
Who is Paul?
RICHARD'S FRIEND.
Had Paul helped Richard?
YES, PAUL LENT MONEY TO RICHARD.
Why didn't Richard pay Paul back?
RICHARD DID NOT KNOW WHERE PAUL WAS.
What was the letter about?
PAUL AND SARAH WERE GETTING A DIVORCE.
Did Paul write Sarah?
NO, IT WASN'T SARAH, IT WAS RICHARD WHO GOT THE
   LETTER.
Why did Paul write to Richard?
PAUL WANTED RICHARD TO BE HIS LAWYER.

Source: Adapted from Lehnert et al., 1983, pp.16–17. Adapted by permission.

The dialogue reveals that BORIS can answer factual questions, such as **Who is Paul?** and **Did Paul write to Sarah?** However, many of BORIS' answers suggest that it possesses intricate knowledge about abstract concepts and categories, and can use this knowledge to answer questions. BORIS understands that **What happened to Richard. . .?** asks about an event or episode. That is, the passage did not need to explicitly state, "Something happened to Richard." Likewise, when asked **Had Paul helped Richard?** BORIS refers to the loan. This indicates that BORIS recognizes the loan of money as an instance of helping.

In fact, the "divorce" story hinges on a variety of complex social conventions and obligations, such as lending, doing favors, and divorce. To permit BORIS to achieve a genuine understanding of the text, the simulation included schemata that represent people's abstract knowledge about such matters. As discussed in chapter 8, these schemata are called Memory Organization Packets, or MOPs (Lehnert et al., 1983; Schank, 1982). Although similar to scripts, MOPs represent a higher level of abstraction, and focus on the goal of a set of actions.

A central theme of the "divorce" story is Paul's loan to Richard. It is likely that, because Richard owes Paul money, Paul feels freer to ask Richard for help, and Richard feels either happy or obligated to provide advice. Therefore, the concept of BORROWING is essential to this story.

Figure 10.2a presents the MOP, M-BORROW (Lehnert et al., 1983). The MOP shows the connections between the main goals, plans, and events of borrowing, such as someone wanting an object and someone else being convinced to lend it. In the BORIS system, each of these MOP concepts is the name of a conceptual dependency network (Schank, 1972). The links among the MOP concepts represent the relations of intention (i), motivation (m), and achievement (a).

Like other types of schemata, MOPs contribute to the integration of the ideas of a message, identify concepts that may fill gaps in the message, and generate expectations that facilitate understanding (Schank, 1982, p. 84). In the course of integrating text ideas in the framework of a MOP, the understander constructs a situation model of the text.

The "divorce" story presents an obvious complication for the M-BORROW MOP. The usual resolution of borrowing is the return of the borrowed object, which in this case is the money. The story suggests, however, that rather than return the money, Richard is going to give Paul legal advice. The reason that this makes sense is a function both of the fact that Richard owes Paul money, and that they are friends. Therefore, Richard feels obligated to return the favor, which can take the form of providing free legal advice.

The relationship between borrowing and doing a favor is addressed at the bottom of Fig. 10.2a. M-BORROW is connected by a FRIENDSHIP

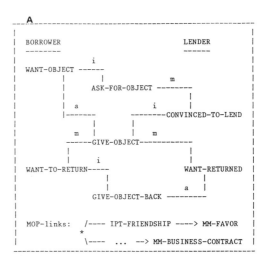

```
A ------------------------------------------------------
|                                                      |
| BORROWER                              LENDER         |
| --------                              ------         |
|                        i                             |
| WANT-OBJECT ------                                   |
|          |        |                 m                |
|          |      ASK-FOR-OBJECT --------              |
|          |        |                    |             |
|          | a                i          |             |
|          |--------        --------CONVINCED-TO-LEND  |
|          |        |        |                         |
|        m |        | m                                |
|        ------GIVE-OBJECT------------                 |
|          |                  |                        |
|          |        i         |                        |
| WANT-TO-RETURN-----         WANT-RETURNED            |
|          |                      |                    |
|          |                    a |                    |
|        GIVE-OBJECT-BACK ---------                    |
|                                                      |
| MOP-links:    /---- IPT-FRIENDSHIP ----> MM-FAVOR    |
|             *                                        |
|             \---- ... --> MM-BUSINESS-CONTRACT       |
-------------------------------------------------------
```

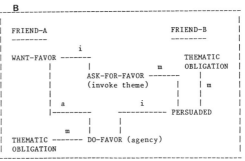

FIG. 10.2. Representations of the Borrow MOP and the Favor meta-MOP. The concepts are linked by the relations of intention (i), motivation (m), and achievement (a). *Source:* Lehnert, Dyer, Johnson, Yang, & Harley, 1983, Figures 2-1 and 2-2, pp. 25–26. Reprinted by permission.

```
B ------------------------------------------------------
|                                                      |
| FRIEND-A                          FRIEND-B           |
| --------                          --------           |
|                   i                                  |
| WANT-FAVOR -------                     THEMATIC      |
|          |        |             m      OBLIGATION    |
|          |      ASK-FOR-FAVOR -------      |         |
|          |      (invoke theme)        |   | m        |
|          | a             i            |   |  |        |
|          |--------        ----------- PERSUADED      |
|          |        |       |                          |
|        m |        |       |                          |
| THEMATIC ------- DO-FAVOR (agency)                   |
| OBLIGATION                                           |
-------------------------------------------------------
```

theme to a more abstract schema, MM-FAVOR, called a meta-MOP (Schank, 1982). MM-FAVOR is shown in more detail in Fig. 10.2b. Like a MOP, this meta-MOP characterizes the relationships among the concepts contributing to the notion of FAVOR. What is important for the present considerations is that when M-BORROW becomes inadequate to accommodate the events described in the story, there is the possibility of invoking an appropriate higher level structure.

Figure 10.2a shows that M-BORROW is also linked via the BUSINESS theme to a meta-MOP called MM-CONTRACT. As Lehnert et al. (1983) pointed out, not all instances of borrowing are favors. If your banker lends you money, it is unlikely that she would accept free legal advice from you in return.

Thus, one aspect of BORIS is that it simulates the sharing of information among a variety of high level knowledge structures. These interactions are reminiscent of the proposal in chapter 8 that story comprehension requires interactions among scripts, text schemata, and plan schemata. Although further demonstrations of the psychological distinctions among scripts, MOPs, and meta-MOPS will be needed, BORIS constitutes an important step toward clarifying how people coordinate information about the human goals, motivations, and intentions that underlie many messages.

CONCLUSIONS

A comprehensive computer understanding system would be a fascinating scientific achievement with many practical benefits. From the perspective of this book, machine understanding also carries many implications about the status of psychological theories of language processes. Simulating language use on the computer provides the theorist with a powerful formal technique for the expression and evaluation of psychological theories.

Simulation modeling has been applied to many levels of language analysis. The coherence graph model emphasized the construction of the text base and macrostructures in discourse. The ATN and connectionist models considered in chapter 3 exemplify the application of the simulation technique to parsing processes. At the other end of the continuum, Kintsch and Greeno (1985) presented a model of the construction of the situation model underlying word arithmetic problems.

Although barely a generation old, the technology of simulation models of language processing is converging, on numerous dimensions, on an accepted set of methods. First, certain formal systems, such as production systems, appear to be particularly useful for capturing the sorts of rules underlying human cognition (e.g., Lehnert et al., 1983; Thibadeau et al., 1982). Second, some categories of solutions to the problems of language processing appear to be more feasible than others. For example, there is growing agreement that human and computer language comprehension requires a left-to-right analysis of the words of a message (e.g., Lehnert et al., 1983; Thibadeau et al., 1982; Winograd, 1972). This contrasts with the approach of traditional linguistics, according to which rules are applied to complete clauses or sentences. Likewise, there is a growing consensus that computer understanding systems require the construction of several levels of representation. However, individual simulations may focus on the theory of one or more levels of language analysis.

Third, simulations of language processing can be evaluated with reference to a battery of tasks of comprehension and production, including fluent reading, recall, paraphrasing, summarizing, and question answering. The models have been created either to perform these tasks, or to generate predictions about human performance.

The interactions between psychology and computer science since 1950 carry some important lessons for the future study of language processes. Computer science provides a rich source of concepts of the processing and representation of information, which may suggest solutions to problems of human cognition. Empirical evidence about human language processes may likewise indicate the preferred plan of attack from a computer science perspective. For example, the findings that people are surprisingly limited in the extent of their elaborative inference processes was consistent with the conclusions of computer scientists that unlimited elaborative inferencing on the part of understanding systems results in an inference explosion that stymies processing.

There are some indications that the psychological and computer science solutions to problems of comprehension may be quite similar. One reason for this may be that the *problem space* (Newell & Simon, 1972) of language processing, which includes the units of language, its rules, and its legal operations, constrains the way in which language comprehension may proceed. Notwithstanding the astounding speed with which computers can execute operations, it may be that the most feasible computer science solutions to certain problems may be ones that are patterned in at least a general way after human information processing. Tentative support for this proposal comes from the preliminary success of connectionist process models (Rumelhart, McClelland, & the PDP Research Group, 1986). These models exhibit extensive parallel and interactive processing, both of which characteristics are presumed to reflect the activities of the human nervous system.

SUMMARY

Early attempts to create machine translation systems failed, alerting computer scientists to the difficulty of programming a computer to understand natural language. Consequently, researchers wrote programs that addressed different subproblems of language processing. These early efforts culminated in the SHRDLU system (Winograd, 1972), which exhibited understanding about the domain of children's building blocks, by integrating the functions of programs of syntax, semantics, reference, and deduction.

Computer understanding systems would have the practical benefit of permitting people to instruct computers without knowledge of technical computer languages. Such systems would also carry important implications for scientific investigation. In particular, a computer understanding system would express a theory of language processes. Computer models that represent human limitations are called simulations of human cognition. This approach to psychological theory has several advantages. First, it requires that the theorist address the fine detail of the task to be simulated, be it chess playing or language understanding. Second, it alerts the theorist to the shortcomings of traditional theories. Third, it requires familiarity with powerful concepts of information processing identified by computer scientists. Fourth, running the program on a high-speed computer identifies implications of the theory that cannot otherwise be detected.

Many influential theories of human language processing have been expressed as computer simulations. In general, each simulation focuses on one or several levels of text analysis, and either draws on existing theory to model other levels, or omits the other levels altogether. The ability to converse with the user is a substantive aspect of some models, but it is not a necessary feature of an understanding system. The READER model of reading processes (Thibadeau et al., 1982) consists of sets of production rules that capture the word-, sentence-, and text-level processes that contribute to discourse understanding. It generates accurate predictions of the time needed to read each word of a text, on the basis of the number of cycles of processing that it requires to analyze each word. Miller & Kintsch (1980) simulated the microprocessing component of the coherence graph model (Kintsch & van Dijk, 1978). The simulation determines the number of processing cycles during which each text proposition occupies working memory. This index is a good predictor of people's text recall. The BORIS system (Lehnert et al., 1983) achieves an in-depth understanding of stories. It includes representations of abstract schemata, including the Memory Operating Packets for complex concepts such as PARTY and BORROWING. These structures permit BORIS to coordinate information about people's goals, motivations, and intentions, and hence to answer complex questions about the story. The coordination of theory in psychology and computer science offers a fruitful path toward understanding discourse processes.

References

Abbott, V., Black, J. B., & Smith, E. E. (1985). The representation of scripts in memory. *Journal of Memory and Language, 24,* 179–199.

Adams, D. (1987). *Dirk Gently's holistic detective agency.* London: Pan Books.

Alba, J. W., Alexander, S. G., Hasher, L., & Caniglia, K. (1981). The role of context in the encoding of information. *Journal of Experimental Psychology: Human Learning and Memory, 7,* 283–292.

Anderson, J. R. (1974a). Verbatim and propositional representation of sentences in immediate and long-term memory. *Journal of Verbal Learning and Verbal Behavior, 13,* 149–162.

Anderson, J. R. (1974b). Retrieval of propositional information from long-term memory. *Cognitive Psychology, 4,* 451–474.

Anderson, J. R. (1975). Item-specific and relation-specific interference in sentence memory. *Journal of Experimental Psychology: Human Learning and Memory, 1,* 249–260.

Anderson, J. R. (1976). *Language, memory, and thought.* Hillsdale, NJ: Lawrence Erlbaum Associates.

Anderson, J. R. (1980). *Cognitive psychology and its implications.* San Francisco: W. H. Freeman.

Anderson, J. R. (1983). *The architecture of cognition.* Cambridge, MA: Harvard University Press.

Anderson, J. R., & Bower, G. H. (1973). *Human associative memory.* Washington, DC: Winston.

Anderson, J. R., & Paulson, R. (1977). Representation and retention of verbal information. *Journal of Verbal Learning and Verbal Behavior, 16,* 439–451.

Anderson, J. R., & Pirolli, P. L. (1984). Spread of activitation. *Journal of Experimental Psychology: Learning, Memory, and Cognition, 10,* 791–798.

Anderson, R. C., & Pichert, J. W. (1978). Recall of previously unrecallable information following a shift in perspective. *Journal of Verbal Learning and Verbal Behavior, 17,* 1–12.

Anderson, R. C., Pichert, J. W., Goetz, E. T., Schallert, D. L., Stevens, K. V., & Trollip,

S. R. (1976). Instantiation of general terms. *Journal of Verbal Learning and Verbal Behavior, 15,* 667–679.

Anderson, R. C., Reynolds, R. E., Schallert, D. L., & Goetz, E. T. (1976, July). *Frameworks for comprehending discourse* (Tech. Rep. No. 12). Laboratory for Cognitive Studies in Education, University of Illinois, Urbana-Champaign, IL.

Anderson, R. C., Spiro, R. J., & Anderson, M. C. (1978). Schemata as scaffolding for the representation of information in connected discourse. *American Education Research Journal, 15,* 433–440.

Asimov, I. (1986). *Foundation and earth.* New York: Ballentine.

Au, T. K. (1986). A verb is worth a thousand words: The causes and consequences of interpersonal events implicit in language. *Journal of Memory and Language, 25,* 104–122.

Auble, P., & Franks, J. J. (1983). Sentence comprehension processes. *Journal of Verbal Learning and Verbal Behavior, 22,* 395–405.

Auel, J. M. (1982). *The valley of horses.* New York: Bantam.

Austin, J. L. (1962). *How to do things with words.* Oxford: Oxford University Press.

Baars, E. J. (1986). *The cognitive revolution in psychology.* New York: Guilford.

Baggett, P. (1986, November). *Learning procedures from interactive videodisc versus passive video.* Paper presented at the annual meeting of the Psychonomic Society, New Orleans.

Bahrick, H. P., Bahrick, P. O., & Wittlinger, R. P. (1975). Fifty years of memory for names and faces: A cross-sectional approach. *Journal of Experimental Psychology: General, 104,* 54–75.

Baker, L. (1978). Processing temporal relationships in simple stories: Effects of input sequence. *Journal of Verbal Learning and Verbal Behavior, 17,* 559–572.

Barsalou, L. W., & Sewell, D. R. (1985). Contrasting the representation of scripts and categories. *Journal of Memory and Language, 24,* 646–665.

Bartlett, F. C. (1932). *Remembering.* Cambridge, England: Cambridge University Press.

Bates, E., Kintsch, W., Fletcher, C. R., & Giuliani, V. (1980). The role of pronominalization and ellipsis in texts: Some memory experiments. *Journal of Experimental Psychology: Human Learning and Memory, 6,* 676–691.

Bates, E., Masling, M., & Kintsch, W. (1978). Recognition memory for aspects of dialogue. *Journal of Experimental Psychology: Human Learning and Memory, 3,* 187–197.

Belmore, S. M. (1981). Age-related changes in processing explicit and implicit language. *Journal of Gerontology, 36,* 316–322.

Belmore, S. M., Yates, J. M., Bellack, D. R., Jones, S. N., & Rosenquist, S. E. (1982). Drawing inferences from concrete and abstract sentences. *Journal of Verbal Learning and Verbal Behavior, 21,* 338–351.

Bever, T. G. (1970). The cognitive basis for linguistic structures. In J. R. Hayes (Ed.), *Cognition and the development of language.* New York: Wiley.

Bierwisch, M. (1970). Semantics. In J. Lyons (Ed.), *New horizons in linguistics* (pp. 166–184). Baltimore, MD: Penguin.

Bisanz, G. L., Laporte, R. E., Vesonder, G. T., & Voss, J. F. (1978). On the representation of prose: New dimensions. *Journal of Verbal Learning and Verbal Behavior, 17,* 337–357.

Black, J. B., & Bern, H. (1981). Causal inference and memory for events in narratives. *Journal of Verbal Learning and Verbal Behavior, 20,* 267–275.

Black, J. B., & Bower, G. H. (1980). Story understanding as problem-solving. *Poetics, 9,* 223–250.

Bloomfield, L. (1933). *Language.* New York: Holt.

Blumenthal, A. L. (1966). Observations with self-embedded sentences. *Psychonomic Science, 6*, 453–454.

Blumenthal, A. L., & Boakes, R. (1967). Prompted recall of sentences: A further study. *Journal of Verbal Learning and Verbal Behavior, 6*, 674–676.

Bobrow, D. G. (1968). Natural language input for a computer problem-solving system. In M. Minsky (Ed.), *Semantic information processing* (pp. 146–226). Cambridge, MA: M.I.T. Press.

Bobrow, D. G., & Norman, D. A. (1975). Some principles of memory schemata. In D. Bobrow & A. Collins (Eds.), *Representation and meaning.* New York: Academic Press.

Bock, J. K. & Brewer, W. F. (1974). Reconstructive recall in sentences with alternative surface structures. *Journal of Experimental Psychology, 103*, 837–843.

Bock, M. (1980). Some effects of titles on building and recalling text structures. *Discourse Processes, 3*, 301–311.

Borland, R., & Flammer, A. (1985). Encoding and retrieval processes in memory for prose. *Discourse Processes, 8*, 305–317.

Bower, G. H. (1972). Mental imagery and associative learning. In L. Gregg (Ed.), *Cognition in learning and memory.* New York: Wiley.

Bower, G. H. (1976). Experiments on story understanding and recall. *Quarterly Journal of Experimental Psychology, 28*, 511–534.

Bower, G. H., Black, J. B., & Turner, T. J. (1979). Scripts in memory for text. *Cognitive Psychology, 11*, 177–220.

Bracewell, R. J., Frederiksen, C. H., & Frederiksen, J. D. (1982). Cognitive processes in composing and comprehending discourse. *Educational Psychologist, 17*, 146–164.

Bradley, D. C., & Forster, K. I. (1987). A reader's view of listening. *Cognition, 25*, 103–134.

Braine, M. D. S., & Wells, R. S. (1978). Case-like categories in children: The actor and some related categories. *Cognitive Psychology, 10*, 100–122.

Bransford, J. D., Barclay, J. R., & Franks, J. J. (1972). Semantic memory: A constructive versus interpretive approach. *Cognitive Psychology, 3*, 193–209.

Bransford, J. D., & Franks, J. J. (1971). The abstraction of linguistic ideas. *Cognitive Psychology, 2*, 331–350.

Bransford, J. D., & Johnson, M. K. (1972). Contextual prerequisites for understanding: Some investigations of comprehension and recall. *Journal of Verbal Learning and Verbal Behavior, 11*, 717–726.

Bransford, J. D., & Johnson, M. K. (1973). Considerations of some problems of comprehension. In W. Chase (Ed.), *Visual information processing.* New York: Academic Press.

Brewer, W. F. (1975). Memory for ideas: Synonym substitution. *Memory & Cognition, 3*, 458–464.

Brewer, W. F., & Dupree, D. A. (1983). Use of plan schema in the recall and recognition of goal-directed actions. *Journal of Experimental Psychology: Learning, Memory, and Cognition, 9*, 117–129.

Brewer, W. F., & Lichtenstein, E. H. (1981). Event schemas, story schemas, and story grammars. In J. Long & A. Baddeley (Eds.), *Attention and performance*, IX. Hillsdale, NJ: Lawrence Erlbaum Associates.

Britton, B. K., Holdredge, T. S., Curry, C., & Westbrook, R. D. (1979). Use of cognitive capacity in reading identical texts with different amounts of discourse level meaning. *Journal of Experimental Psychology: Human Learning and Memory, 5*, 262–270.

Britton, B. K., Meyer, B. J., Hodge, M. H., & Glynn, S. M. (1980). Effects of the organization of text on memory: Tests of retrieval and response criterion hypotheses. *Journal of Experimental Psychology: Human Learning and Memory, 6*, 620–629.

Britton, B. K., Meyer, B. J., Simpson, R., Holdredge, T. S., & Curry, C. (1979). Effects of the organization of text on memory: Tests of two implications of a selective attention hypothesis. *Journal of Experimental Psychology: Human Learning and Memory, 5,* 496–506.

Broadbent, D. E. (1958). *Perception and communication.* New York: Pergamon Press.

Brooks, L. R. (1968). Spatial and verbal components of the act of recall. *Canadian Journal of Psychology, 22,* 349–367.

Brown, A. L., & Day, J. D. (1983). Macrorules for summarizing texts: The development of expertise. *Journal of Verbal Learning and Verbal Behavior, 22,* 1–14.

Brown, A. L., & Smiley, S. S. (1977). Rating the importance of structural units of prose passages: A problem of metacognitive development. *Child Development, 48,* 1–8.

Bulgeski, B. R. (1968). Images as mediators in one-trial paired-associate learning. II: Self-timing in successive lists. *Journal of Experimental Psychology, 77,* 328–334.

Camp. C. J., Lachman, J. L., & Lachman, R. (1980). Evidence for direct-access and inferential retrieval in question–answering. *Journal of Verbal Learning and Verbal Behavior, 19,* 583–596.

Caplan, D. (1972). Clause boundaries and recognition latencies for words in sentences. *Perception and Psychophysics, 12,* 73–76.

Caramazza, A., Grober, E., Garvey, C., & Yates, J. (1977). Comprehension of anaphoric pronouns. *Journal of Verbal Learning and Verbal Behavior, 16,* 601–609.

Carbonnell, J. Q. Jr. (1978). Politics: Automated ideological reasoning. *Cognitive Science, 2,* 27–51.

Carpenter, P. A., & Just, M. A. (1975). Sentence comprehension: A psycholinguistic model of verification. *Psychological Review, 82,* 45–73.

Carpenter, P. A., & Just, M. A. (1977). Reading comprehension as eyes see it. In M. Just and P. Carpenter (Eds.), *Cognitive processes in comprehension.* Hillsdale, NJ: Lawrence Erlbaum Associates.

Carpenter, P. A., & Just, M. A. (1983). What your eyes do while your mind is reading. In K. Rayner (Ed.), *Eye movements in reading: Perceptual and language processes.* New York: Academic Press.

Carrithers, C., & Bever, T. G. (1984). Eye-fixation patterns during reading confirm theories of language comprehension. *Cognitive Science, 8,* 157–172.

Carroll, J. M. (1978). Sentence perception units and levels of syntactic structure. *Perception & Psychophysics, 23,* 506–514.

Carroll, L. (1960). *Alice in Wonderland and other favourites.* New York: Washington Square Press.

Chafe, W. L. (1970). *Meaning and the structure of language.* Chicago: University of Chicago Press.

Charniak, E. (1975, June). Organization and inference in a frame-like system of common sense knowledge. In R. Schank & B. Nash-Webber (Eds.), *Theoretical issues in natural language processing.* An interdisciplinary workshop, Massachusetts Institute of Technology, Cambridge, MA.

Chase, W. G., & Simon, H. A. (1973). Perception in chess. *Cognitive Psychology, 4,* 55–81.

Chomsky, N. (1957). *Syntactic structures.* The Hague: Mouton.

Chomsky, N. (1965). *Aspects of the theory of syntax.* Cambridge: M.I.T.

Christie, A. (1967). *Destination unknown.* London: Fontana Books.

Cirilo, R. K. (1981). Referential coherence and text structure in story comprehension. *Journal of Verbal Learning and Verbal Behavior, 20,* 358–367.

Cirilo, R. K., & Foss, D. J. (1980). Text structure and reading time for sentences. *Journal of Verbal Learning and Verbal Behavior, 19,* 96–109.

Clark, H. H. (1969). Linguistic processes in deductive reasoning. *Psychological Review*, 76, 387–404.

Clark, H. H. (1977). Inferences in comprehension. In D. LaBerge & S. J. Samuels (Eds.), *Perception and comprehension*. Hillsdale, NJ: Lawrence Erlbaum Associates.

Clark, H. H. (1982). Making sense of nonce sense. In G. Flores d'Arcais & R. Jarvella (Eds.), *The process of language understanding*. New York: Wiley.

Clark, H. H., & Chase, W. G. (1972). On the process of comparing sentences against pictures. *Cognitive Psychology*, 3, 472–517.

Clark, H. H., & Clark, E. V. (1977). *Psychology and language*. New York: Harcourt Brace Jovanovich.

Clark, H. H., & Haviland, S. E. (1977). Comprehension and the given–new contract. In R. Freedle (Ed.), *Discourse production and comprehension*. Hillsdale, NJ: Lawrence Erlbaum Associates.

Clark, H. H., & Marshall, C. R. (1981). Definite reference and mutual knowledge. In A. Joshi, B. Webber, & I. Sag (Eds.), *Elements of discourse understanding*. Cambridge: Cambridge University Press.

Clark, H. H., & Schunk, D. (1980). Polite responses to polite requests. *Cognition*, 8, 111–143.

Clark, H. H., & Sengul, C. J. (1979). In search of referents for nouns and pronouns. *Memory & Cognition*, 7, 33–41.

Clifton, C. Jr., Frazier, L., & Connine, C. (1984). Lexical expectations in sentence comprehension. *Journal of Verbal Learning and Verbal Behavior*, 23, 696–708.

Cohen, G. (1979). Language comprehension in old age. *Cognitive Psychology*, 11, 412–429.

Collins, A., Brown, J. S., & Larkin, K. M. (1980). Inference understanding. In R. Spiro, B. Bruce, & B. Brewer (Eds.), *Theoretical issues in reading comprehension*. Hillsdale, NJ: Lawrence Erlbaum Associates.

Conrad, F. G., & Rips, L. J. (1986). Conceptual combination and the given/new distinction. *Journal of Memory and Language*, 25, 255–278.

Cooper, L. A., & Shepard, R. N. (1973). Chronometric studies of the rotation of mental images. In W. Chase (Ed.), *Visual information processing*. New York: Academic Press.

Corbett, A. T. (1984). Prenominal adjectives and the disambiguation of anaphoric nouns. *Journal of Verbal Learning and Verbal Behavior*, 23, 683–695.

Corbett, A. T., & Chang, F. R. (1983). Pronoun disambiguation: Accessing potential antecedents. *Memory & Cognition*, 11, 283–294.

Corbett, A. T., & Dosher, B. A. (1978). Instrument inferences in sentence encoding. *Journal of Verbal Learning and Verbal Behavior*, 17, 479–492.

Craik, F. I. M. (1981). Encoding and retrieval effects in human memory: A partial review. In J. Long & A. Baddeley (Eds.), *Attention and performance*, IX. Hillsdale, NJ: Lawrence Erlbaum Associates.

Craik, F. I. M., & Byrd, M. (1981). Aging and cognitive deficits: The role of attentional processes. In F. Craik & S. Trehub (Eds.), *Aging and cognitive processes*. New York: Plenum.

Craik, F. I. M., & Lockhart, R. S. (1972). Levels of processing: A framework for memory research. *Journal of Verbal Learning and Verbal Behavior*, 11, 671–684.

Craik, F. I. M., & Simon, E. (1980). Age differences in memory: The role of attention and depth of processing. In L. Poon, J. Fozard, L. Cermak, D. Arenberg, & W. Thompson (Eds.), *New directions in memory and aging*. Hillsdale, NJ: Lawrence Erlbaum Associates.

Craik, F. I. M., & Watkins M. J. (1973). The role of rehearsal in short term memory. *Journal of Verbal Learning and Verbal Behavior*, 12, 599–607.

Crain, S., & Steedman, M. (1985). On not being led up the garden path: The use of context by the psychological syntax processor. In D. Dowty, L. Karttunen, & A. Zwicky (Eds.), *Natural language parsing: Psychological, computational and theoretical perspectives.* Cambridge, England: Cambridge University Press.

Crowder, R. G. (1982). *The psychology of reading: An introduction.* New York: Oxford University Press.

Cutler, A., & Fodor, J. A. (1979). Semantic focus and sentence comprehension. *Cognition, 7,* 49–59.

Danks, J. H. (1986). Identifying component processes in text comprehension: Comment on Haberlandt and Graesser. *Journal of Experimental Psychology: General, 115,* 193–197.

Dixon, P. (1982). Plans and written directions for complex tasks. *Journal of Verbal Learning and Verbal Behavior, 21,* 70–84.

Dixon, R. A., Hultsch, D. F., Simon, E. W., & von Eye, A. (1984). Verbal ability and text structure effects on adult age differences in text recall. *Journal of Verbal Learning and Verbal Behavior, 23,* 569–578.

Dooling, D. J., & Lachman, R. (1971). Effects of comprehension on retention of prose. *Journal of Experimental Psychology, 88,* 216–222.

Dosher, B. A., & Corbett, A. T. (1982). Instrument inferences and verb schemata. *Memory & Cognition, 10,* 531–539.

Downey, D. M. (1979). *The role of motivational inferences in story comprehension.* Unpublished manuscript, Department of Communication Disorders and Speech Science, University of Colorado, Boulder.

Eamon, D. B. (1977, May). *Thematization of concepts in a four-term series problem.* Paper presented at the annual meeting of the Midwestern Psychological Association, Chicago.

Eamon, D. B. (1978–79). Selection and recall of topical information in prose by better and poorer readers. *Reading Research Quarterly, 14,* 244–257.

Ebbinghaus, H. (1885). *Uber das gedachtnis: Untersuchungen zur experimentellen psychologie.* Leipzig: Duncker and Humboldt. (Translated by H. A. Ruger & C. E. Bussenius, 1913, and reissued by Dover Publications, 1964.)

Ehrlich, K. (1980). The comprehension of pronouns. *Quarterly Journal of Experimental Psychology, 32,* 247–256.

Ehrlich, K., & Johnson-Laird, P. N. (1982). Spatial descriptions and referential continuity. *Journal of Verbal Learning and Verbal Behavior, 21,* 296–306.

Ehrlich, K., & Rayner, K. (1983). Pronoun assignment and semantic integration during reading: Eye movements and immediacy of processing. *Journal of Verbal Learning and Verbal Behavior, 22,* 75–87.

Erickson, T. D., & Mattson, M. E. (1981). From words to meaning: A semantic illusion. *Journal of Verbal Learning and Verbal Behavior, 20,* 540–551.

The Fate of the Sun. (1987, March 23). *Time,* p. 65.

Ferreira, F., & Clifton, C. Jr. (1986). The role of context in resolving syntactic ambiguity. *Journal of Memory and Language, 25,* 348–368.

Feigenbaum, E. A. (1963). The simulation of verbal learning behavior. In E. A. Feigenbaum & J. Feldman (Eds.), *Computers and thought* (pp. 297–309). New York: McGraw-Hill.

Feigenbaum, E. A., & McCorduck, P. (1984). *The fifth generation: Artificial intelligence and Japan's computer challenge to the world.* New York: NAL.

Fillmore, C. J. (1968). The case for case. In E. Bach & R. T. Harms (Eds.), *Universals of linguistic theory.* New York: Holt, Rinehart and Winston.

Fletcher, C. R. (1984). Markedness and topic continuity and discourse processing. *Journal of Verbal Learning and Verbal Behavior, 23,* 487–493.

Fodor, J. A. (1983). *The modularity of mind.* Cambridge, MA: M.I.T. Press.

Fodor, J. A., & Bever, T. G. (1965). The psychological reality of linguistic segments. *Journal of Verbal Learning and Verbal Behavior, 4,* 414–420.

Fodor, J. A., Bever, T. G., & Garrett, M. F. (1974). *The psychology of language: An introduction to psycholinguistics and generative grammar.* Toronto: McGraw-Hill.

Fodor, J. A., & Garrett, M. F. (1967). Some syntactic determinants of sentential complexity. *Perception and Psychophysics, 2,* 289–296.

Fodor, J. A., Garrett, M. F., Walker, E. C., & Parkes, C. H. (1980). Against definition. *Cognition, 8,* 263–367.

Forster, K. I. (1979). Levels of processing and the structure of the language processor. In W. Cooper & E. Walker (Eds.), *Sentence processing: Psychological studies presented to Merrill Garrett.* Hillsdale, NJ: Lawrence Erlbaum Associates.

Frazier, L., & Fodor, J. D. (1978). The sausage machine: A new two-stage parsing model. *Cognition, 6,* 291–325.

Frazier, L., & Rayner, K. (1982). Making and correcting errors during sentence comprehension: Eye movements in the analysis of structurally ambiguous sentences. *Cognitive Psychology, 14,* 178–210.

Frederiksen, C. H. (1975). Acquisition of semantic information from discourse: Effects of repeated exposures. *Journal of Verbal Learning and Verbal Behavior, 14,* 158–169.

Frederiksen, C. H. (1985). Cognitive models and discourse analysis. In C. Cooper & S. Greenbaum (Eds.), *Written communication annual. Volume I: Linguistic approaches to the study of written discourse.* Beverly Hills, CA: Sage.

Frederiksen, J. R. (1981). Understanding anaphora: Rules used by readers in assigning pronominal referents. *Discourse Processes, 4,* 323–347.

Frege, G. (1892). Uber Sinn und Bedeutung. *Zeitschrift fur Philosophie und Philosophische Kritik, 100,* 20–25. Translated in P. T. Geach and M. Black (Eds.) (1952). *Philosophical writings of Gottlob Frege.* Oxford: Blackwell.

Galambos, J. A., & Black, J. B. (1985). Using knowledge of activities to understand and answer questions. In A. Graesser & J. Black (Eds.), *The psychology of questions.* Hillsdale, NJ: Lawrence Erlbaum Associates.

Galambos, J. A., & Rips, L. J. (1982). Memory for routines. *Journal of Verbal Learning and Verbal Behavior, 21,* 260–281.

Garnham, A. (1982). Testing psychological theories about inference making. *Memory & Cognition, 10,* 341–349.

Garrett, M. F., Bever, T. G., & Fodor, J. A. (1966). The active use of grammar in speech perception. *Perception and Psychophysics, 1,* 30–32.

Garrod, S., & Sanford, A. (1977). Interpreting anaphoric relations: The integration of semantic information while reading. *Journal of Verbal Learning and Verbal Behavior, 16,* 77–90.

Gee, J. P., & Grosjean, F. (1984). Empirical evidence for narrative structure. *Cognitive Science, 8,* 59–85.

Gentner, D., & Collins, A. (1981). Studies of inference from lack of knowledge. *Memory & Cognition, 9,* 434–443.

Gentner, D., & Grudin, J. (1985). The evolution of mental metaphors in psychology: A 90-year retrospective. *American Psychologist, 40,* 181–192.

Gernsbacher, M. A. (1985). Surface information loss in comprehension. *Cognitive Psychology, 17,* 324–363.

Glanzer, M., Dorfman, D., & Kaplan, B. (1981). Short-term storage in the processing of text. *Journal of Verbal Learning and Verbal Behavior, 20,* 656–670.

Glanzer, M., & Ehrenreich, S. L. (1979). Structure and search of the internal lexicon. *Journal of Verbal Learning and Verbal Behavior, 18,* 381–398.

Glenn, C. G. (1978). The role of episodic structure and of story length in children's recall of simple stories. *Journal of Verbal Learning and Verbal Behavior, 17,* 229–247.

Glowalla, U., & Colonius, H. (1982). Toward a model of macrostructure search. In A. Flammer & W. Kintsch (Eds.), *Advances in psychology 8: Discourse processing* (pp. 111–123). Amsterdam: North-Holland.

Glucksberg, S., & McCloskey, M. (1981). Decisions about ignorance: Knowing that you don't know. *Journal of Experimental Psychology: Human Learning and Memory, 7,* 311–325.

Goetz, E. T. (1977, July). *Inferences in the comprehension of and memory for text* (Tech. Rep. No. 49). Center for the Study of Reading, University of Illinois at Urbana-Champaign.

Goetz, E. T. (1979). Inferring from text: Some factors influencing which inferences will be made. *Discourse Processes, 2,* 179–195.

Goldman, S. R. (1985). Inferential reasoning in and about narrative texts. In A. Graesser & J. Black (Eds.), *The psychology of questions.* Hillsdale, NJ: Lawrence Erlbaum Associates.

Gough, P. B. (1965). Grammatical transformations and speed of understanding. *Journal of Verbal Learning and Verbal Behavior, 4,* 107–111.

Gough, P. B. (1966). The verification of sentences: The effects of delay of evidence and sentence length. *Journal of Verbal Learning and Verbal Behavior, 5,* 492–496.

Graesser, A. C., & Clark, L. F. (1985). *Structure and procedures of implicit knowledge.* Norwood, NJ: Ablex.

Graesser, A. C., Gordon, G. E., & Sawyer, J. D. (1979). Recognition memory for typical and atypical actions in scripted activities: Tests of a script pointer + tag hypothesis. *Journal of Verbal Learning and Verbal Behavior, 18,* 319–332.

Graesser, A. C., Haberlandt, K. F. & Koizumi, D. (1987). How is reading time influenced by knowledge-based inferences and world knowledge? In B. Britton & S. M. Glynn (Eds.), *Executive control processes in reading.* Hillsdale, NJ: Lawrence Erlbaum Associates.

Graesser, A. C., Higgenbotham, M. W., Robertson, S. P., & Smith, W. R. (1978). A natural inquiry into the National Enquirer: Self-induced versus task-induced reading comprehension. *Discourse Processes, 1,* 355–372.

Graesser, A. C., Hoffman, N. L., & Clark, L. F. (1980). Structural components of reading time. *Journal of Verbal Learning and Verbal Behavior, 19,* 135–151.

Graesser, A. C., Koizumi, D., Vamos, G., & Elofson, C. S. (1985). A model of question answering. In *Proceedings of the seventh annual conference of the Cognitive Science Society* (288–292). Hillsdale, NJ: Lawrence Erlbaum Associates.

Graesser, A. C., & Murachver, T. (1985). Symbolic procedures of question answering. In A. Graesser & J. Black, *The psychology of questions.* Hillsdale, NJ: Lawrence Erlbaum Associates.

Graesser, A. C., Robertson, S. P., & Anderson, P. A. (1981). Incorporating inferences in narrative representations: A study of how and why. *Cognitive Psychology, 13,* 1–26.

Graesser, A. C., Robertson, S. P., Lovelace, E. R., & Swinehart, D. M. (1980). Answers to why-questions expose the organization of story plot and predict recall of actions. *Journal of Verbal Learning and Verbal Behavior, 19,* 110–119.

Graf, R., & Torrey, J. W. (1966). Perception of phrase structure in written language. In *American Psychological Association Convention Proceedings* (pp. 83–84).

Greenberg, J. H. (1963). Some universals of grammar with particular reference to the order of meaningful elements. In J. H. Greenberg (Ed.), *Universals of language*. (58–90) Cambridge, MA: M.I.T. Press.

Grice, H. P. (1957). Meaning. *Philosophical Review, 66*, 377–88. Reprinted in Steinberg & Jakobovits (1971), 53–59.

Grice, H. P. (1975). William James Lectures, Harvard University, 1967. Published in part as "Logic and conversation." In P. Cole & J. L. Morgan (Eds.), *Syntax and Semantics*, Vol. III: *Speech acts* (pp. 41–58). New York: Seminar Press.

Guilford, J. P., Fruchter, B., & Zimmerman, W. S. (1952). Factor analysis of the Army Air Force's battery of experimental aptitude tests. *Psychometrika, 17*, 45–68.

Guindon, R., & Kintsch, W. (1984). Priming macropropositions: Evidence for the primacy of macropropositions in the memory for text. *Journal of Verbal Learning and Verbal Behavior, 23*, 508–518.

Haberlandt, K. F., Berian, C., & Sandson, J. (1980). The episode schema in story processing. *Journal of Verbal Learning and Verbal Behavior, 19*, 635–650.

Haberlandt, K., & Bingham, G. (1984). The effect of input direction on the processing of script statements. *Journal of Verbal Learning and Verbal Behavior, 23*, 162–177.

Haberlandt, K. F., & Graesser, A. C. (1985). Component processes in text comprehension and some of their interactions. *Journal of Experimental Psychology: General, 114*, 357–374.

Haberlandt, K. F., Graesser, A. C., Schneider, N. J., & Kiely, J. (1986). Effects of task and new arguments on word reading times. *Journal of Memory and Language, 25*, 314–322.

Halliday, M. A. K. (1967). Notes on transitivity and theme in English, (Part 2). *Journal of Linguistics, 3*, 177–244.

Halliday, M. A. K. (1970). Language structure and language function. In J. Lyons (Ed.), *New horizons in linguistics*. Harmondsworth: Penguin.

Halliday, M. A. K., & Hasan, R. (1976). *Cohesion in English*. London: Longman.

Harris, R. J. (1973). Answering questions containing marked and unmarked adjectives and adverbs. *Journal of Experimental Psychology, 97*, 399–401.

Harris, R. J. (1974). Memory and comprehension of implications and inferences of complex sentences. *Journal of Verbal Learning and Verbal Behavior, 13*, 626–637.

Harris, R. J., & Monaco, G. E. (1978). The psychology of pragmatic implication: Information processing between the lines. *Journal of Experimental Psychology: General, 107*, 1–22.

Hart, J. T. (1967). Memory and the memory-monitoring process. *Journal of Verbal Learning and Verbal Behavior, 6*, 685–691.

Hasher, L., & Griffin, M. (1978). Reconstructive and reproductive processes in memory. *Journal of Experimental Psychology: Human Learning and Memory, 4*, 318–330.

Haviland, S. E., & Clark, H. H. (1974). What's new? Acquiring new information as a process in comprehension. *Journal of Verbal Learning and Verbal Behavior, 13*, 512–521.

Hayes, J. R., & Simon, H. A. (1974). Understanding written problem instructions. In L. Gregg (Ed.), *Knowledge and cognition* (pp. 167–200). Hillsdale, NJ: Lawrence Erlbaum Associates.

Hayes-Roth, B., & Hayes-Roth, F. (1977). The prominence of lexical information in memory representations of meaning. *Journal of Verbal Learning and Verbal Behavior, 16*, 119–136.

Hayes-Roth, B., & Thorndyke, P. W. (1979). Integration of knowledge from text. *Journal of Verbal Learning and Verbal Behavior, 18*, 91–108.

Hebb, D. O. (1949). *The organization of behavior*. New York: Wiley.

Herriot, P. (1969). The comprehension of active and passive sentences as a function of pragmatic expectations. *Journal of Verbal Learning and Verbal Behavior, 8,* 166–169.

Hidi, S., & Baird, W. (1986). Interestingness—A neglected variable in discourse processing. *Cognitive Science, 10,* 179–194.

Hobbs, J. R. (1979). Coherence and coreference. *Cognitive Science, 3,* 67–90.

Hockett, C. F. (1958). *A course in modern linguistics.* New York: Macmillan.

Hornby, P. A. (1972). The psychological subject and predicate. *Cognitive Psychology, 3,* 632–642.

Hornby, P. A. (1974). Surface structure and presupposition. *Journal of Verbal Learning and Verbal Behavior, 13,* 530–538.

Hunt, E. B. (1978). Mechanics of verbal ability. *Psychological Review, 85,* 109–130.

Jarvella, R. J. (1971). Syntactic processing of connected speech. *Journal of Verbal Learning and Verbal Behavior, 10,* 409–416.

Jarvella, R. J. (1979). Immediate memory and discourse processing. In G. H. Bower (Ed.), *The psychology of learning and motivation* (Vol. 13). New York: Academic Press.

Johnson, M. K., Bransford, J. D., & Solomon, S. K. (1973). Memory for tacit implications of sentences. *Journal of Experimental Psychology, 98,* 203–205.

Johnson, W., & Kieras, D. (1983). Representation—saving effects of prior knowledge in memory for simple prose. *Memory & Cognition, 11,* 456–486.

Johnson-Laird, P. N. (1980). Mental models in cognitive science. *Cognitive Science, 4,* 71–116.

Johnson-Laird, P. N. (1983). *Mental models.* Cambridge, MA: Harvard University Press.

Just, M. A., & Carpenter, P. A. (1978). Inference processes during reading: Reflections from eye fixations. In J. W. Senders & R. A. Monty (Eds.), *Eye movements and the higher psychological functions.* Hillsdale, NJ: Lawrence Erlbaum Associates.

Just, M. A., & Carpenter, P. A. (1980). A theory of reading: From eye fixations to comprehension. *Psychological Review, 87,* 329–354.

Just, M. A., & Carpenter, P. A. (1984). Reading skills and skilled reading in the comprehension of text. In H. Mandl, N. Stein, & T. Trabasso (Eds.), *Learning and comprehension of text.* Hillsdale, NJ: Lawrence Erlbaum Associates.

Just, M. A., & Carpenter, P. A. (1987). *The psychology of reading and language comprehension.* (pp. 261–272) Newton, MA: Allyn and Bacon.

Just, M. A., Carpenter, P. A., & Woolley, J. D. (1982). Paradigms and processes in reading comprehension. *Journal of Experimental Psychology: General, 111,* 228–238.

Kahneman, D. (1973). *Attention and effort.* Englewood Cliffs, NJ: Prentice-Hall.

Kaplan, R. M. (1972). Augmented transition networks as psychological models of sentence comprehension. *Artificial Intelligence, 3,* 77–100.

Katz, J. J., & Fodor, J. A. (1963). The structure of a semantic theory. *Language, 39,* 170–210.

Keenan, J. M. (1978). Psychological issues concerning comprehension: Comments on "Psychology of pragmatic implication. Information between the lines" by Harris and Monaco. *Journal of Experimental Psychology: General, 107,* 23–27.

Keenan, J. M., Baillet, S. D., & Brown, P. (1984). The effects of causal cohesion on comprehension and memory. *Journal of Verbal Learning and Verbal Behavior, 23,* 115–126.

Keenan, J. M., MacWhinney, B., & Mayhew, D. (1977). Pragmatics in memory: A study of natural conversation. *Journal of Verbal Learning and Verbal Behavior, 16,* 549–560.

Kemper, S. (1982). Filling in the missing links. *Journal of Verbal Learning and Verbal Behavior, 21,* 99–107.

Kieras, D. E. (1978). Good and bad structure in simple paragraphs: Effects on apparent theme, reading time, and recall. *Journal of Verbal Learning and Verbal Behavior, 17,* 13–28.

Kieras, D. E. (1980). Initial mention as a signal to thematic content in technical passages. *Memory & Cognition, 8,* 345–353.

Kieras, D. E. (1981a). Component processes in the comprehension of simple prose. *Journal of Verbal Learning and Verbal Behavior, 20,* 1–23.

Kieras, D. E. (1981b). Topicalization effects in cued recall of technical prose. *Memory & Cognition, 9,* 541–549.

Kieras, D. E. (1981c). The role of major referents and sentence topics in the construction of passage macrostructure. *Discourse Processes, 4,* 1–15.

Kimball, J. (1973). Seven principles of surface structure parsing in natural language. *Cognition, 2,* 15–47.

King, D. R. W., & Anderson, J. R. (1976). Long term memory search: An intersecting activation process. *Journal of Verbal Learning and Verbal Behavior, 15,* 587–605.

Kintsch, W. (1972). Notes on structure of semantic memory. In E. Tulving & W. Donaldson (Eds.), *Organization of memory.* New York: Academic Press.

Kintsch, W. (1974). *The representation of meaning in memory.* Hillsdale, NJ: Lawrence Erlbaum Associates.

Kintsch, W. (1977). On comprehending stories. In M. Just & P. Carpenter (Eds.), *Cognitive processes in comprehension.* Hillsdale, NJ: Lawrence Erlbaum Associates.

Kintsch, W. (1980). Learning from text, levels of comprehension, or: Why would anyone read a story anyway. *Poetics, 9,* 7–98.

Kintsch, W. (1988). The role of knowledge in discourse comprehension: A construction–integration model. *Psychological Review, 95,* 163–182.

Kintsch, W., & Bates, E. (1977). Recognition memory for statements from a classroom lecture. *Journal of Experimental Psychology: Human Learning and Memory, 3,* 150–159.

Kintsch, W., & Greeno, J. G. (1985). Understanding and solving word arithmetic problems. *Psychological Review, 92,* 109–129.

Kintsch, W., & Keenan, J. (1973). Reading rate and retention as a function of the number of propositions in the base structure of sentences. *Cognitive Psychology, 5,* 257–274.

Kintsch, W., Kozminsky, E., Streby, W. J., McKoon, G., & Keenan, J. M. (1975). Comprehension and recall of text as a function of context variable. *Journal of Verbal Learning and Verbal Behavior, 14,* 158–169.

Kintsch, W., & van Dijk, T. A. (1978). Toward a model of text comprehension and production. *Psychological Review, 85,* 363–394.

Kintsch, W., & Vipond, D. (1979), Reading comprehension and readability in educational practice and psychological theory. In L. G. Nilsson (Ed.), *Perspectives on memory research.* Hillsdale, NJ: Lawrence Erlbaum Associates.

Kintsch, W., & Young, S. R. (1984). Selective recall of decision-relevant information from texts. *Memory & Cognition, 12,* 112–117.

Kolodner, J. L. (1983). Reconstructive memory: A computer model. *Cognitive Science, 7,* 281–328.

Kozminsky, E. (1977). Altering comprehension: The effect of biasing titles on text comprehension. *Memory & Cognition, 5,* 482–490.

Kucera, H., & Francis, W. N. (1967). *Computational analysis of present-day English.* Providence, RI: Brown University Press.

Ladefoged, P. (1967). *Three areas of experimental phonetics.* London: Oxford University Press.

Lashley, K. S. (1951). The problem of serial order in behavior. In L. A. Jeffress (Ed.), *Cerebral mechanisms in behavior: The Hixon Symposium.* New York: Wiley.

Lehnert, W. (1977). Human computational question answering. *Cognitive Science, 1*, 47–73.

Lehnert, W. G. (1978). *The process of question answering.* Hillsdale, NJ: Lawrence Erlbaum Associates.

Lehnert, W. G., Dyer, M. G., Johnson, P. N., Yang, C. J., & Harley, S. (1983). Boris—An experiment in in-depth understanding of narratives. *Artificial Intelligence, 20*, 15–62.

Lesgold, A. M., Roth, S. F., & Curtis, M. E. (1979). Foregrounding effects in discourse comprehension. *Journal of Verbal Learning and Verbal Behavior, 18*, 291–308.

Lichtenstein, E. H., & Brewer, W. F. (1980). Memory for goal-directed events. *Cognitive Psychology, 12*, 412–445.

Light, L. L., & Anderson, P. A. (1983). Memory for scripts in young and older adults. *Memory & Cognition, 11*, 435–444.

Lindsay, P. H., & Norman, D. A. (1972). *Human information processing: An introduction to psychology.* New York: Academic Press.

Loftus, E. F. (1975). Leading questions and the eyewitness report. *Cognitive Psychology, 7*, 560–572.

Loftus, E. F., & Palmer, J. C. (1974). Reconstruction of automobile destruction: An example of the interaction between language and memory. *Journal of Verbal Learning and Verbal Behavior, 13*, 585–589.

Loftus, E. F., & Zanni, G. (1975). Eyewitness testimony: The influence of the wording of a question. *Bulletin of the Psychonomic Society, 5*, 86–88.

Lorch, R. F. Jr., Lorch, E. P., & Matthews, P. D. (1985). On-line processing of the topic structure of a task. *Journal of Memory and Language, 24*, 350–362.

Lorch, R. F. Jr., Lorch, E. P., & Morgan, A. M. (1987). Task effects and individual differences in on-line processing of the topic structure of a text. *Discourse Processes, 10*, 63–80.

Lyons, J. (1968). *Introduction to theoretical linguistics.* Cambridge, England: Cambridge University Press.

Lyons, J. (1977). *Semantics,* Vol. 2. Cambridge: Cambridge University Press.

MacLeod, C. M., Hunt, E. B., & Mathews, N. N. (1978). Individual differences in the verification of sentence picture relationships. *Journal of Verbal Learning and Verbal Behavior, 17*, 493–507.

MacNamara, J. T. (1987). [Review of *Language development in the pre-school years*]. *Canadian Psychology, 28*, 304–305.

Malt, B. C. (1985). The role of discourse structure in understanding anaphora. *Journal of Memory and Language, 24*, 271–289.

Mandler, J. M. (1987). On the psychological reality of story structure. *Discourse Processes, 10*, 1–29.

Mandler, J. M., & Johnson, N. S. (1977). Remembrance of things parsed: Story structure and recall. *Cognitive Psychology, 9*, 111–151.

Mandler, J. M., & Murachver, T. (1985, November). *Script activation and lexical processing.* Presented at the annual meeting of the Psychonomic Society, Boston.

Mani, K., & Johnson-Laird, P. N. (1982). The mental representation of spatial descriptions. *Memory & Cognition, 10*, 181–187.

Marcus, M. P. (1980). *A theory of syntactic recognition for natural language.* Cambridge, MA: M.I.T. press.

Masson, M. E. J. (1984, November). *Priming work identification with rapidly presented sentences.* Paper presented at the annual meeting of the Psychonomic Society, San Antonio.

Mathews, N. N., Hunt, E. B., & MacLeod, C. M. (1980). Strategy choice and strategy training in sentence-picture comparison. *Journal of Verbal Learning and Verbal Behavior, 19*, 531–548.

Matthews, A., & Chodorow, M. S. (1988). Pronoun resolution in two-clause sentences: Effects of ambiguity, antecedent location, and depth of embedding. *Journal of Memory and Language, 27,* 245–260.

Mayer, R. E., & Cook, L. K. (1981). Effects of shadowing on prose comprehension. *Memory & Cognition, 9,* 101–109.

McClelland, J. L., & Kawamoto, A. H. (1986). Mechanics of sentence processing: Assigning roles to constituents. In D. E. Rumelhart & J. L. McClelland and the PDP Research Group (Eds.), *Parallel distributed processing: Explorations in the microstructure of cognition,* Vol. 1. Cambridge, MA: M.I.T. Press.

McClelland, J. L., Rumelhart, D. E., & Hinton, G. E. (1986). The appeal of parallel distributed processing. In D. E. Rumelhart, J. L. McClelland & the PDP Research Group (Eds.), *Parallel distributed processing: Explorations in the microstructure of cognition,* Vol. 1. Cambridge, MA: M.I.T. Press.

McCloskey, M. & Bigler, K. (1980). Focused memory search in fact retrieval. *Memory & Cognition, 8,* 253–264.

McConkie, G. W., & Rayner, K. (1975). The span of the effective stimulus during a fixation in reading. *Perception and Psychophysics, 17,* 578–586.

McKoon, G. (1977). Organization of information in text. *Journal of Verbal Learning and Verbal Behavior, 16,* 247–260.

McKoon, G., & Ratcliff, R. (1980a). Priming in item recognition: The organization of propositions in memory for text. *Journal of Verbal Learning and Verbal Behavior, 19,* 369–386.

McKoon, G., & Ratcliff, R. (1980b). The comprehension processes and memory structures involved in anaphoric reference. *Journal of Verbal Learning and Verbal Behavior, 19,* 668–682.

McKoon, G., & Ratcliff, R. (1986). Inferences about predictable events. *Journal of Experimental Psychology: Learning, Memory, and Cognition, 12,* 82–91.

McMahon, L. E. (1963). *Grammatical analysis as part of understanding a sentence.* Unpublished doctoral dissertation, Harvard University.

Meyer, B. J. F. (1975). *The organization of prose and its effects on memory.* Amsterdam: North-Holland Publishing.

Meyer, D. E., & Schvaneveldt, R. W. (1971). Facilitation in recognizing pairs of words: Evidence of a dependence between retrieval operations. *Journal of Experimental Psychology, 90,* 227–234.

Miller, G. A. (1956). The magical number seven, plus or minus two. Some limits on our capacity for processing information. *Psychological Review, 63,* 81–97.

Miller, G. A. (1981). *Language and speech.* San Francisco: W. H. Freeman.

Miller, G. A., & Isard, S. (1963). Some perceptual consequences of linguistic rules. *Journal of Verbal Learning and Verbal Behavior, 2,* 217–228.

Miller, G. A., & McKean, K. O. (1964). A chronometric study of some relations between sentences. *Quarterly Journal of Experimental Psychology, 16,* 297–308.

Miller, J. R. (1980). *The role of knowledge and text structure in prose comprehension.* Unpublished manuscript, Department of Psychology, University of Colorado, Boulder.

Miller, J. R. (1985). A knowledge-based model of prose comprehension: Applications to expository texts. In B. K. Britton & J. B. Black (Eds.), *Understanding expository text: A theoretical and practical handbook for analyzing explanatory text* (pp. 199–226). Hillsdale, NJ: Lawrence Erlbaum Associates.

Miller, J. R., & Kintsch, W. (1980). Readability and recall of short prose passages: A theoretical analysis. *Journal of Experimental Psychology: Human Learning and Memory, 6,* 335–354.

Minsky, M. (1975). A framework for representing knowledge. In P. Winston (Ed.), *The psychology of computer vision.* New York: McGraw-Hill.

Mitchell, D. C., & Holmes, V. M. (1985). The role of specific information about the verb in parsing sentences with local structural ambiguity. *Journal of Memory and Language, 24,* 542–559.

Morris, C. D., Bransford, J. D., & Franks, J. J. (1977). Levels of processing versus transfer appropriate training. *Journal of Verbal Learning and Verbal Behavior, 16,* 519–534.

Morrow, D. G. (1985). Prominent characters and events organize narrative understanding. *Journal of Memory and Language, 24,* 304–319.

Morrow, D. G., Greenspan, S. L., & Bower, G. H. (1987). Accessibility and situation models in narrative comprehension. *Journal of Memory and Language, 26,* 165–187.

Morton, J. (1969). Interaction of information in word recognition. *Psychological Review, 76,* 165–178.

Murphy, G. L. (1985). Processes of understanding anaphora. *Journal of Memory and Language, 24,* 290–303.

Myers, J. L., O'Brien, E. J., Balota, D. A., & Toyofuku, M. L. (1984). Memory search without interference: The role of integration. *Cognitive Psychology, 16,* 217–242.

Nakamura, G. V., Graesser, A. C., Zimmerman, J. A., & Rhia, J. (1985). Script processing in a natural situation. *Memory & Cognition, 13,* 140–144.

Neely, J. H. (1977). Semantic priming and retrieval from lexical memory: Roles of inhibitionless spreading activation and limited-capacity attention. *Journal of Experimental Psychology: General, 106,* 226–254.

Neisser, U. (1976). *Cognition and reality: Principles and implication of cognitive psychology.* San Francisco: W. H. Freeman.

Nelson, T. O., Gerler, D., & Narens, L. (1984). Accuracy of feeling-of-knowing judgments for predicting perceptual identification and relearning. *Journal of Experimental Psychology: General, 113,* 282–300.

Nelson, T. O., Leonesio, R. J., Shimamura, A. P., Landwehr, R. F., & Narens, L. (1982). Overlearning and the feeling of knowing. *Journal of Experimental Psychology: Learning, Memory and Cognition, 8,* 279–288.

Nelson, T. O., & Narens, L. (1980). Norms of 300 general information questions: Accuracy of recall, latency of recall, and feeling of knowing ratings. *Journal of Verbal Learning and Verbal Behavior, 19,* 338–368.

Newell, A., & Simon, H. A. (1972). *Human problem solving.* Englewood Cliffs, NJ: Prentice Hall.

Newell, A., Shaw, J. C., & Simon, H. A. (1958). Elements of a theory of human problem solving. *Psychological Review, 65,* 151–166.

Nezworski, T., Stein, N. L., & Trabasso, T. (1982). Story structure versus content in children's recall. *Journal of Verbal Learning and Verbal Behavior, 21,* 196–206.

Norman, D. A. (1973). Memory, knowledge, and the answering of questions. In R. Solso (Ed.), *Contemporary Issues in Cognitive Psychology: The Loyola Symposium.* Washington DC: V. H. Winston.

Norman, D. A., & Bobrow, D. G. (1975). On data-limited and resource limited processes. *Cognitive Psychology, 7,* 44–64.

Norman, D. A., & Rumelhart, D. E. (1975). *Explorations in cognition.* San Francisco: W. H. Freeman.

O'Brien, E. J., Duffy, S. A., & Myers, J. L. (1986). Anaphoric inference during reading. *Journal of Experimental Psychology: Learning, Memory, and Cognition, 12,* 346–352.

Offir, C. E. (1973). Recognition memory for presuppositions of relative clause sentences. *Journal of Verbal Learning and Verbal Behavior, 12,* 636–643.

Omanson, R. C. (1982). The relation between centrality and story category variation. *Journal of Verbal Learning and Verbal Behavior, 21,* 326–337.

Paivio, A. (1971). *Imagery and verbal processes.* New York: Holt, Rinehart, and Winston.

Palmer, S. E. (1977). Hierarchical structure in perceptual representation. *Cognitive Psychology, 9,* 441–474.

Paris, S. G., & Lindauer, B. K. (1976). The role of inference in children's comprehension and memory for sentences. *Cognitive Psychology, 8,* 217–227.

Perfetti, C. A., & Goldman, S. R. (1974). Thematization and sentence retrieval. *Journal of Verbal Learning and Verbal Behavior, 13,* 70–79.

Perfetti, C. A., & Goldman, S. R. (1976). Discourse memory and reading comprehension skill. *Journal of Verbal Learning and Verbal Behavior, 14,* 33–42.

Perrig, W., & Kintsch, W. (1985). Propositional and situational representations of text. *Journal of Memory and Language, 24,* 503–518.

Peterson, L. R., & Peterson, M. J. (1959). Short-term retention of individual verbal items. In D. L. Hintzman, *The psychology of learning and memory.* San Francisco: W. H. Freeman.

Pompi, F. P., & Lachman, R. (1967). Surrogate processes in the short-term retention of connected discourse. *Journal of Experimental Psychology, 75,* 143–151.

Posner, M. I., & Snyder, C. R. R. (1975). Attention and cognitive control. In R. L. Solso (Ed.), *Information processing and cognition: The Loyola Symposium.* Hillsdale, NJ: Lawrence Erlbaum Associates.

Post, T. A., Greene, T., & Bruder, G. (1982, November). *"On-line" text processing in high- and low-knowledge individuals.* Paper presented at the annual meeting of the Psychonomic Society, Minneapolis, MN.

Potts, G. R. (1972). Information processing strategies used in the encoding of linear orderings. *Journal of Verbal Learning and Verbal Behavior, 11,* 727–740.

Potts, G. R., Keenan, J. M., & Golding, J. M. (1988). Assessing the occurrence of elaborative inferences: Lexical decision versus naming. *Journal of Memory and Language, 27,* 399–415.

Potts, G. R., & Peterson, S. B. (1985). Incorporation versus compartmentalization in memory for discourse. *Journal of Memory and Language, 24,* 107–118.

Quillian, M. R. (1967). A revised design for an understanding machine. *Machine Translation, 7.*

Quillian, M. R. (1968). Semantic memory. In M. Minsky (Ed.), *Semantic information processing* (pp. 227–270). Cambridge, MA: M.I.T. Press.

Raphael, B. (1968). SIR: Semantic information retrieval. In M. Minsky (Ed.), *Semantic information processing* (pp. 33–145). Cambridge: M.I.T. Press.

Ratcliff, R., & McKoon, G. (1978). Priming in item recognition. *Journal of Verbal Learning and Verbal Behavior, 17,* 403–417.

Ratcliff, R., & McKoon, G. (1981a). Automatic and strategic priming in recognition. *Journal of Verbal Learning and Verbal Behavior, 20,* 204–215.

Ratcliff, R., & McKoon, G. (1981b). Does activation really spread? *Psychological Review, 88,* 454–462.

Rayner, K. (1977). Visual attention in reading: Eye movements reflect cognitive processes. *Memory & Cognition, 4,* 443–448.

Rayner, K. (Ed.). (1983a). *Eye movements in reading: Perceptual and language processes.* New York: Academic Press.

Rayner, K. (1983b). The perceptual span and eye movement control during reading. In K. Rayner (Ed.), *Eye movements in reading: Perceptual and language processes.* New York: Academic Press.

Rayner, K., Carlson, M., & Frazier, L. (1983). The interaction of syntax and semantics during sentence processing: Eye movements in the analysis of semantically biased sentences. *Journal of Verbal Learning and Verbal Behavior, 22*, 358–374.

Reber, A. S., & Anderson, J. R. (1970). The perception of clicks in linguistic and nonlinguistic messages. *Perception and Psychophysics, 8*, 81–89.

Reder, L. M. (1982). Plausibility judgements versus fact retrieval: Alternative strategies for sentence verification. *Psychological Review, 89*, 250–280.

Reder, L. M. (1987). Strategy-selection in question answering. *Cognitive Psychology, 19*, 90–134.

Reder, L. M., & Anderson, J. R. (1980). A partial resolution of the paradox of interference: The role of integrating knowledge. *Cognitive Psychology, 12*, 447–472.

Reder, L. M., & Ross, B. H. (1983). Integrated knowledge in different tasks: The role of retrieval strategy on fan effects. *Journal of Experimental Psychology: Learning, Memory, and Cognition, 9*, 55–72.

Reder, L. M. & Wible, C. (1984). Strategy use in question answering: Memory strength and task constraints on fan effects. *Memory & Cognition, 12*, 411–419.

Reinhart, T. (1982). Pragmatics and linguistics: An analysis of sentence topics. *Philosophica, 27*.

Reiser, B. J., Black, J. B., & Abelson, R. P. (1985). Knowledge structures in the organization and retrieval of autobiographical memories. *Cognitive Psychology, 11*, 89–137.

Reitman, J. (1974). Without surreptitious rehearsal, information in short-term memory decays. *Journal of Verbal Learning and Verbal Behavior, 13*, 365–377.

Revlin, R., Bromage, B., & Van Ness, M. (1981). Thematic contribution to overgeneralization in memory for quantified discourse. *Journal of Experimental Psychology: Human Learning and Memory, 7*, 227–230.

Reynolds, A. G., & Flagg, P. W. (1976). Recognition memory for elements of sentences. *Memory & Cognition, 4*, 422–432.

Rickheit, G., Schnotz, W., & Strohner, H. (1985). The concept of inference in discourse comprehension. In G. Rickheit & H. Strohner (Eds.), *Inferences in text processing*. Amsterdam: Elsevier Science Publishers.

Rieger, C. (1975, June). The commonsense algorithm as a basis for computer models of human memory, inference, belief, and contextual language comprehension. In R. Schank & B. Nash-Webber (Eds.), *Theoretical issues in natural language processing*. An interdisciplinary workshop. Cambridge, MA: M.I.T.

Riesbeck, C. (1975). Conceptual analysis. In R. C. Schank, *Conceptual information processing*. Amsterdam: North-Holland.

Rips, L. J., Shoben, E. J., & Smith, E. E. (1973). Semantic distance and the verification of semantic relations. *Journal of Verbal Learning and Verbal Behavior, 12*, 1–20.

Rule, B. G., & Bisanz, G. L. (1987). Goals and strategies of persuasion: A cognitive schema for understanding social events. In M. P. Zanna, J. M. Olson, & C. P. Herman (Eds.), *Social influence: The Ontario Symposium*, Vol 5. Hillsdale, NJ: Lawrence Erlbaum Associates.

Rumelhart, D. E. (1977). Understanding and summarizing brief stories. In D. G. Bobrow & A. M. Collins (Eds.), *Representations and understanding: Studies in cognitive science*. New York: Academic Press.

Rumelhart, D. E. (1977). Understanding and summarizing brief stories. In D. Laberge & S. J. Samuels (Eds.), *Basic processes in reading: Perception and comprehension*. Hillsdale, NJ: Lawrence Erlbaum Associates.

Rumelhart, D. E., McClelland, J. L., and the PDP Research Group. (1986). *Parallel distributed processing: Explorations in the microstructure of cognition*, (Vol. I). Cambridge, MA: Bradford Books.

Rumelhart, D. E., & Ortony, A. (1977). The representation of knowledge in memory. In R. Anderson, R. Spiro, & W. Montague (Eds.), *Schooling and the acquisition of knowledge*. Hillsdale, NJ: Lawrence Erlbaum Associates.

Sachs, J. D. (1967). Recognition memory for syntactic and semantic aspects of connected discourse. *Perception and Psychophysics, 2,* 437–442.

Sag, I. A. & Hankamer, J. (1984). Toward a theory of anaphoric processing. *Linguistics and Philosophy, 7,* 325–345.

Sanford, A. (1985). Aspects of pronoun interpretation: Evaluation of search formulations of inference. In G. Rickheit and H. Strohner (Eds.), *Inferences in text processing.* Amsterdam: Elsevier Science Publishers.

Schacter, D. L. (1983). Feeling of knowing in episodic memory. *Journal of Experimental Psychology: Learning, Memory and Cognition, 9,* 39–54.

Schallert, D. L. (1976). Improving memory for prose: The relationship between depth of processing and context. *Journal of Verbal Learning and Verbal Behavior, 15,* 621–632.

Schank, R. C. (1972). Conceptual dependency: A theory of natural language understanding. *Cognitive Psychology, 3,* 552–631.

Schank, R. C. (1976). The role of memory in language processing. In C. Cofer (Ed.), *The nature of human memory.* San Francisco: W. H. Freeman.

Schank, R. C. (1979). Interestingness: Controlling inferences. *Artificial Intelligence, 12,* 273–297.

Schank, R. C. (1982). *Dynamic memory.* Cambridge, England: Cambridge University Press.

Schank, R. C., & Abelson, R. (1977). *Scripts, plans, goals, and understanding.* Hillsdale, NJ: Lawrence Erlbaum Associates.

Schmalhofer, F., & Glavanov, D. (1986). Three components of understanding a programmer's manual: Verbatim, propositional, and situation representations. *Journal of Memory and Language, 25,* 279–294.

Schneider, W., & Shiffrin, R. M. (1977). Controlled and automatic human information processing: Detection, search and attention. *Psychological Review, 84,* 1–66.

Schvaneveldt, R. W., Meyer, D. E., & Becker, C. A. (1976). Lexical ambiguity, semantic context, and visual word recognition. *Journal of Experimental Psychology: Human Perception and Performance, 2,* 243–256.

Schwarz, M. N. K., & Flammer, A. (1981). Text structure and title-effects on comprehension and recall. *Journal of Verbal Learning and Verbal Behavior, 20,* 61–66.

Searle, J. R. (1975). Indirect speech acts. In P. Cole and J. L. Morgan (Eds.), *Syntax and semantics,* Vol. 3: Speech Acts, (pp. 59–82). New York: Seminar Press.

Segalowitz, N. S. (1982). The perception of semantic relations. *Memory & Cognition, 10,* 381–388.

Seidenberg, M. S., & Tanenhaus, M. K. (in press). Modularity and lexical access. In Gopnik (Ed.), *Proceedings of the McGill cognitive science workshops.* Norwood NJ: Ablex.

Sells, P. (1985). *Lectures on contemporary syntactic theories.* Stanford, CA: Center for the Study of Language and Information.

Sharkey, N. E., & Mitchell, D. C. (1985). Word recognition in a functional context: The use of scripts in reading. *Journal of Memory and Language, 24,* 253–270.

Shepard, R. N., & Chipman, S. (1970). Second-order isomorphism of internal representations: Shapes of states. *Cognitive Psychology, 1,* 1–17.

Shepard, R. N., & Metzler, J. (1971). Mental rotation of three-dimensional objects. *Science, 171,* 701–703.

Simon, H. A. (1972). What is visual imagery? An information processing interpretation. In L. Gregg (Ed.), *Cognition in learning and memory.* New York: Wiley.

Simon, H. A. (1974). How big is a chunk? *Science, 183,* 482–488.

Simon, H. A. (1975). The functional equivalence of problem solving skills. *Cognitive Psychology, 7*, 268–288.

Simon, H. A., & Newell, A. (1971). Human problem solving: The state of the theory in 1970. *American Psychologist, 26*, 145–159.

Singer, M. (1976). Thematic structure and the integration of information. *Journal of Verbal Learning and Verbal Behavior, 15*, 549–558.

Singer, M. (1979a). Temporal locus of inference in the comprehension of brief passages: Recognizing and verifying implications about instruments. *Perceptual and Motor Skills, 49*, 539–550.

Singer, M. (1979b). Processes of inference in sentence encoding. *Memory & Cognition, 7*, 192–200.

Singer, M. (1980). The role of case-filling inferences in the coherence of brief passages. *Discourse Processes, 3*, 185–201.

Singer, M. (1981). Verifying the assertions and implications of language. *Journal of Verbal Learning and Verbal Behavior, 20*, 46–60.

Singer, M. (1982). Comparing memory for natural and laboratory reading. *Journal of Experimental Psychology: General, 111*, 331–347.

Singer, M. (1984). Toward a model of question answering: Yes-no questions. *Journal of Experimental Psychology: Learning, Memory, and Cognition, 10*, 285–297.

Singer, M. (1985). Mental operations of question answering. In A. Graesser & J. Black (Eds.), *The psychology of questions*. Hillsdale, NJ: Lawrence Erlbaum Associates.

Singer, M. (1986). Answering yes-no questions about causes: Question acts and question categories. *Memory & Cognition, 14*, 55–63.

Singer, M., & Ferreira, F. (1983). Inferring consequences in story comprehension. *Journal of Verbal Learning and Verbal Behavior, 22*, 437–448.

Singer, M., & Rosenberg, S. T. (1973). The role of grammatical relations in the abstraction of linguistic ideas. *Journal of Verbal Learning and Verbal Behavior, 12*, 273–284.

Slobin, D. I. (1966). Grammatical transformations and sentence comprehension in childhood and adulthood. *Journal of Verbal Learning and Verbal Behavior, 5*, 219–227.

Smith, D. A., & Graesser, A. C. (1981). Memory for actions in scripted activities as a function of typicality, retention interval, and retrieval task. *Memory & Cognition, 9*, 550–559.

Smith, E. E. (1981, May). *Studying on-line comprehension of stories*. Paper presented at the Cognitive Science Colloquium, Yale University, New Haven, CT.

Soli, S. D., & Balch, W. R. (1976). Performance biases and recognition memory for semantic and formal changes in connected discourse. *Memory & Cognition, 4*, 673–676.

Sperber, D. & Wilson, D. (1986). *Relevance: Communication and cognition*. Cambridge, MA: Harvard University Press.

Sperling, G. (1963). A model for visual memory tasks. *Human Factors, 5*, 19–31.

Spilich, G. J., Vesonder, G. T., Chiesi, H. L., & Voss, J. F. (1979). Text processing of domain-related information for individuals with high and low domain knowledge. *Journal of Verbal Learning and Verbal Behavior, 18*, 275–290.

Spiro, R. J. (1980). Accommodative reconstruction in prose recall. *Journal of Verbal Learning and Verbal Behavior, 19*, 84–95.

Spiro, R. J., & Esposito, J. (1981). Superficial processing of explicit inferences in text. *Discourse Processes, 4*, 313–322.

Springston, F. J. (1975). *Some cognitive aspects of presupposed coreferential anaphora*. Unpublished doctoral dissertation, Stanford University.

Stein, N. L., & Glenn, C. G. (1979). An analysis of story comprehension in elementary school children. In R. Freedle (Ed.), *New directions in discourse processing*. Norwood, NJ: Ablex.

Sternberg, S. (1969). The discovery of processing stages: Extensions of Donder's method. In W. Koster (Ed.), *Attention and performance, II. Acta psychologica, 30*, 412–431.

Strawson, P. F. (1952). *Introduction to logical theory*. New York: Wiley.

Strawson, P. F. (1964). Intention and convention in speech acts. *Philosophical review, 73*, 439–60.

Strohner, H., & Nelson, K. E. (1974). The young child's development of sentence comprehension: Influence of event probability, nonverbal context, syntactic form and strategies. *Child Development, 45*, 567–576.

Sulin, R. A., & Dooling, D. J. (1974). Intrusion of a thematic idea in retention of prose. *Journal of Experimental Psychology, 103*, 255–262.

Swinney, D. A. (1979). Lexical access during sentence comprehension: (Re)consideration of context effects. *Journal of Verbal Learning and Verbal Behavior, 18*, 545–569.

Thibadeau, R., Just, M. A., & Carpenter, P. A. (1982). A model of the time course and content of reading. *Cognitive Science, 6*, 157–203.

Thorndyke, P. W. (1976). The role of inferences in discourse comprehension. *Journal of Verbal Learning and Verbal Behavior, 15*, 437–446.

Thorndyke, P. W. (1977). Cognitive structures in comprehension and memory of narrative discourse. *Cognitive Psychology, 9*, 77–110.

Thorndyke, P. W. (1979). Knowledge acquisition from newspaper stories. *Discourse Processes, 2*, 95–112.

Till, R. E., & Walsh, D. A. (1980). Encoding and retrieval factors in adult memory for implicational sentences. *Journal of Verbal Learning and Verbal Behavior, 19*, 1–16.

Tolman, E. C. (1948). Cognitive maps in rats and men. *Psychological Review, 55*, 189–208.

Townsend, D. T., & Bever, T. G. (1982). Natural units of representation interact during sentence comprehension. *Journal of Verbal Learning and Verbal Behavior, 21*, 688–703.

Trabasso, T., Rollins, H., & Shaughnessy, E. (1971). Storage and verification stages in processing concepts. *Cognitive Psychology, 2*, 239–289.

Trabasso, T., Secco, T., & van den Broek, P. (1984). Causal cohesion and story coherence. In H. Mandl, N. Stein, & T. Trabasso (Eds.), *Learning and comprehension of text*. Hillsdale, NJ: Lawrence Erlbaum Associates.

Trabasso, T., & Sperry, L. L. (1985). Causal relatedness and importance of story events. *Journal of Memory and Language, 24*, 595–611.

Trabasso, T., & van den Broek, P. (1985). Causal thinking and the representation of narrative events. *Journal of Memory and Language, 24*, 612–630.

Treisman, A. M. (1960). Contextual cues in selective listening. *Quarterly Journal of Experimental Psychology, 12*, 242–248.

Turing, A. M. (1963). Computing machinery and intelligence. In E. A. Feigenbaum & J. Feldman (Eds.), *Computers and thought* (pp. 11–35). New York: McGraw-Hill.

Turner, A., & Greene, E. (1978). Construction and use of a propositional text base. *JSAS Catalog of Selected Documents in Psychology, 8*, 58. (Ms. No. 1713).

van Dijk, T. A. (1977). Semantic macro-structure and knowledge frame in discourse comprehension. In M. A. Just and P. A. Carpenter (Eds.), *Cognitive processes in comprehension*. Hillsdale, NJ: Lawrence Erlbaum Associates.

van Dijk, T. A., & Kintsch, W. (1983). *Strategies of discourse comprehension*. New York: Academic Press.

Vipond, D. (1980). Micro- and macroprocesses in text comprehension. *Journal of Verbal Learning and Verbal Behavior, 19*, 276–296.

Vonk, W. (1985). The immediacy of inferences in the understanding of pronouns. In G. Rickheit & H. Strohner (Eds.), *Advances in psychology, 29: Inferences in text processing* (pp. 205–218). Amsterdam: North-Holland.

Walker, C. H., & Meyer, B. J. F. (1980). Integrating different types of information in text. *Journal of Verbal Learning and Verbal Behavior, 19*, 263–275.

Walker, C. H., & Yekovich, F. R. (1984). Script based inferences: Effects of text and knowledge variables on recognition memory. *Journal of Verbal Learning and Verbal Behavior, 2*, 357–370.

Waltz, D. N., & Pollack, J. B. (1985). Massively parallel parsing: A strongly interactive model of natural language interpretation. *Cognitive Science, 9*, 51–74.

Wanner, E. (1980). The ATN and the sausage machine: Which one is baloney? *Cognition, 8*, 209–25.

Wanner, E., & Maratsos, M. (1978). An ATN approach to comprehension. In M. Halle, J. Bresnan, & G. Miller (Eds.), *Linguistic theory and psychological reality*. Cambridge, MA: M.I.T. Press.

Warren, R. M., & Warren, R. P. (1970). Auditory illusions and confusions. *Scientific American, 223*, 30–36.

Wason, P. C. (1961). Response to affirmative and negative binary statements. *British Journal of Psychology, 52*, 133–142.

Wason, P. C. (1965). The contexts of plausible denial. *Journal of Verbal Learning and Verbal Behavior, 4*, 7–11.

Watergate transcripts. (1974, May 1). *Chicago Tribune*, p. 33.

Waters, H. S. (1983). Superordinate-subordinate structure in prose passages and the importance of propositions. *Journal of Experimental Psychology: Learning, Memory & Cognition, 9*, 294–299.

Weizenbaum, J. (1968). Contextual understanding by computers. In P. A. Kolers & M. Eden (Eds.), *Recognizing patterns: Studies in living and automatic systems*. Cambridge, MA: M.I.T. Press.

Winograd, T. (1972). *Understanding natural language*. New York: Academic Press.

Winston, P. H. (1984). *Artificial intelligence*, Second Edition. Reading, MA: Addison Wesley.

Woods, W. A. (1968). Procedural semantics for a question-answer machine. In *Proceedings of fall joint computer conference*. New York: Spartan.

Woods, W. A. (1970). Transition network grammars for natural language analysis. *Communications of the Association for Computing Machinery, 13*, 591–606.

Woods, W. A. (1973). An experimental parsing system for transition network grammars. In R. Rustin (Ed.), *Natural language processing*. Englewood Cliffs, NJ: Prentice-Hall.

Yekovich, F. R., & Thorndyke, P. W. (1981). An evaluation of alternative functional models of narrative schemata. *Journal of Verbal Learning and Verbal Behavior, 20*, 454–469.

Yekovich, F. R., Walker C. H., & Blackman, H. S. (1979). The role of presupposed and focal information in integrating sentences. *Journal of Verbal Learning and Verbal Behavior, 18*, 535–548.

Young, R. M. (1973). *Children's seriation behavior: A production-system analysis*. Unpublished Ph.D. dissertation, Department of Psychology, Carnegie-Mellon University.

Author Index

Subject Index

Acknowledgments and Copyrights

Table 1.2, p. 7. From Bower et al., 1979, Table 1, p. 179. Copyright © 1979 by the American Psychological Association. Reprinted by permission.

Table 1.4, p. 16. From Winograd, 1972, pp. 8–13. Copyright © 1972 by Academic Press, Inc. Reprinted by permission.

Figure 2.3, p. 38. From Kintsch & Keenan, 1973, Figure 1, p. 262. Copyright © 1973 by Academic Press, Inc. Adapted by permission.

Table 2.1, p. 40. Kintsch et al., 1975, Table 2, p. 198. Copyright © 1975 by Academic Press, Inc. Adapted by permission.

Figure 2.4, p. 41. From Kintsch et al., 1975, Figure 2, p. 203. Copyright © 1975 by Academic Press, Inc. Adapted by permission.

Figure 2.5, p. 45. From Anderson & Paulson, 1977, Figure 3, p. 445. Copyright © 1977 by Academic Press, Inc. Adapted by permission.

Figure 3.5, p. 76. From Frazier & Rayner, 1982, Figures 1 and 2, p. 181. Copyright © 1982 by Academic Press, Inc. Reprinted by permission.

Figure 3.6, p. 78. From Kimball, 1973, Example 4, p. 17. Copyright © 1973 by Elsevier Science Publishers B. V. (North Holland). Adapted by permission.

Figure 3.7, p. 80. From Rumelhart et al., 1986, Figure 2, p. 8. A Bradford book, Copyright © 1986 by the Massachusetts Institute of Technology. Reprinted by permission.

Figure 3.8, p. 82. From Waltz & Pollack, 1985, Figure 1b, p. 58. Copyright © 1985 by Ablex Publishing Corp. Reprinted with permission from D. L. Waltz and J. B. Pollack, 1985. Also appears in D. L. Waltz and J. Feldman, eds., *Connectionist models and their implications*, chapter 7, pp. 181–204, Ablex Publishing Corp., 1988.

Figure 3.9, p. 84. From Wanner & Maratsos, 1978, Figure 3.1, p. 124. Copyright © 1986 by the Massachusetts Institute of Technology. Reprinted by permission.

Table 4.3, p. 97. From Miller, 1980. Reprinted by permission of the author.

Figure 4.1, p. 102. From Kintsch & van Dijk, 1978, Figure 5, p. 385. Copyright © 1978 by the American Psychological Association. Adapted by permission.

Figure 5.2, p. 141. From Kieras, 1978, Figure 1 and Table 1, p. 16. Copyright © 1978 by Academic Press, Inc. Adapted by permission.

Table 6.1, p. 152. From *Memory & Cognition*, 8, pp. 345–353, by D. E. Kieras, Table 4. Reprinted by permission of the Psychonomic Society, Inc., Copyright © 1980.

Table 6.2, p. 155. From Kintsch et al., 1975, Table 2, p. 198. Copyright © 1975 by Academic Press, Inc. Adapted by permission.

Table 6.3, p. 158. From Graesser et al., 1981, Table 1, p. 8. Copyright © 1981 by Academic Press, Inc. Adapted by permission.

Figure 6.1, p. 159. From Graesser et al., 1981, Figure 1, p. 9. Copyright © 1981 by Academic Press, Inc. Adapted by permission.

Chapter 7. Some content based on: Singer, M. (1988). Inferences in reading comprehension. In M. Daneman, G. MacKinnon, and G. Waller, eds., *Reading research: Advances in theory and practice*, Vol. 6. Copyright © 1988 by Academic Press, Inc. Reprinted by permission.

Table 7.1, p. 173.   Reprinted with permission of publisher. From: Singer, M. (1979a). Temporal locus of inference in the comprehension of brief passages: Recognizing and verifying implications about instruments. *Perceptual and Motor Skills, 49,* 539–550, Table 1.

Table 8.1, p. 192.   From Mandler & Johnson, 1977, Table 2, p. 121. Copyright 1977 by Academic Press, Inc. Adapted by permission.

Table 8.2, p. 193.   From Thorndyke, 1977, Table 1, p. 79. Copyright © 1977 by Academic Press, Inc. Adapted by permission.

Figure 8.2, p. 198.   From Trabasso et al., 1984, Figure 3.9, p. 99. Copyright © 1984 by Lawrence Erlbaum Associates. Reprinted by permission.

Figure 8.3, p. 205.   From Abbott et al., 1985, Figure 1, p. 183. Copyright © 1985 by Academic Press, Inc. Reprinted by permission.

Table 8.3, p. 213.   From Graesser et al., 1979, Table 1, p. 323, and Table 2, p. 327. Copyright © 1979 by Academic Press, Inc. Adapted by permission.

Table 8.4, p. 214.   From *Memory & Cognition, 9,* pp. 550–559, by D. A. Smith & A. C. Graesser, 1981, Table 1. Reprinted by permission of the Psychonomic Society, Inc., Copyright © 1981.

Table 8.5, p. 216.   From Walker & Yekovich, 1984, Table 1, p. 361 and Table 2, p. 363. Copyright © 1984 by Academic Press, Inc. Reprinted by permission.

Table 9.1, p. 228.   From Reder, 1982, Table 1, p. 259. Copyright © 1982 by the American Psychological Association. Adapted by permission.

Figure 9.3, p. 236.   From Clark & Chase, 1972, Table 1, p. 480. Copyright © 1972 by Academic Press, Inc. Adapted by permission.

Table 9.3, p. 237.   From Clark & Chase, 1972, Table 2, p. 482. Copyright © 1972 by Academic Press, Inc. Adapted by permission.

Figure 9.4, p. 238.   From Mathews et al., 1980, Figure 1, p. 538. Copyright © 1980 by Academic Press, Inc. Reprinted by permission.

Figure 9.5, p. 242.   From Anderson, 1976, Figure 8.7a, p. 278. Copyright © 1976 by Lawrence Erlbaum Associates. Adapted by permission.

Table 10.2, p. 252.   From Winograd, 1972, pp. 8–13. Copyright © 1972 by Academic Press, Inc. Reprinted by permission.

Figure 10.1, p. 262–263.   From Miller & Kintsch, 1980, Appendix, pp. 353–354. Copyright © 1980 by the American Psychological Association. Adapted by permission.

Table 10.3, p. 265.   From Lehnert et al., 1983, pp. 16–17. Copyright © 1983 by Elsevier Science Publishers B. V. (North Holland). Reprinted by permission.

Figure 10.2, p. 267.   From Lehnert et al., 1983, Figures 2–1 and 2–2, pp. 25–26. Copyright © 1983 by Elsevier Science Publishers B. V. (North Holland). Reprinted by permission.